Why Smart People Can Be So Stupid

Why Smart People Can Be So Stupid

EDITED BY ROBERT J. STERNBERG

 YALE UNIVERSITY PRESS *New Haven & London*

Published with assistance from
the Mary Cady Tew Memorial Fund

Set in Monotype Garamond and Meta types
by Keystone Typesetting, Inc.
Printed in the United States of America by
R. R. Donnelley & Sons.

Library of Congress Cataloging-in-Publication Data
Why smart people can be so stupid /
edited by Robert J. Sternberg.
     p.   cm.
Includes bibliographical references and index.
ISBN 0-300-09033-1 (alk. paper)
1. Intellect. 2. Stupidity. 3. Errors—Psychological aspects.
4. Conduct of life. I. Sternberg, Robert J.
BF431. W535 2002
153.9—dc21   2001005846

A catalogue record for this book is available
from the British Library.

The paper in this book meets the guidelines for permanence
and durability of the Committee on Production Guidelines for
Book Longevity of the Council on Library Resources.

10 9 8 7 6 5 4 3 2 1

CONTENTS

PREFACE

Those who have wondered *if* smart people can be stupid do not have to look very far, nor do they have to look through the lenses of any particular ideology.

- A president of the United States, graduate of Yale Law School, and Rhodes Scholar showed behavior so "stupid" that few people can understand why he did what he did. Beyond any hormonally motivated behavior on his part, the whole world wondered how a trained lawyer could have allowed himself to become entangled in such a legal nightmare.
- A seasoned prosecutor and judge with a reputation for some brilliance damaged his good name among much of the U.S. population with his apparent vendetta against a president. His campaign left many people convinced that the prosecutor was more interested in "winning" than in pursuing any reasonable legal case.
- A U.S. congressman known for being ideological but balanced and wise left the fray with his reputation in tatters when he and his fellow House "managers" pursued a case they could not win.
- A former prosecutor and state's attorney general in Delaware was sentenced to death for murdering a girlfriend who jilted him.
- A world-renowned geologist, while being investigated for and charged with storing child pornography, involved himself with a boy whom he was later accused of molesting.

Whether one believes in a single intelligence (*g* or IQ) or multiple intelligences or anything in between, the behavior of the individuals mentioned above (and, indeed, at times, our own behavior) seems inexplicable in terms of what we know about intelligence. Why do people think and behave in such stupid ways that they end up destroying their livelihood or even their lives?

This book is devoted to addressing these questions, which the vast majority of theories in psychology, including theories of intelligence, seem to neglect. The world supports a multi-million-dollar industry in intelligence and ability research and testing to determine who has the intelligence to succeed, but it devotes virtually nothing to determine who will best use this intelligence and who will squander it by engaging in amazing, breathtaking acts of stupidity.

"Stupidity" here does not refer to mental retardation, learning disability, or any of the usual labels assigned to people who perform poorly on one or another conventional test. Many of these people function well in their everyday lives. Rather, the focus here is on those who demonstrate the kind of stupidity that can take one's breath away.

Clearly, this is not a book about stupidity in the conventional, IQ-based sense. But stupidity in the conventional sense is almost never the kind that destroys people's lives or the lives of those around them. Rather, the book deals with the kind of stupidity that has left countries in the nearly perpetual throes of wars that no one ever seems to win and where it often is not clear what is at stake or how the battle lines have been drawn.

In order to achieve coherence, the contributors to this book were asked to address the following issues:

- The nature of the attribute of stupidity
- The proposed theory of the attribute
- How stupidity relates to intelligence
- How stupidity contributes to stupid behavior
- Whether stupidity is measurable
- Whether stupidity is modifiable (in order to make a person less stupid)

This book will be of special interest to readers for several reasons. First, the topic is particularly timely, as Americans watch political leaders at all points in the political spectrum behaving in ways that, to outsiders at least, appear breathtakingly stupid. Second, although many books address intelligence in its various forms, relatively few tackle the topic of stupidity. The majority of such books are simplistic "how-to" books that eschew both psychological theory and empirical research. Although the book does contain information on how people can avoid behaving stupidly in their own lives, that information is supplied from the standpoint that anyone can benefit from gaining insights into why people act as stupidly as they do. Third, and finally, this book includes a variety of perspectives on stupidity, providing readers with a range of sources for that behavior.

ACKNOWLEDGMENTS

I am grateful to Sai Durvasula and Cynthia Blankenship for assistance in the preparation of the manuscript, to Susan Arellano for contracting the book, and to my colleagues at the Center for the Psychology of Abilities, Competencies, and Expertise (PACE Center) at Yale for their collaborations, which have helped immeasurably in the development of my thinking about stupidity.

Preparation of this book was supported in part by Grant REC-9979843 from the National Science Foundation and a government grant under the Javits Act Program (Grant No. R206R000001) as administered by the Office of Educational Research and Improvement, U.S. Department of Education. Grantees undertaking such projects are encouraged to express freely their professional judgment. This book, therefore, does not necessarily represent the positions or policies of the U.S. government and no official endorsement should be inferred.

RAY HYMAN

1 Why and When Are Smart People Stupid?

The Issue

The title of this book, *Why Smart People Can Be So Stupid,* assumes that smart people at least sometimes do stupid things. In addition, the title implies that such stupid behavior needs explaining. The first challenge to anyone who tries to provide an explanation is that the title is phrased in terms from the common vernacular. The key words *smart* and *stupid* belong to folk psychology. As such, their meanings are vague, ambiguous, and shift with person and context.

The term *smart* can be equated with the psychological concept of *intelligence*. This, in fact, is what the contributors to this volume seem to have done. Indeed, this may be the one matter upon which all these authors are in agreement. Unfortunately, the term *stupid* seems to have no obvious technical counterpart in psychological theory. One consequence is that the authors differ greatly on how they treat this concept.

The title makes it clear that smartness is a property of people. It is an enduring property of a person. A person who is "smart" today is expected to be smart tomorrow and into the foreseeable future. Of course, at least some of the authors make it clear that they do not consider intelligence to be fixed. People can, with effort and proper instruction, improve their intelligence. However, quick changes and major fluctuations in intelligence are rare.

Stupidity, on the other hand, can be a property of an act, behavior, state, or person. We might believe that the act of smoking is stupid regardless of the intent, motivations, and construals of the people doing the smoking. Although I believe that many people apply the label of "stupid" to acts in this way, I suspect that none of the contributors to this book consider this usage. The hint of a paradox in this book's title resides in the possibility that "stupid" is being used as a property of a person. Because, with one exception, all the authors treat *stupid* as the opposite of *smart;* handling both these terms as properties of the person implies that the same person is both smart and stupid at the same time. So, at first blush, the title seems to pose a paradox. This, in turn, suggests a puzzle to be solved.

One way to resolve this paradox is implicit in the chapters by Wagner, Sternberg, and possibly a few others. This resolution is to treat intelligence and stupidity as domain-dependent. Thus, the same person could be smart in her professional life and stupid in her personal affairs. A more interesting way to dissolve the apparent paradox is to treat stupidity as a state or a property of behavior. This would allow for a person who is generally smart in her professional life to occasionally behave stupidly in that same professional life. Indeed, it is this latter scenario that most of the contributors to this book seem to have in mind.

All the authors focus on the behavior of smart people. This leaves open the question of whether dumb (unintelligent) people can be stupid. This is both tricky and nontrivial. I think it is fair to say that most of the contributors treat stupidity as a failure of the actor to optimally use her abilities or cognitive capacity. Although this makes sense, it also seems to be at variance with the common assumption that stupidity is a manifestation of low intelligence. If stupidity is treated as a discrepancy between actual and potential behavior, then it cannot be the case that a person who behaves in a maladaptive fashion and who is using the full potential of her low intellectual abilities is acting stupidly.

Points of Agreement and Disagreement

Most of the authors accept the challenge of answering the question of why smart people can be stupid. Both Perkins and Ayduk and Mischel deal with the matter as a failure of self-regulation. Stupid behavior, in their treatments, comes about when activity is triggered at an inappropriate time in an inappropriate situation or when the actor fails to suppress an immediate gratification in the pursuit of a more important, but longer-range, objective. For Dweck, stupidity follows from failure to fully use one's capabilities and failure to exploit opportunities for learning. These failures, in turn, seem to follow from a belief in fixed intelligence and a defensive avoidance of tackling tasks that could lead to poor performance. Both Stanovich and Austin and Deary look for causes of stupidity in personality and other dispositional aspects of the individual, independent of intelligence. Both Wagner and Grigorenko and Lockery also find stupidity at the level of social systems. Halpern attributes the stupidity of Bill Clinton's handling of the revelation of his affair with Monica Lewinsky to his failure to recognize changes in the environment and his reliance on old habits (mindlessness).

Three strikingly different ways of resolving the apparent paradox are evident in the chapters by Stanovich, Moldoveanu and Langer, and Sternberg, respectively. While most of the authors treat "stupid" as the opposite of "smart" (intelligent), Stanovich argues for the advantages of treating stupid as the opposite of rational. Following the lead of some other cognitive scientists, Stanovich considers mental functioning at three levels. The first, or biological level, deals with the "hardware" or implementation of activity. The second level, algorithmic, corresponds to the cognitive capabilities of the system. Stanovich locates smartness or intelligence at this level. The third level, the intentional one, is where thinking dispositions, goal setting, coping styles, and the like are found. Here is where it makes sense to speak of rational or stupid behaviors. Stupidity, in this analysis, follows from a failure to use the cognitive abilities at level two in the pursuit of goals (pragmatic or epistemic).

Moldoveanu and Langer focus on the inappropriate use of the label "stupid." They argue that many apparent cases of stupidity result from the mindless labeling of actors by observers. They also discuss apparent stupidity stemming from mindless interactive pursuits of scripts (such as teacher-pupil scripts), and from the mindless assimilation by the actor of social biases. They argue that most, if not all, the research in which subjects fail to act according to normative standards does not justify the implication that the subjects' behavior is "irrational" or that humans are "cognitive cripples." Such implications merely reflect the failure of mindless experimenters to recognize that their subjects might be processing the given information differently from the way they do. Moldoveanu and Langer believe that when proper consideration of the way subjects have construed the problem is taken into account, their rationality will be vindicated. They propose that if we substitute the mindful/mindless continuum for the intelligent/nonintelligent one, the temptation to label people and behaviors as stupid will vanish.

Sternberg dissolves the paradox by simply denying that smart people can be stupid. Instead, in contrast to Stanovich, Sternberg seems to accept that stupid is the opposite of smart. However, he changes the issue from *why smart people can be so stupid* to *why smart people can be so foolish*. In this context, foolish is the opposite of wise. This enables him to bring to bear his balance theory of wisdom and his imbalance theory of foolishness. In this light,

Clinton's behavior in the Lewinsky aftermath might not have been stupid, but it certainly was foolish. Sternberg agrees with Halpern, that Clinton's inappropriate behavior ("stupid" in Halpern's story and "foolish" in Sternberg's account) resulted from defects in reading situational cues.

Moldoveanu and Langer stand out as the only authors to reject the ecological validity of the heuristics and biases research. They imply that this research has no bearing upon real-world behavior. Stanovich, on the other hand, lists several examples of how these same laboratory-discovered biases operate in the real world—physicians' diagnoses, risk assessment, legal issues, and so on. Wagner, Halpern, and Grigorenko and Lockery explicitly acknowledge the reality of these biases in real life, while the other contributors seem to implicitly accept this extension.

The apparent disagreements among the authors can be traced, in part, to the ambiguities in the terms *smart* and *stupid*. The authors differ in just how they define and map these terms onto psychological constructs. The major source of apparent disagreement, however, results from the different exemplars, contexts, and examples that the authors use as their referents for stupidity. Most of them dismiss examples of "stupidity" resulting from lack of information, momentary lapses, fatigue, and simple "performance" executions as uninteresting. Some impulsive actions, such as a truck driver who tries to beat a train at a railroad crossing, and the failure of children to postpone gratification, are the focus of at least two chapters. The Clinton-Lewinsky affair receives prominent attention in two other chapters. Managerial incompetence, the Iran-Contra affair, smoking, Chechnya, teacher-student perceptions, stereotyping of learning disabilities, and social follies such as Vietnam and the Rodney King affair are other examples used by different authors in their explorations of stupidity.

Adaptive and maladaptive behaviors occur in an enormous variety of contexts and situations. Each of these contexts can raise a variety of different issues. In all of them, some behaviors seem to be so irresponsible, heedless, thoughtless, negligent, or outrageous that they invite the label "stupid." Perhaps, as Moldoveanu and Langer imply, it would be better if we avoided using this pejorative label. However, if we abandon it, I suspect we will find that we will need some equivalent way to identify those acts that go beyond mere mindlessness. Not all goofs are created equal.

In his classic *The Mentality of Apes*, Wolfgang Köhler (1959) identified three kinds of errors in his extensive observations of chimpanzees solving problems:

1. *"Good errors."* "In these, the animal does not make a stupid, but rather an almost favourable impression, if only the observer can get

right away from preoccupation with human achievements, and concentrate only on the nature of the behaviour observed."

2. *"Errors caused by complete lack of comprehension of the conditions of the task."* "This can be seen when the animals, in putting a box higher up, will take it from a statically good position and put it into a bad one. The impression one gets in such cases is that of a certain innocent limitation."

3. *"Crude stupidities arising from habit."* "In situations which the animal ought to be able to survey.... Such behaviour is extremely annoying— it almost makes one angry, . . . This kind of behaviour never arises unless a similar procedure often took place beforehand as a real and genuine solution. The stupidities are not accidental 'natural' fractions, from which *primarily* apparent solutions can arise . . . they are the *after-effects* of former genuine solutions, which were often repeated, and so developed a tendency to appear *secondarily* in later experiments, without much consideration for the special situation. The preceding conditions for such mistakes seem to be drowsiness, exhaustion, colds, or even excitement" (pp. 173–174).

Köhler was a staunch defender of animal intelligence. His book is a spirited rebuttal to Thorndike's attempt to account for all animal "reasoning" in terms of blind trial and error. Yet, we see that Köhler feels compelled to label some chimpanzee behaviors as "stupid." Indeed, he needs this label precisely because he recognizes that other chimpanzee behavior can be insightful and intelligent in the context of the chimpanzee's world. Likewise, we do not defame human cognition by recognizing some cognitive actions as stupid. It is only because we acknowledge that human cognition is usually rational and adaptive that we can identify some departures from this rational and adaptive behavior as stupid.

I previously mentioned how the apparent differences in the approaches to stupidity by the various contributor to this book are due to their use of different referents. So it might be helpful to briefly discuss a few more examples of goofs or maladaptive behavior to strengthen our grasp of the many issues arising from this consideration of why smart people can be so stupid.

Some Additional Candidates for Stupid Behavior

At times a patently smart person can blunder or go badly astray. Every field of human activity provides a multitude of examples of such behavior. Each example, in turn, suggests a number of possible reasons for departures from rational or sensible behavior. Here, I look at some examples beyond those discussed by the contributors to this volume in order to see how their discussions might help us understand these additional cases.

On September 23, 1846, astronomers Galle and d'Arrest, both from Berlin, announced the discovery of a new planet, which was later named Neptune. The remarkable thing about this discovery was that the astronomers made their discovery by aiming their telescope at a location in the sky based on the mathematical calculations of the French astronomer Urbain Jean Joseph Leverrier. Leverrier had become interested in the problem of the orbit of the recently discovered planet Uranus. The perceived sightings of Uranus seemed to deviate somewhat from the orbit calculated from Newtonian mechanics. Some contemporary astronomers proposed various possibilities to account for this discrepancy such as unseen satellites or other planets. Some even suggested that Newton's inverse square law might not hold for the farther reaches of space. As a strict Newtonian, Leverrier began his attack on the problem with the firm belief that Newton's laws were inviolate (Grosser 1979; Hanson 1962).

The problem became one of squaring the reported locations of Uranus with the orbit predicted by Newtonian theory. Leverrier reexamined both the old and later sightings of Uranus. He recalculated the orbits from the data and discovered that previous astronomers had made several errors. Nevertheless, after correcting for these errors, he still found a small but real discrepancy between the observed and predicted locations for the planet. After considering and eliminating several possibilities, he surmised that the observed perturbation of the orbit was due to a previously undetected planet farther away from the sun than Uranus. His task then became to determine the size and orbit of this possible planet. This problem was inherently difficult because of several unknowns. After time-consuming and enormously difficult and sophisticated calculations, Leverrier announced the size, distance from the sun, orbit, and predicted locations for this hypothetical planet.

At first he could not persuade the major French and British observatories to look for his predicted planet. He finally convinced Galle to look for it where his calculations predicted it should be. A few days after receiving the coordinates from Leverrier, Galle and his colleague looked and found the new planet very close to where Leverrier had predicted it to be. Some luck was involved because Leverrier's orbit deviated in parts from Neptune's actual orbit. However, at the time of the sighting, Neptune's actual orbit and Leverrier's predicted orbit overlapped. With the discovery of Neptune,

Leverrier became an instant celebrity. He was lionized as the second New-ton and was honored by the major scientific societies throughout Europe. What especially intrigued his scientific colleagues was that Leverrier had made this important discovery without himself making any observations. The famous French astronomer Claude Flammarion wrote that Leverrier "discovered a star with the tip of his pen, without other instrument than the strength of his calculations alone" (quoted in Baum and Sheehan 1997, p. 2).

Leverrier was thirty-five years old when he achieved one of the greatest triumphs for Newtonian mechanics. To discover Neptune, he relied on Newton's theory and almost superhuman mathematical calculations. Prior to the discovery of Neptune, Leverrier had discovered a perturbation in the orbit of Mercury. The discrepancy was very small, but he could not explain it away as simply an error. Fresh from his triumph of reconciling the perturba-tion in Uranus' orbit with Newtonian mechanics, Leverrier set about to do the same for the disturbance in Mercury's orbit. He worked on this problem another thirteen years before he was ready to announce his prediction of a new planet closer to the sun than Mercury. This planet would help to ac-count for the perturbations in Mercury's orbit (Baum & Sheehan 1997; Fernie 1994; Fontenrose 1973; Hanson 1962).

Leverrier announced his new theory about a hidden planet inside Mer-cury's orbit on September 12, 1859. On December 22 of that same year, Edmonde Lescarbault, a physician and amateur astronomer from the rural district of Orgères, wrote a letter to Leverrier claiming that he had observed the very same planet described by Leverrier in March of that year. Leverrier visited Lescarbault, unannounced, and questioned him carefully to judge his honesty and competence. Although Leverrier discovered that Lescarbault had used crude instrumentation and had carelessly kept his records, he decided that Lescarbault was honest and sufficiently competent to have spotted the previously hidden planet. Leverrier arranged to have Lescar-bault receive the Legion of Honor. He also named the new planet Vulcan.

The announcement of the discovery of Vulcan created a sensation. This was considered a second great triumph for the genius Leverrier. Leverrier made new calculations regarding the size and orbit of Vulcan and advised the astronomical world when and where to look to best view this new planet. At the appointed time, astronomers—both professional and amateur— around the world looked for Vulcan and failed to find it. Leverrier made new calculations and sent out new advisories about where and when to look. Again, no credible sightings occurred. During the next several years, this drama kept repeating itself. Leverrier would make new calculations and send out new instructions. Astronomers would aim their telescopes at the new coordinates and find nothing. On occasion, one or two professional astronomers and some amateurs did report sighting what they believed was the planet Vulcan. In most cases, the reports were inconsistent with one another and with Leverrier's calculations.

Leverrier issued his last alert in 1877, the same year he died. He strongly maintained his belief in the reality of Vulcan right up to his death. By that time, however, most of the astronomical world no longer believed that either Vulcan or any other planetary matter lay between Mercury and the sun. Nevertheless, the problem of the perturbation in Mercury's orbit persisted. Finally, in 1915, Einstein published his general theory of relativity, which triumphantly accounted for the orbit of Mercury. Hanson (1962) succinctly encapsulates Leverrier's rise to fame and descent to ignomy in the following words:

> Who else can be said to have raised a scientific theory to its pinnacle of achievement—and then shortly later, to have discovered those discrepancies which dashed the theory to defeat? By pressing Newton's mechanics to the limit of its capacities to explain and predict, Leverrier revealed Uranus' aberrations as intelligible; he also predicted the existence of the then-unseen planet Neptune, which has just those properties required dynamically to explain Uranus' misbehavior. In history few have approached Leverrier's achievement as a human resolution of an intricate natural problem. When he detected a somewhat analogous misbehavior in Mercury, Leverrier naturally pressed the same pattern of explanation into service. He calculated, via the law of gravitation, the elements of some as-yet-unseen planet which would do for Mercury just what Neptune had done for Uranus. In this Leverrier failed. In a sense, his failure was one for Newtonian mechanics itself. (p. 359)

Halpern's analysis of why President Clinton believed he could have an affair with Monica Lewinsky and remain unscathed can be applied to why Leverrier went so wrong in his advocacy for the reality of Vulcan. His resounding success in predicting the existence of Neptune set the stage for his prediction of Vulcan. He went through the same process of carefully delineating the precise anomaly in each case that required explanation. In both cases, he then went through the painstaking calculations to find a previously unseen planet that would have just the right size, orbit, and other properties to account for the anomalous behavior of each planet. This procedure was brilliantly validated in the case of Neptune.

Neptune's discovery was uncontroversial. It was made by a major observatory, and immediately other astronomers could confirm the sighting and also retroactively find Neptune in photographs made earlier of that part of the sky. Confirmation for Vulcan was less clearcut. The first evidence came from an amateur with crude instruments and no prior record of contributions to astronomy. However, given that his procedure had been so successful with Neptune, Leverrier did not need such strong evidence to convince himself that his calculations had borne fruit again. During his remaining seventeen years, the overwhelming majority of attempts to observe Vulcan were negative. However, sporadic reports did keep reaching Leverrier—mostly from amateurs—of alleged sightings of Vulcan. Such partial reinforcement is all that Leverrier apparently needed to maintain his unwavering belief in the reality of Vulcan.

With hindsight, we can find several indications that should have alerted Leverrier to the fact that Vulcan did not exist. In terms of Sternberg's theory, we could conclude that Leverrier was foolish in not recognizing the clues that made the Vulcan affair importantly different from the Neptune situation. However, one can also, in the spirit of Moldoveanu and Langer, create scenarios that, given Leverrier's background and perception of the situation, would make Leverrier normatively correct in his belief in Vulcan. In Köhler's sense, one could argue that Leverrier made a "good error."

So, was Leverrier's blunder an example of stupidity? Even many of his contemporaries believed he had gone too far in his defense of Vulcan. I find it easier to excuse his initial belief in Vulcan based on his calculations and his trust in Lescarbault. However, to stubbornly persist in his belief during the next seventeen years when every major observatory consistently failed to find evidence for the planet's existence was at least foolish if not stupid. When should we describe a smart person's behavior as stupid? If we can imagine a possible scenario under which the maladaptive behavior has normative or quasi-normative status, does this mean that the behavior has to be accepted as rational and reasonable? Given this strong principle of charity (Thagard & Nisbett 1983), must we then treat all blunders as equally rational and reasonable?

PILTDOWN MAN

In December 1918, Arthur Smith Woodward and Charles Dawson announced the discovery of a fossil skull and jaw belonging to an early Pleistocene primitive human whom they called *Eoanthropous* (The Dawn Man) (Weiner 1980). The pieces of the skull were clearly human, but the part of the accompanying jaw seemed clearly ape-like. These fossils had been found together in a gravel deposit at Piltdown in Sussex, England. Dawson, a country lawyer and amateur archaeologist, had earlier brought fragments of skull bones to Smith Woodward in the Department of Geology of the

British Natural History Museum. Woodward and Dawson did some more digging in the pit and uncovered more pieces of the brain case and the jaw. All the pieces were iron-stained, which was appropriate for fossils having been buried in the Piltdown gravels. The fossils were judged to be from the early Pleistocene period because of the presumed age of the gravel pit and the fossil remains of ancient animals that were also found in close proximity.

Piltdown Man, as the assumed creature who belonged to the skull and bone fragments came to be called, was considered sufficiently ancient to be a viable candidate for Darwin's missing link between ape-like ancestors and modern man. Woodward's reconstruction of the skull further emphasized this possibility. Although the skull was clearly human, Woodward's reconstruction resulted in a brain that was clearly larger than that of any known ape but definitely smaller than that of any known human. The jaw, however, was clearly ape-like. The portion of the jaw that was preserved had two molar teeth that were worn flat. Such worn molars can occur only in humans because the canine teeth in apes prevent their jaws from moving from side to side, which would be necessary for the flat molars. In his reconstruction, Woodward assumed that such a jaw would have a large canine tooth. However, he re-created the canine such that it would jut out to allow the jaw to move from side to side and, as a result, would have unusual wear.

Woodward's reconstruction was significant for two key reasons. When the discovery of Piltdown Man was first announced, some scientists openly expressed skepticism that the skull and jaw could belong to the same individual. They suggested that somehow the jaw and the skull fragments accidentally had drifted together. The defenders of Piltdown countered this argument by stating that it was highly unlikely to find in close proximity fragments of a human skull with no other human-like remains and fragments of a jawbone with no other ape remains. In addition, Woodward was able to point to the flattened molar teeth, which had never been seen in an ape. Shortly afterward, a tooth was found in the Piltdown gravel pit that just happened to have the peculiar wear pattern that Woodward had predicted in his reconstruction. This striking confirmation of Woodward's unusual prediction silenced most skeptics. Later, in 1915, Dawson reported finding further fragments of a skull and a molar tooth that apparently belonged to the Piltdown jaw some few miles from the original Piltdown site. This additional conjunction of a human-like skull and ape-like jaw, for practical purposes, ended opposition to the idea that the jaw and skull came from the same individual.

Many reasons have been cited for the acceptance of the Piltdown artifacts as representing an ancient human ancestor. Some key British scientists had developed theories about ancient humans that each, for his own reasons, saw confirmed in Piltdown Man. Piltdown Man clearly suggested that our ancestors had first developed a big brain and then shed their ape-like features. In addition, several scientists believed that Piltdown Man fit the missing link predicted by Charles Darwin. Most historians of the Piltdown saga attribute national pride as a major factor. Fossil evidence of prehistoric man had been found on the continent in Germany and France, but not in Britain, the home of Darwin. Indeed, the French scientists openly taunted the British on this score. So it was a source of national pride when fossil evidence of what could be the direct ancestor of modern man was found on British soil.

Although Piltdown Man was accepted as a legitimate member of the human family tree for forty years after its discovery, questions about its central role in our evolution began to accumulate. Piltdown Man implied that modern humans had evolved from ancestors who first acquired a big brain and then shed their ape-like features. However, as more and more fossil evidence of prehistoric humans began to accumulate, Piltdown's status began to change. All the subsequent fossil finds since 1912 indicated that prehistoric humans first shed their ape-like features and then developed the larger brain—just the opposite of what Piltdown implied. The scientists and the textbooks handled this apparent paradox by assuming there were two major evolutionary branches from early ape-like ancestors: one branch, apparently the more successful one, involved those creatures that first shed their ape-like appearance and then acquired a big brain; the other branch, including Piltdown, developed a big brain first. The branch represented by Piltdown was an evolutionary dead end.

Around 1950, Kenneth Oakly applied the fluorine test to both the jaw and skull fragments of the Piltdown fossils. The test was not as sophisticated as later tests for determining the age of fossils. It could not, for example, detect any difference in age between the jaw and skull. However, it was sufficiently accurate to clearly determine that the fragments could not be from the early Pleistocene era. At best, they did not go back beyond the later Pleistocene era. This created a perplexing situation. If the fluorine tests were correct, then Piltdown Man—this creature that was part human and part ape—was wandering around at the same time that modern humans were. Furthermore, this peculiar creature had no known ancestors and no known descendants. Clearly, something was amiss!

In 1953, Oxford University anatomist J. S. Weiner, after some discussions at a scientific meeting, asked himself why he and other scientists had accepted the proposition that the Piltdown jaw and skull belonged to the same creature. His answer was the flat molars in the jaw. What if, he asked himself, someone had deliberately faked and planted the fossils?

But there appeared to be one main objection to this startling suggestion—the flat wear of the molar teeth at such an early stage of attrition (a type of wear not found in any of the modern apes). Dr. Weiner then took a chimpanzee jaw, filed down the molar teeth to form flat biting surfaces and stained them with potassium permanganate. When he showed the results of his experiment to me [the renowned Oxford anatomist, Walter Le Gros Clark] the next morning I looked at the teeth with amazement, for they reproduced so exactly the appearance of the unusual type of wear in the Piltdown molars. We therefore took the first opportunity to visit the Natural History Museum in London in order to examine the original Piltdown specimens with the possibility in mind that the teeth had been flattened by artificial abrasion. But first we had to consider what were the features by which the effects of natural wear of a tooth might be expected to differ from the effects of artificial abrasion. A study of a large series of human and ape teeth showed us that there were a certain number of features on which we would probably place reliance, and *when we inspected the Piltdown molars in the light of this experience the evidences of artificial abrasion immediately sprang to the eye. Indeed, so obvious did they seem that it may well be asked—how was it that they had escaped notice before? The answer is really quite simple—they had never been looked for. The history of scientific discovery is replete with examples of the obvious being missed because it had not been looked for, and the present instance is just one more example; nobody previously had ever examined the Piltdown jaw with the idea of a possible forgery in mind.* [Italics added] (Clark 1955, p. 145)

Walter Le Gros Clark lists the five criteria for identifying normal wear in lower molar teeth. Just glancing at the Piltdown molars quickly revealed that their pattern of wear violated all five criteria. In addition, new X-ray photographs showed that, contrary to the original report, the roots of the molars were more similar to ape than to human roots. Finally, "close inspection of the biting surfaces of the molars with a binocular microscope reveals that they are scored with criss-cross scratches; apparently the result of the application of an abrasive of some sort" (p. 146). These findings alone suffice to prove the fossils were fabricated. Weiner, Clark, and others quickly found other evidence for forgery. Indeed, the case for forgery was overwhelming.

In the context of this book, the question raised by Piltdown Man is: How can so many of the world's best scientists have been taken in by this hoax for forty years? Clark provides one answer. He acknowledges that the evidence of a hoax was immediately evident upon inspection. His answer is that none of the original scientists saw the obvious signs of fraud because none of them were looking at the evidence with the hypothesis of fraud in mind. Other commentators have argued that the hoaxer must have been sufficiently scientifically knowledgeable and intelligent to have successfully fooled these great minds. Neither answer makes sense. The hoax was clearly rather crude. Almost all the signs of fraud were obvious. Just about all the original Piltdown scientists were—or should have been—aware of the many indicators of normal wear in lower molar teeth. For example, dentine wears faster than enamel, so that normally flattened molars show a concave surface. The Piltdown molars were flat, revealing the abnormal situation in which the dentine and enamel wore at the same rate. Also, the margins of normally worn molars are rounded and beveled. The Piltdown molars had sharp edges. All the other indicators of fraud were equally evident.

A better answer to how this crude hoax could have succeeded is found in the dynamics hypothesized to account for bystander apathy. Similar factors occurred in the Home-Stake oil swindle (McClintick 1977), in which prominent celebrities and executives of major financial institutions were lured into a tax deduction scheme that promised them 400 percent return on their investments. From the inadequately, and even illegally, prepared prospectuses to the outlandish promises of impossible returns, all the signs of fraud were obvious to any investor who took time to read the literature. Each of the prominent financial experts could have, and should have, easily detected these signs. Just as virtually the entire scientific community failed to detect the indications of fraud in the Piltdown hoax, these knowledgeable investors failed to follow the advice they routinely gave their clients. One reason the financial experts were successfully conned was that each one assumed the others had properly checked out the details. In like manner, each of the Piltdown experts simply assumed that the other experts had checked the teeth and the other evidence.

With each person mindlessly assuming that the others had mindfully looked into the important details, it turned out that no expert had actually done the obvious, mundane checks relevant to his or her domain. Many of the factors discussed by the contributors to this volume can help us understand how the Piltdown scientists fell for such a crude hoax. Confirmation bias and other biases and heuristics can easily apply. As we consider additional cases, however, we keep uncovering principles and issues not brought up in these chapters. To me, this says that we have a long way to go before we can piece together the full story of why smart people can go badly astray.

Were the Piltdown scientists stupid? Were they foolish? Yes, we can conjure up scenarios to account for or "excuse" their blunder. Such scenarios, however, seem more strained than the ones we can generate to account for Leverrier's blunder. It seems to me even more inexcusable for the Piltdown scientists to have overlooked obvious evidence of forgery for such a long time. Still, I can imagine that those who preach the principle of charity would not condone calling the Piltdown scientists foolish, let alone stupid. There-fore, I've chosen my final two examples to define more precisely what I think ought to be called foolish or stupid.

ALFRED RUSSEL WALLACE AND S. J. DAVEY

During the 1880s, S. J. Davey carried out a series of experiments that probably constitute the first systematic investigation of the fallacies of eye-witness testimony (Davey 1887; Hodgson 1887; Hodgson 1892). Davey instigated these experiments because of his personal experiences with spiri-tualism. In 1883 he was startled by a vision of a friend who had recently died. As a result he began reading extensively in the literature of spiritualism and psychical research. In 1884 he began attending seances conducted by the British medium Eglinton. One of Eglinton's specialities was producing writ-ing on slates, allegedly originating from spirits in the other world. Davey wrote glowing reports of Eglinton's powers to various journals. Davey came to believe he also had mediumistic powers. "One afternoon in September, 1884, I took two slates and determined to experiment alone. I held them together with a small pencil grain between. I was in my library; the slates were taken out of a private box by myself; I glanced at them and placed them in the position above described. In the course of some few minutes I lifted up the slates and examined them, and found the word 'Beware' written in large characters across the under side of the upper slate" (Davey 1887, p. 406). Experiences such as this convinced Davey that he himself pos-sessed mediumistic powers. Sometime afterward he discovered that these previously inexplicable experiences were hoaxes played upon him by his friends.

Davey continued having seances with Eglinton until 1885 when a friend claimed he had seen Eglinton cheating during one of the seances. This inspired Davey to see how much of Eglinton's and other mediums' feats he could duplicate by trickery. When he demonstrated some of his spiritualistic tricks he was surprised by how the onlookers reacted.

> I noticed that many persons made statements concerning my perfor-mances, as to the conditions of the production of the writing, which were just as emphatic as I made in my own reports about Eglinton, and I also noticed that nearly all these statements were entirely wrong. Even when I sometimes revealed the fact that I was merely a conjurer, the reply which I frequently received was something of this kind: 'Yes, you may say it is conjuring, but it could not have been done by that means when I did so-and-so' (describing a supposed test) 'and yet we got the writing all the same.'" (Davey 1887, p. 408)

To systematically explore such reactions, Davey developed a seance consisting of a fixed sequence of demonstrations. He then conducted a series of seances, each one for a small group of individuals including scholars, spiritualists, skeptics, and others. He tried to carry out each seance exactly the same as the others according to his script. After each seance, he requested the attendees to write out, as fully as they could, exactly what they had experienced. Many of these reports are given in full and form the basis for what can still be considered one of the most exhaustive analyses of the fallacies of eye-witness testimony ever undertaken (Davey 1887; Hodgson 1887; Hodgson 1892).

Just about all the distortions of memory and testimony that subsequent psychological research has documented are found in these accounts. Before Davey's experiments had been done, almost everyone, including skeptics and believers, accepted the testimony of ordinary people as being generally credible. Richard Hodgson, in his article introducing Davey's report, described the situation in 1887 in this way:

> Concerning; the physical phenomena of Spiritualism, Mr. A. R. Wallace has said:—"They have all, or nearly all, been before the world for 20 years; the theories and explanations of reviewers and critics do not touch them; they have been tested and examined by sceptics of every grade of incredulity, men in every way qualified to detect imposture or to discover natural causes—trained physicists, medical men, lawyers, and men of business— but in every case the investigators have either been baffled, or become converts." . . . It has indeed been considered by perhaps the majority of Spiritualists, not only that the recorded testimony to these physical phenomena is enough to establish their genuineness, but that any honest investigator might establish their genuineness to his own satisfaction by personal experience. I agreed in great measure with this opinion when, some ten years ago, I attended my first seance; but hitherto my personal experiences, though not by any means extensive, have been almost precisely of the same nature as Mrs. Sidgwick's . . . the physical phenomena which I have witnessed were clearly ascertained by my friends and myself to be fraudulent, or they were inconclusive and accompanied by circumstances which strongly suggested trickery. . . ." (Hodgson 1887, p. 381)

Alfred Russel Wallace, whose quotation begins Hodgson's introduction, was by any standards a smart person and one of the great scientists of all time. In addition to being the co-founder of the theory of evolution by natural selection, Wallace made many outstanding contributions to anthropology and biology in his long career (Kottler 1974; Williams-Ellis 1966). Wallace was also a maverick who supported a variety of controversial political, social,

Why and When Are Smart People Stupid? : 15

and scientific positions (Kottler 1974; Wallace 1875; Williams-Ellis 1966). He was an ardent foe of vaccination and a strong proponent of phrenology. As a result of his experiences at some seances when he returned to England from his long sojourn in the East Indies, Wallace—to the dismay of his scientific colleagues—became a firm supporter of spiritualism. Indeed, he defended even those mediums who had been caught cheating.

As a naturalist, Wallace trusted not only his own observations of alleged psychic phenomena but also those of witnesses. So when many sitters reported seeing their dead relatives materialize at seances, Wallace accepted their testimonies without question. He reported that he had witnessed a medium materialize a six-foot sunflower during a seance and insisted there was no possibility for trickery (Wallace, 1875, 1898). So it is interesting to see how he responded to the original publication of Davey's experiments in the *Journal for the Society for Psychical Research*. The thrust of Davey's report was that a conjuror doing simple tricks could elicit the same testimonials to psychic phenomena that were obtained from seances with allegedly true mediums. At the time that Davey first published his results he did not reveal the secrets of how he had accomplished his seance demonstrations. Davey withheld the explanation of his methods because he intended to continue conducting more experiments. It is in this context that Wallace wrote his letter to the editor of the *Journal for the Society for Psychical Research:*

> SIR,—In the January number of the *Journal* the death of Mr. S. J. Davey is announced, with a complimentary reference to his "experiments," recorded in Vol. IV. of the *Proceedings*. I, and many other Spiritualists, thought at the time that to publish those experiments without any elucidation of them other than Mr. Davey's assertion, that they were all "tricks," was an unscientific and unfair proceeding, since it accepted as evidence in his case a mere personal statement which it has always refused to consider of the slightest value when made by Spiritualists.
>
> Now, however, that further secrecy is unnecessary, I trust that Mrs. Sidgwick, Mr. Hodgson, and other persons to whom . . . Mr. Davey communicated "the details of his methods," will give a full account of them, in order that we who believe that there are genuine phenomena of which Mr. Davey purported to give "trick" imitations, may be able to judge how far this claim is supported by the actual facts of the case.
>
> If such experiments as those recorded at Sittings 11 and 12, and at the materialisation seance are clearly and fully explained as mechanical or sleight-of-hand tricks, available under the conditions usually adopted by professed mediums, it will do more to weaken the evidence for Spiritualistic phenomena than anything that has yet been adduced by dis-

believers. As one of the witnesses says: "I believe that a full explanation of his methods would 'fire a shot heard round the world' in almost every civilised community where the phenomena of so-called 'Spiritualism' are perplexing, and often madden true and good people." . . . But to have this effect it will not do to explain *some* of the phenomena by trick, leaving the more mysterious unsolved. They are claimed to be *all* trick, and unless *all* can be so explained many of us will be confirmed in our belief that Mr. Davey was really a medium as well as a conjurer, and that in imputing all his performances to "trick" he was deceiving the Society and the public. (Wallace 1891, p. 43)

Hodgson (1892) described in detail the methods used by Davey. In the same article, he responds to Wallace's letter. Hodgson points out that in the person of Wallace "there is no more illustrious name than his upon the roll of adherents to a belief in Spiritualism; and his reply is substantially a confession that he cannot distinguish between Mr. Davey's performances and ordinary 'mediumistic' phenomena. But strangely enough . . . Mr. Wallace's conclusions seems to be, not that the analogous phenomena which have been reported about 'mediums' were due to trickery, but that Mr. Davey's performances were 'mediumistic'! . . . we are asked to prove that Mr. Davey was not a medium!" (pp. 254–255).

Even after Hodgson fully revealed the methods by which Davey was able to successfully simulate spiritualistic phenomena, Wallace never wavered in his staunch defense of mediumistic phenomena. He was indefatigable in rebutting every skeptical argument against the reality of spiritualistic and psychic phenomena. Rereading his many interchanges with skeptics today, I am impressed with his ingenuity and cleverness in finding weaknesses in his opponents' arguments. He always found ways to rationalize exposures, confessions, and other actions of alleged psychics and mediums that were embarrassing even to other believers.

We can find reasons for his adherence to otherwise discredited beliefs in the chapters of this book. It is easy to cite personality factors, his prior history with unfair attacks on novel claims, his long isolation from Victorian society, his lack of formal education, and so on. Even using the principle of charity, however, I find it difficult to excuse his support of discredited mediums and his insistence that Davey, despite his claims to the contrary, was really a medium. Even many of Wallace's fellow spiritualists and believers in the paranormal often felt that Wallace was wrong in his support of even the most disreputable medium.

So, can we say that Wallace was a smart person who acted stupidly in this domain? Do we have here an example of expertise that is highly domain-dependent? In the domain of biology and finding and identifying new plants and animals, Wallace had acquired the appropriate tacit knowledge and wisdom. In the domain of psychical research, however, he was certainly foolish in Sternberg's sense and perhaps stupid in the everyday sense.

One new issue that arises, especially with Wallace, is the possibility that smart people can be stupid *just because they are smart*. I conjecture that if Wallace had been somewhat less intelligent and ingenious, he might not have been able to deflect the otherwise strong arguments and evidence against his strong beliefs in spiritualism and phrenology. His intelligence enabled him to devise clever ways to disarm and deflect any attacks on his cherished beliefs.

ARTHUR CONAN DOYLE AND THE FAIRIES

Arthur Conan Doyle was the creator of Sherlock Holmes, arguably the most famous fictional detective of all time. Holmes was the master of careful observation and logical deduction. On the few occasions when he encountered something allegedly paranormal, he managed to debunk it and provide a perfectly mundane explanation. His creator, while sharing many of Holmes's qualities, also differed in important ways (Stashower 1999). Doyle spent almost all the last part of his life promoting the cause of spiritualism and related psychical matters. His two-volume *History of Spiritualism* (1975) competes with Wallace's writings for the reputation of being the most supportive treatises of every spiritualistic claim. Like Wallace, Doyle defended the reality of even those mediums who had been caught in blatant trickery. And, like Wallace, Doyle used his intelligence and cleverness to dismiss all counterarguments.

As is well known, Doyle did not like his fictional detective (Stashower 1999). He felt that the popularity of Sherlock Holmes was interfering with his desire to be known as a serious author of historical fiction. Twice, Doyle actually tried to get rid of Holmes by having him killed in the stories. The public outcry was so great, however, that each time Doyle was forced to resurrect his protagonist. Some commentators believe that in attempting to kill Holmes, Doyle was actually trying to suppress that part of his personality that was skeptical and that stood in the way of his fully believing in psychic and other unlikely phenomena.

Perhaps Doyle's most striking departure from rationality was his support for the reality of fairies. His book *The Coming of the Fairies* (1972) tells the story of two teenage girls who were able to obtain photographic images of fairies while alone in the woods. Doyle includes reproductions of these photos and, in good Sherlock Holmes style, argues for the reality of these fairies.

In another example of perhaps being too "smart" for one's own good,

Doyle wrote a fascinating chapter, in his book *The Edge of the Unknown,* "The Riddle of Houdini" (1970), soon after Houdini died in 1928. In this chapter, Doyle tries to come to grips with what he considered to be both the virtues and vices of this famous magician and spiritualist debunker. In what appears to be the type of argument his famous detective might make, Doyle, step by step, describes Houdini's famous escapes as well as his unrelenting attacks on mediums. From Doyle's viewpoint, Houdini unfairly included genuine mediums along with fake mediums in his attacks. Gradually, and with Holmesian thoroughness, Doyle attempts to show that Houdini had powers that went beyond those of conjuring—that Houdini was in fact a true psychic medium who could accomplish his famous escapes by dematerializing and rematerializing himself. Why, if Houdini possessed such psychic powers, did he devote so much of his life to denying the existence of such powers? The ingenuity of Doyle (Holmes) comes to the rescue. As Doyle develops his case, it appears that Houdini did not want people to know that true psychic powers exist and that he, Houdini, possessed them. If people realized that Houdini was a psychic, they would not give him credit for being a clever conjurer. According to Doyle, Houdini's vanity was such that he wanted to receive credit for being a clever magician. So he denied paranormal powers in both himself and others. Thus Doyle was able to use his smartness to outsmart himself—that is, to maintain his cherished beliefs in spiritualism and fairies.

Conclusions

The question of why smart people can be (or seem to be) so stupid raises a multitude of issues. The chapters in this book are a good start toward bringing up many of these facets. But stupidity is a complex, ambiguous, and vague notion. It is also emotionally charged and socially sensitive. As my additional examples show—and these represent only a minute fraction of the possibilities—as we widen our sample of exemplars, more and more new issues crop up. Despite the fact that this book is only a first attempt to take a serious look at stupidity, and that the contributors differ among themselves on some of the issues, I have a sense that at least some partial consensus and some themes can be found among the chapters, either explicitly or implicitly. I list some of these themes here.

1. *Stupidity contains both cognitive and moral implications.* Recall Köhler's description of how he responds to watching a chimpanzee make a bad or

stupid error. He admits feeling frustrated and angry. Similarly, Dweck and other contributors to this book seem to be implying that stupid behavior is somehow morally wrong because the actor is failing to use her existing abilities to full advantage. The failure or departure for optimal behavior is inexcusable given the knowledge and cognitive capacities of the actor.

2. *Justifiable mistakes and blunders should not be labeled "stupid."* At least some of the authors explicitly or implicitly subscribe to a principle of charity that requires us to withhold attributing stupidity to maladaptive acts for which we can find plausible justification. Moldoveanu and Langer, for example, take the strong position that if we can imagine an alternative construction of the situation for which the given behavior would be normatively correct, then we should consider that behavior rational or reasonable even if that behavior violates the normative standards for the way the observer represents the situation. I suggest that this stance is overly strong for at least two reasons. The first is that our ability to *imagine* a possible scenario in which the actor's behavior is rational does not guarantee that the actor, in fact, was acting according to the alternative representation. Second, even if we can generate multiple representations for a given problem, it does not mean that all representations are equally reasonable. Intelligence and rationality might include the ability to generate the representation that the problem poser has in mind.

3. *Many acts of stupidity, or seeming stupidity, result from mindlessness.* While this seems trivially obvious, we have to be careful about how we explicate this principle. As Perkins and others have noted, because of the limitations of controlled processing, we cannot be mindful of all our actions. Indeed, the overwhelming activity of the brain and cognitive processing occurs outside of conscious control. Some aspects of wisdom, as Sternberg envisions it, and expertise are prototypically automatic, unconscious and "mindless." To preserve our limited mindful processing capacity for important matters, we have no choice but to automate as many mundane processes as possible.

One could argue that it would be stupid to try to be mindful about every situation that we confront. Intelligence and/or wisdom might consist in knowing what to be mindful about and when to delegate processing to mindlessness. Perkins makes the interesting suggestion that it might be possible to develop mindless procedures that actually prevent the sort of folly he discusses.

4. *Many acts of apparent stupidity result from limited or inadequate information and*

resources. The authors who explicitly make this point do not necessarily deny that stupidity can stem from inadequate information and resources. They find such causes uninteresting. However, it would be within the spirit of least some of the contributions to deny the label of "stupidity" to such acts. After all, this can be seen as a justifiable or excusable reason for behaving in a maladaptive way.

Again, we have to be cautious in mindlessly accepting this principle. When Franz Joseph Gall created what later became phrenology, he validated his hypotheses about what function goes with which bump on the skull by observing people under a wide range of settings (Gall 1835). For example, when he thought that the size of a certain place on the skull indicated acquisitiveness, he then looked for people with large bumps in that area and tried to see if they were acquisitive. He also looked for people who had small bumps to see if they were lacking in acquisitiveness. So far as I can tell, Gall kept no written tallies of the results. He relied on his memory to decide whether the correlation between bumps and function existed. When Gall did his research, there was no correlation coefficient, the constructs and procedures for evaluating reliability and validity had not yet been developed, the notion of random and representative sampling as opposed to biased sampling was not available, the need for double-blind procedures was unknown, and the many biases of observation, memory, and testimony had not yet been discovered by psychologists. Gall was badly mistaken in his findings of correlations between function and bumps, but we would not call him stupid because the information and methodologies he needed were simply not available to him.

Many otherwise smart people today find correlations between what alleged psychics say and the events in their lives. They believe these correlations are real despite the fact that the best psychological research consistently finds no validity to what the alleged psychics say. Most of these people also lack the required information to know how their perceived correlations are illusory. It is not so easy to justify their mistakes in this area as it is to justify, for example, Gall's mistakes. Many people today might falsely believe psychics because they lack the necessary information—but such information is available and, at least in some cases, we might argue that they *should* know about it.

5. *Dumb people cannot do stupid things.* None of the authors explicitly state such a principle. I find it implicit in many of their discussions. For example, according to Stanovich, stupid or irrational behavior occurs when an individual violates normative principles in spite of the fact

that she has adequate cognitive capacities for successfully coping with the problem. The irrationality here stems from thinking dispositions and coping styles of the kind discussed by Austin and Deary. Although this is probably inconsistent with folk usage, the implication is that a person who performs a maladaptive act because she has inadequate cognitive capacities is not stupid so long as she is doing the best she can with what she has.

6. *Smart people can be stupid just because they are smart.* I have used the examples of Alfred Russel Wallace and Arthur Conan Doyle to make this point.

Obviously, there is much more to be said about smartness, wisdom, stupidity, and foolishness. This collection of chapters is a welcome start.

REFERENCES

Baum, R., & W. Sheehan (1997). *In search of planet Vulcan: The ghost in Newton's clockwork universe.* New York: Plenum Trade.

Clark, W. Le Gros (1955). The exposure of the Piltdown forgery. *Proceedings of the Royal Institution of Great Britain, 36* (part 1, no. 162), 138–151.

Davey, S. J. (1887). Experimental investigation. *Proceedings of the Society for Psychical Research, IV,* 405–495.

Doyle, A. C. (1970). *The edge of the unknown.* New York: Berkeley [reprint of 1930 publication].

——. (1972). *The coming of the fairies.* New York: Samuel Weiser [reprint of the 1922 edition].

——. (1975). *The history of spiritualism.* New York: Arno Press [originally published in two volumes in 1926].

Fernie, J. D. (1994). In pursuit of Vulcan. *American Scientist, 82,* 412–415.

Fontenrose, R. (1973). In search of Vulcan. *Journal for the History of Astronomy, 4,* 145–158.

Gall, F. J. (1835). *On the origin of the moral qualities and intellectual faculties of man and the conditions of their manifestation.* Boston: Marsh, Capen, & Lyon (in six volumes).

Grosser, M. (1979). *The discovery of Neptune.*

New York: Dover (reprint of 1962 Harvard Press edition).

Hanson, N. R. (1962). Leverrier: The zenith and nadir of Newtonian mechanics. *Isis, 53* (part 3, no. 173), 359–378.

Hodgson, R. (1887). Davey's imitations by conjuring of phenomena sometimes attributed to spiritual agent: The possibilities of mal-observation and lapse of memory from a practical point of view. *Proceedings of the Society for Psychical Research, IV,* 381–404.

——. (1892). *Proceedings of the Society for Psychical Research, VIII,* 253–310.

Köhler, W. (1959). *The mentality of apes.* New York: Vintage Books (translated from the second revised edition of 1927).

Kottler, M. J. (1974). Alfred Russel Wallace, the origin of man, and spiritualism. *Isis, 65,* 145–192.

McClintick, D. (1977). *Stealing from the rich: The Home-Stake oil swindle.* New York: M. Evans.

Stashower, D. (1999). *Teller of tales: The life of Arthur Conan Doyle.* New York: Holt.

Thagard, P., & R. E. Nisbett (1983). Rationality and charity. *Philosophy of Science, 50,* 250–265.

Wallace, A. R. (1875). *On miracles and modern spiritualism: Three essays.* London: James Burns.

——. (1891). Correspondence: Mr. S. J. Davey's experiments. *Journal of the Society for Psychical Research, 5*, 43.

——. (1898). *The wonderful century: Its successes and its failures*. New York: Dodd, Mead.

Weiner, J. S. (1980). *The Piltdown forgery*. New York: Dover (republication of the Oxford University Press 1955 edition).

Williams Ellis, A. (1966). *Darwin's moon: A biography of Alfred Russel Wallace*. London: Blackie & Son, Ltd.

CAROL S. DWECK

2 Beliefs That Make Smart People Dumb

For many years I have studied the beliefs that make smart people dumb—beliefs that make them do dumb things, and also cause them to fall behind intellectually over time. In fact, this has been the central issue in my research: why people who have all the ability one could wish for often don't use it when they need it most and can even lose it (relative to their initially less able peers).

The reason for this, ironically, lies in the very fact that many smart people become too invested in being smart. They think of smartness as something that they have and others don't—as something that makes them special and worthy. As a result, they become too focused on being smart and looking smart rather than on challenging themselves, stretching and expanding their skills, becoming smarter. In other words, they focus on the trait of intelligence and on proving that they have it, rather than on the *process* of learning and growing over time.

As we will see, this mind-set can be self-defeating in the short run and in the long run. In this chapter, I will spell out both the beliefs that make smart people dumb and the more adaptive beliefs that can make people "smarter." I will also cite research in the field of creativity to suggest that many prodigies fizzle out and that many of our most revered creative geniuses, contrary to popular belief, did not start off being particularly smart.

Let us begin by looking at the beliefs that are at the core of smart and dumb behavior.

The Belief That Intelligence Is a Fixed Trait versus a Potential That Can Be Developed

Different people have different views of intelligence (see Dweck 1999). Some think of it as a fixed trait, with each person having a certain finite amount. Some, lucky, people are smart and other, less fortunate, people are not. Since intelligence is usually a highly valued commodity, most people with this view hope they rank among the intelligent.

Other people, in contrast, view intelligence as a potential that can be developed over time. It's not that they see everyone as being the same; they simply emphasize the idea that everyone can become smarter by developing their intellectual potential. For them, then, it's not about ranking among some intellectual elite; it's about working hard, taking on challenges, striving to learn—things that will allow them to grow intellectually.

Which view is correct? As many of you know, psychologists have championed both views. Herrnstein and Murray (1994), in their book *The Bell Curve,* take the position that intelligence is highly resistant to change. But many other traditional and contemporary psychologists (Binet 1909/1973; Brown & Campione 1996; Perkins 1994; Resnick 1983; Sternberg 1985) see much of intelligence as a repertoire of intellectual abilities that can be cultivated over time. Again, these psychologists do not deny the individual differences in intellectual propensities and abilities that exist, but discuss (and show through their research) how intellectual abilities can grow, both through education and personal striving.

The focus of this chapter, however, is not on the true nature of intelligence. It's on the profound consequences of what people *believe* about their intelligence. Once people believe their intelligence is fixed, a number of things start happening, for although they believe their intelligence is fixed, they do not know *at what level* it is fixed. Is it really high or is it disappointingly low?

So they look to their performance outcomes to tell them—but they must try to ensure that every outcome they look at will be an unqualified success. As will be seen, this sets in motion a variety of defensive and self-defeating behaviors, such as a tendency to sacrifice valuable learning opportunities that might expose inadequacies, even when these opportunities may be vital to their long-term success.

In contrast, once people believe that their intelligence is a potential that can be developed, they start focusing, not on the short-term outcomes that might make them look good, but on the effort and strategies that will lead to learning and long-term achievement. I turn now to research that supports and illuminates these ideas.

What Does Performance Measure?

Strictly speaking, performance on an intellectual task, any task, simply measures your performance on that task—the particular skills you brought to bear on those questions or problems at that point in time. It might reflect your actual skill level at that time, but it may have nothing to do with your broader intellectual abilities and it may have even less to do with your intellectual potential, your ability to expand your skills in the future. It certainly has little to do with your worth as a person.

Yet people who believe in fixed intelligence tend to invest many intellectual tasks with the power to tell them about not only their current skills, but also their global intelligence, their future intelligence, and their overall worth.

Those who believe in intelligence as a potential that can be developed (that is, those who believe in *malleable* intelligence) stick closer to the facts. They see their performance on an intellectual task as simply reflecting the specific skills required by the task, as well as the effort and strategies they put into it.

Interestingly, those who believe in fixed versus malleable intelligence do not differ in their basic intelligence, however you wish to define it. Really smart people can hold either belief. Also, most people tend to hold one belief or the other—about 85 percent of people will clearly endorse either fixed intelligence or malleable intelligence. The rest are either undecided or hold a hybrid belief.

The Belief That Performance Measures Intelligence and Self-Worth

Wenjie Zhao, Claudia Mueller, and I conducted a study to find out what bright students thought their academic performance measured. In this study, we gave college students at an Ivy League university some vivid scenarios about intellectual failures and asked them to imagine that these things were happening to them. In one of the scenarios, the student wanted very much to go to graduate school but obtained a really poor score on the Graduate Record Exam; in another the student had searched for a major, found one that he or she really liked, but did badly in a critical course; and in the third, the student performed very poorly on a class presentation in an important class after classmates had done splendidly on theirs. After each, we asked: How would you feel, what would you think, and what would you do? That is, we asked them what the failure would mean to them and what it would do to them.

We then compared the answers given by students who believed in fixed intelligence with those given by students who believed in malleable intelligence. Students who held the view that their intelligence is fixed told us, to a significantly greater extent, that the failure would mean that they were dumb. In other words they would infer that they were intellectually inferior, even though they may have had a lifetime of academic success up to that point. More significantly, many said they would feel "worthless" or "like a complete loser." Not surprisingly, this group, far more than those believing in malleable intelligence, said that they would be devastated and would give up all hope of success in the area.

The students who believed in malleable intelligence reacted very differently. They were certainly not happy about the poor showing and freely expressed their grave disappointment. However, instead of condemning their intellect and their worth, they questioned the way they had prepared for the tasks, they said they would seek information where possible about why they had fared so poorly, and they planned ways in which they could overcome the failures and reach their goal. For them, the failures told them about their current skill level, their strategies, and their effort. Failure meant to them that they needed to do something different in the future to succeed— and, indeed, that is what they intended to do.

Given these dramatic differences in the way these groups responded to the same situation, it is very important to understand the ways in which the two groups were not different. They did not differ in their basic current intellectual skills (which we sampled in a separate session), they did not differ in their confidence in their intelligence when they entered our study, nor did they differ in their overall self-esteem or their level of optimism beforehand. However, in response to the failures (even though these were imagined failures), those who believed in fixed intelligence seemed to lose confidence in themselves and lose heart. Those who believed in an intelligence that could be developed recognized clearly the ways in which they had fallen short, but also saw ways in which they might develop in the future.

Another study, which I conducted with Melissa Kamins (Kamins & Dweck 2000), looked even more directly at the link between the belief in fixed intelligence and the belief that your intellectual performance measures your worth. In this study, again with students at a top university, those who believed in fixed intelligence were highly likely to say directly that they view their academic performance as reflecting their worth as a person. For example, they tended to agree with such statements as: "To be honest, if I didn't do as well in school as I hoped, I'd think less of myself as a person." Those who believed in malleable intelligence tended to disagree with these kinds of statements.

In other words, when people believe that intelligence is a fixed trait, they often see poor performance as indicating that they lack intelligence, and they often see lacking intelligence as signaling low worth as a person. In this way they generalize from an academic outcome to intelligence to worth. In this framework, then, doing well and having intelligence makes you a special and worthy person (perhaps better than others), but doing poorly puts you in the category of the unworthy.

What if we told students directly that a task measured only a specific skill, albeit an important one? Would this prevent them from generalizing from that task to their global intelligence? In a study by Jeremy Stone and me (Stone & Dweck 1998), we examined this question with younger (preadolescent) students. We told them that a task we had brought for them to work on measured *an* important intellectual ability. Later on in the session we questioned them further about what they thought the task measured: that particular ability, their overall intelligence, or their future intelligence. Those who believed in fixed intelligence tended to endorse all three. They said that the task would tell them not only how good they were at those kinds of tasks, but also how smart they were in general, as well as how smart they would be when they grew up. In other words, they were investing the task with the power to measure their enduring intellectual ability even though we had told them no such thing.

In contrast, those students who believed in intelligence as a more dynamic potential that could be developed over time saw the task as telling them only about their current skills on those specific kinds of tasks, but not about their global intelligence and certainly not about their adult intelligence.

Teaching a Belief in Malleable Intelligence

What if we taught people a malleable theory of intelligence? Would this prevent them from seeing a failure as reflecting on their global ability, and instead focus them on effort? Ying-Yi Hong, C. Y. Chiu, Derek Lin, Wendy Wan, and I examined this question in a study of college students at a top university in Hong Kong (Hong et al. 1999). In this study we gave students "scientific" articles that espoused either a fixed or a malleable view of intelligence. Each article described research projects and case histories, but in the fixed intelligence article they were used to document the view of intelligence as a trait that cannot be altered, whereas in the malleable intelligence article they were used to show how intelligence is a potential that can be developed. Half the students read one article, while the other half read the other.

After they finished the article and wrote about it, students went on to another task, one that was quite challenging. How would they think about the fact that this task was quite difficult for them?

The results were clear. Compared to the students who were focused on the idea of fixed intelligence, those who had been taught to focus on malleable intelligence now saw their difficulty as reflecting on their effort and were more persistent in their pursuit of task mastery. This study also showed that the belief in fixed intelligence could be changed and that when it is, people begin to think differently about what their setbacks mean.

In studies with students at Stanford University, Aronson and his colleagues (Aronson 1998; Aronson & Fried 1998) obtained even more dramatic findings. Teaching students the malleable theory of intelligence not only aided their performance in the face of obstacles on an individual intellectual task, it actually raised their college grade point average and their commitment to school.

This means that students who focus on the malleable view of intelligence not only feel better about themselves when they confront challenging work, they also do better. Indeed, in two studies that followed students across a challenging transition to junior high school (see Dweck & Sorich 1999), students who confronted the transition holding a malleable view of intelligence earned higher grades and higher achievement test scores than did their classmates who held the fixed view. This was true even though the two groups of students had entered with equal academic skills (and equal self-esteem).

How does this happen? How does holding a fixed view of intelligence turn into poorer performance and loss of academic standing over time? Let's take a look at some of the ways this occurs.

Sacrificing the Chance to Learn: The Belief That Learning Is Risky

One of the dumbest things people with the fixed view of intelligence do is to sacrifice important learning opportunities when those opportunities contain a risk of revealing ignorance or making errors. Of course, the very idea of learning implies that there is something you don't already know. Yet people who hold the fixed view of intelligence feel they cannot afford to reveal their ignorance and make errors because, as we saw, this can call their intelligence and even their worth into question.

Indeed, we have often asked students to tell us when it is that they feel smart. While people with the malleable view say they feel smart when they are striving to learn or understand something new, people with the fixed view say they feel smart when they are doing something they're already good at (and doing it better than others) (see Dweck 1999).

In many studies, students with the fixed view have told us and showed us that they prefer a safe task on which they can look smart over a more personally challenging task from which they could learn something important (Dweck & Leggett 1988; Stone & Dweck 1998). Even some of the most talented college students with the fixed view, when we ask them, have told us plainly: "If I knew I wasn't going to do well at a task, I probably wouldn't do it even if I might learn a lot from it" (Mueller & Dweck 1998).

Perhaps the most dramatic evidence of this and its maladaptive consequences comes from a study by Hong, Chiu, Dweck, Lin, and Wan (1999). This study was conducted at the University of Hong Kong, which, as I mentioned above, is a top university in Hong Kong. All courses at that university are conducted in English, and all exams and papers are in English. This means that proficiency in English is crucial to academic success, and students there care greatly about academic success.

Yet not all the students arrive at the university with a high level of English proficiency. Naturally, then, the smartest thing would be for students to do everything in their power to make sure their English is good enough for them to succeed academically.

In our study, we surveyed social science students at the University of Hong Kong who were embarking on their first year. They had all taken an English proficiency test, and we knew their scores. We then told them that the faculty of the university was considering offering an English course for students who needed to improve their English skills, and asked them how likely they would be to take such a course were it to be offered.

Of course, the students who were already proficient in English were not highly interested. But what about the students who were deficient in their English skills? What did they say they would do? Well, of the nonproficient students, those who held the malleable theory of their intellectual skills, quite reasonably said they were eager to take the course. However, the students who held the fixed view, even when they needed to take the course, were not eager to do so. They expressed a surprisingly low degree of interest in this opportunity; in fact, their interest was no higher than that of their fellow students who were already proficient.

In short, students who held a fixed view of their intelligence were not willing to take steps to remedy their deficiency even though their success in college might be at stake. How could this be? Perhaps they were not willing to publicly display their deficiency by joining a remedial class. Perhaps they did not consider themselves to be "good at languages" and were not optimistic about doing well in such a course. Whatever the reason, I think we can agree that they were not willing to pursue the smart course of action.

In a second study, we again showed that students who embrace a fixed view of intelligence are not willing to pursue actions that are necessary for their success. They again avoided confronting their deficiency. However, when students were *taught* the malleable view of intelligence, they were then willing to take the steps that were necessary to turn poor skills into better ones.

To summarize, students who hold a fixed view of their intelligence care so much about looking smart that they act dumb, for what could be dumber than giving up a chance to learn something that is essential for your own success? If a valuable learning opportunity contains the risk of errors or requires them to confront a deficiency, they may well sacrifice that opportunity. I believe that this is one of the major ways that smart people can become relatively less smart over time. If others are availing themselves of these learning opportunities and you are simply displaying over and over again the skills you already have, then you will almost certainly lose your edge.

Denying the Power of Effort: The Belief That Effort Is Only for the Incompetent

Many people who hold the fixed view of intelligence hold yet another belief that makes them do dumb things. It is the belief that if you're truly intelligent, you don't need effort. (Or that if you need effort, you're not intelligent.)

Specifically, people who hold a fixed theory of their intelligence agree more with statements like these: "If you're really smart at something, you shouldn't have to work hard at it." "Things come easily to people who are true geniuses." They also agree that " If you have to work hard at something, you're probably not very good at it." In contrast, those students who hold the malleable theory agree instead with statements declaring that even geniuses have to work hard to arrive at their great discoveries or creations (Dweck 1999; Dweck & Leggett 1988).

What's wrong with believing that intelligence makes effort unnecessary? Why is this such a bad belief? Isn't it true that smart people do things more easily than people who are not smart? What is true is that if two people do the same exact task and one requires less effort to do it, that person is probably more skilled at that task at that time.

However, most important tasks in life at some point require a great deal of effort no matter how smart you are. Moreover, as we will see, the experts agree on one thing: motivation (engagement, effort, persistence) is the key to creative accomplishment and even creative genius. Those who believe that smart people shouldn't have to work hard may not put in the work required to accomplish what they're really capable of. That is, they may fail to fulfill their potential.

Indeed, the belief that effort is not necessary for smart people and that needing effort is a sign of incompetence will lead to a host of self-defeating behavior. First, it means that when confronted with a challenge that requires their effort, people who believe in fixed intelligence will start to worry about their intelligence. Just when they need all their resources to figure out how to solve the problem, they will be distracted by concerns about their adequacy.

Second, they may well do something defensive, and unfortunately many defensive things they might do to save face are things that are likely to compromise their performance. For example, they might decide to slacken or withhold their effort, perhaps pretending not to care. While this choice may prevent a "true" assessment of their ability (since, after all, you can't judge the intelligence of someone who didn't really try), it may doom their performance.

This phenomenon is called self-handicapping (Berglas 1990), and it is the tendency to do things that will prevent you from looking like you have low ability, even if these are things that jeopardize your performance. When people self-handicap, it means that they care more about looking smart (or avoiding looking dumb) than about accomplishing something. The more important this something really is, the more we can say that this tendency is truly self-defeating.

Rhodewalt (1994) asked the question: Who are the people who care so much about appearing intelligent that they will actually withhold their effort when these efforts count most? To answer this question, he gave people a self-handicapping questionnaire that asked them how likely they were to do things like not studying enough for a test or leaving important things to the last minute. He also assessed their views of their intelligence. As you might expect, he found that those people who had fixed views of their intelligence were the ones who did these things. It is not that they care less about success. It is simply that they care so much about being intelligent that they do not wish to risk looking dumb by working hard.

Earlier in this chapter we saw that people who believe in fixed intelligence will sacrifice important learning opportunities that might put their sense of their intelligence on the line. Here, we see that people who believe in fixed intelligence sometimes directly sabotage their accomplishments by withholding effort.

Even aside from the fact that effort is nearly always a key ingredient in important, long-term successes, effort is something people should enjoy.

Missing Out on the Pleasure of Effort

Working toward valued goals in life, whether for ourselves or for important others, is something that should be a source of gratification. In fact, when you think about it, being deeply involved in things you believe in—being committed to them—and striving to make them happen gives life much of its meaning.

Yet, in our studies, those who hold a fixed view of their intelligence say not only that they think working hard means a person is dumb, but also that they don't like it. In fact they tell us that one of their main goals is to avoid working hard (Dweck & Sorich 1999). This is no surprise, for if effort undermines your sense of intelligence and even worth, it is bound to become aversive.

I worry about these people. I worry that they will not know the pleasure that can come from sustained commitment and sustained hard work in the service of valued goals. I worry about them when their lives are going well, but I especially worry about them when their lives are not going well—for example, when they are depressed. Most people at some point experience a period of depression, and one of the main characteristics of depression is that everything feels like a tremendous effort. If effort is unpleasant to start with, how much more unpleasant will it be at such times? Some of my current research (with Allison Baer) is looking at just this question: Do people with a belief in fixed intelligence have a harder time getting out of a depression because they cannot make themselves do the things that keep their lives functioning?

I also worry that there are many things in American society that promote the view that smart people don't need to expend effort, for example, the word *gifted*. The word *gifted* implies that some people simply have a gift that makes them able to do things that other people can't: Things should just come naturally to someone who is gifted. Nowhere in this notion is the idea that these people still need to work hard to stretch themselves and fulfill their potential. I am concerned that students who are so labeled will want low-effort tasks, tasks that they can do easily and perfectly, so they can keep proving that they deserve this label. We need a new label, one that still recognizes students who are exceptional but that energizes them to take intellectual and creative risks rather than encouraging them to play it safe.

In summary, people who believe in fixed intelligence often believe that effort is not necessary if you're intelligent and tell us that effort is something they wish to minimize. As we have seen, this may cause self-defeating behavior and may rob them of the gratification that comes from long-term effort in the service of things they value.

Never Knowing What You Could Have Been or Done

Perhaps worst of all, this view of intelligence can rob people of the opportunity to fulfill their potential. If geniuses were simply born and not (also) made, maybe people's theories about themselves wouldn't matter. The ones who were born smart or talented would make the contributions, and the ones who weren't wouldn't. However, as I noted above, creativity researchers agree that motivation is *the* key ingredient in creative contribution and creative genius (Runco, Nemiro, & Walberg 1998; see also Nickerson 1999; Perkins 1994; Weisberg 1999). By "motivation," they mean just what we have been talking about: the ability to commit to a valued goal, the ability to sustain that commitment over time—even in the face of obstacles—and the ability to enjoy the effort and engagement. Let us look more deeply into this.

Converting Intelligence into Genius—Or Not

American society tends to believe that geniuses are born and not made—that people are born with special talents, that these talents are evident early, and that they more or less naturally blossom forth over time. Our great poets, philosophers, composers, and scientists, we believe, were poetic, philosophical, musical, or scientific babies. In fact, we've built whole mythologies about the wondrous things our favorite geniuses did as tots.

The problem is that although some of this may be true, much of it is not. Many of our most hailed geniuses appeared somewhat ordinary as children (Howe 1999). In fact, Charles Darwin's father was disappointed in how ordinary his son seemed as a child (Simonton 1999); yet, as we know, Darwin through his dedication went on to become one of the greatest scientific geniuses of all time. According to Howe (1999), Tolstoy, William James, John Stuart Mill, and Norbert Wiener were also considered to be unexceptional children.

Studies of brilliant musicians reveal a similar pattern. For example, a study of exceptional pianists then in their thirties (Sosniak 1985) asked the question of what set them apart from their peers in their earlier years. The answer was that there were no early indications that they would be the ones to succeed. Indeed, in adolescence their progress had in most cases been no better than that of hundreds of other young pianists. In another study of promising young violinists (Ericcson, Krampe, & Klemens 1993), it was the number of hours of practice, not "innate talent" that predicted skill level. Indeed the literature is full of accounts of talented young people who fizzled out (see, e.g., Howe 1999), yet another testimony to the role of motivation in the development and perpetuation of talent.

Although some of the stories of incredibly precocious feats are true, it turns out that some oft-repeated tales have been fabricated. Moreover, when we identify true instances of child prodigies, we typically find that they had put in thousands of hours of practice. In fact, creativity researchers have come up with what they call the "ten-year rule"—the idea that no truly great creative contributions come without at least ten years of intense effort and preparation (Hayes 1989; see Weisberg 1986). Actually, as Hayes (1989) points out, it often takes ten years for people such as painters, poets, or composers to master the technical expertise of their field and then another ten to arrive at the point where they can make an extraordinary creative contribution (see also Policastro & Gardner 1999).

Mozart is always trotted out as an example of the precocity of great geniuses and while Mozart may have been a performing prodigy, he was by many accounts not a composing prodigy (Bloom 1985; Gutman 2000; Hayes 1989; Weisberg 1999). Although it is wonderful that he was composing anything at an early age, his early compositions were neither original nor noteworthy. They were often pastiches of other composers' efforts, and this is fine, for he was learning the tools of the trade. It is not until the age of twenty-one that his compositions were "Mozart" pieces, ones that are considered masterworks today. This is in no way meant to deny the unique and amazing genius of Mozart; it is simply meant to argue that most of the world's great revolutionary geniuses did not make their contributions without years of previous preparation.

In the same way that early Mozarts were not true Mozarts, we find that early Cezannes were not what we think of as Cezanne, nor were early Coleridges what we think of as Coleridge, and so on. There was a long, intense, obsessive learning period that made these people who they became.

We also tend to think of creative contributions as emerging full-blown from the mind or hands of the creator. Many a cartoon has shown Einstein simply scribbling his immortal equation or Beethoven pouring out his immortal symphonies. Yet, Einstein thought intensely and had frequent meetings with many other scientists for years before his insights took shape (Gruber & Wallace 1999). And Beethoven talked about the long period of time he carried his musical ideas with him, revising them again and again before even starting to write them down (Gruber & Wallace 1999).

Thus creative geniuses were often ordinarily smart or talented people who went for it—who became enraptured or obsessed with something and devoted themselves to it—be it music, science, poetry, or philosophy. They were not people who shrank from challenge or held back their effort for fear of revealing ignorance or low ability. Nor were they people who were daunted by the inevitable obstacles that arise in the pursuit of anything difficult. Instead their extraordinary commitment converted their talent into genius.

In short, a belief in fixed intelligence by creating a concern with repeatedly proving one's ability and one's worth and by fostering the avoidance of challenge, the minimizing of effort, and the withdrawal from difficulty would surely work against the conversion of intelligence into genius. And, once more, what could be dumber than to limit your potential in the areas you care about most?

Making People Dumb by Telling Them They're Smart

Society puts a premium on achievement and the fulfillment of potential. Indeed, countless self-help books have counseled people how to make the most of their talents, and countless childrearing guides have counseled parents how to promote the flowering of their children's abilities. One prevalent view in American culture is that by praising people's abilities or intelligence, one can boost their confidence, increase their motivation, and raise their achievement level.

Although this sounds sensible, we have just seen that people who are too focused on their intelligence can be vulnerable to underachievement. Perhaps the act of praising intelligence when people succeed, rather than boosting self-confidence and achievement, might focus them on measuring their intelligence, worrying about its adequacy, avoiding risk, and questioning their intelligence when they fail. We set out to test this hypothesis.

In a series of studies with preadolescent students, Claudia Mueller and I (Mueller & Dweck 1998) gave students a challenging task to work on. All students succeeded on the first set of problems, and all were praised for their success. However, they were praised in different ways. Some students were praised for their intelligence on the task, some students were praised for their effort (since, as we have seen, achievers are often people who focus on effort), and some were simply praised for their excellent performance. This last group was the "control group," and it usually fell between the other two groups; the first two groups were the ones of greatest interest, and I will focus on these.

It is hard to believe that simply praising differently on one occasion could have much effect, but it had a dramatic effect on students' subsequent thoughts, feelings, and performance. Let's take a look at the many ways it affected them.

First, after their success, students were offered a choice of what they wanted to work on later in the session. Did they want a task that offered an opportunity to learn something new and important, but was quite challenging? Or did they want a safer task, one that ensured success? Most of the students who were praised for their intelligence wanted the latter—the sure thing. They were willing to sacrifice a meaningful chance to learn in order to make sure that they would keep on looking smart. In contrast, 90 percent of the students who were praised for their effort chose the challenging learning task. They were willing to risk mistakes and confusion, for they valued learning over self-protection.

Next, students were given a second set of problems, ones that were much harder. They did far more poorly on these than they had on the first set. How did this difficulty affect them? How did it affect their enjoyment of the task? How did they now feel about their abilities? And how well did they perform on a subsequent set of problems (ones that were very much like the first set)? Again the groups looked very different.

The students who were praised for their intelligence showed a steep decline in their enjoyment of the task once they hit difficulty. They also showed a sharp drop in their desire to take the problems home to practice (which is reminiscent of the students in our previous studies who were not eager to take actions to remedy their deficiencies). In contrast, when students were praised for their effort, they showed *no* decline in their enjoyment of the task despite their experiencing difficulty. In fact, many of them liked the task even better, now that they found it more challenging. Moreover, these students were eager to take the problems home to practice. Some even requested that the researcher write down the name of the task so their parents could get it for them. Thus, when performance is said to be about intelligence, enjoyment rapidly wanes when performance turns poor. When it is simply about effort, enjoyment and engagement remain high.

What did the poorer performance mean to the students in this study? The students who were praised for their intelligence now told us that they thought they were *not* smart and *not* good at the task. In other words, if success told them they were smart, failure was now telling them they were dumb. They had learned to read their intelligence from their performance, just like the vulnerable students we discussed earlier. In contrast, the students who were praised for effort thought their poorer performance simply called for more effort in the future. They did not doubt themselves or their intelligence, but simply concluded that a harder task called for something more from them.

Finally, we gave all students a third set of problems to work on, problems that were equal in difficulty to the first set of problems, on which they had succeeded admirably. The students who had been praised for their intelligence showed a significant decline in their performance from the first set to this third set, and now showed the worst performance of any group. Whether they were defensively holding back their effort or were simply discouraged and debilitated, their performance was dramatically impaired. In some real sense, they were less able than they had been before.

The students who had received praise for their effort showed a significant increase in their performance from the first set to the third, and now showed the best performance of the three groups. Unlike their intelligence-praised classmates, they were inspired by the setback.

We were so startled by the strength of these findings that we repeated the study four times, and got virtually the same results each time.

A few more findings from these studies are worth mentioning. In one of the studies we asked students to write a short paragraph to an unknown student in another school about their experiences in the study. We also asked them to include their scores on the problems. To our amazement, 40 percent of the students who had been praised for their intelligence lied about their score, adjusting it upward in their report to the other student. Very few of the students in the other groups did so. This means that for the intelligence-praised students, their score was such an important reflection of themselves that they felt compelled to enhance it. Again, this is reminiscent of those people we discussed before who equated their performance with their worth.

In two of the studies, we assessed students' beliefs about their intelligence. The question for us here was whether intelligence praise conveyed to students that their intelligence is a fixed trait—that what was being assessed from their performance was their deep, abiding, underlying intellectual skills. In both of those studies we indeed found that students who had been praised for their intelligence believed intelligence was a fixed trait to a significantly greater extent than did students who had been praised for their effort.

Although these were short-term experiments, they demonstrate the dramatic effects that certain key beliefs can have on motivation and performance. Intelligence praise taught students that intelligence is a fixed quality and that it can be measured from their performance. They quickly became afraid of challenge, they sacrificed learning, and they stopped enjoying effort. Not surprisingly, their skills suffered.

In contrast, praise that focused on effort seemed to convey that the task skills were acquirable through effort. These students relished the challenge, wanted to learn more, and sought continued effort. Their task skills, not surprisingly, flourished.

In summary, contrary to popular belief, praising people's intelligence does not fortify them. It might buoy them up temporarily, but it instills beliefs that make them vulnerable. Focusing people on "process," such as their effort or their strategies, is what seems to fortify them. That is, it motivates them in a way that allows them to withstand and even thrive on setbacks. These experiments thus encapsulate the theme of this chapter: an undue focus on intelligence can make smart people dumb; a focus on effort can make people smarter.

Conclusion

In this chapter I have spelled out the beliefs that can make smart people dumb: the belief that intellectual ability is fixed; the idea that current performance measures long-term potential; and the belief that people who are truly gifted don't need effort for their achievements. I have shown how these beliefs can stunt intellectual growth.

I have also spelled out the beliefs that foster the growth of talent and even genius over time: the belief that intellectual potential can be developed; the idea that current performance simply tells you where you are and what you need to do now; and the belief that *everyone* needs sustained effort to realize their potential and make truly noteworthy contributions.

What this really means is that people are, to a large extent, in charge of their own intelligence. Being smart—and staying smart—is not just a gift, not just a product of their genetic good fortune. It is very much a product of what they put into it. It means that being smart is a long process of self-development and self-discovery.

REFERENCES

Aronson, J. (1998). The effects of conceiving ability as fixed or improvable on responses to stereotype threat. Unpublished manuscript, University of Texas.

Aronson, J., & C. Fried (1998). Reducing stereotype threat and boosting academic achievement of African Americans: The role of conceptions of intelligence. Unpublished manuscript, University of Texas.

Berglas, S. (1990) Self-handicapping: Etiological and diagnostic considerations. In R. L. Higgins (Ed.), *Self-handicapping: The paradox that isn't* (pp. 151–186). New York: Plenum.

Binet, A. (1909/1973). *Les idées modernes sur les enfants* [Modern ideas on children]. Paris: Flamarion.

Bloom, B. S. (1985). *Developing talent in young people.* New York: Ballantine.

Brown, A. L., & J. C. Campione (1996). Psychological theory and the design of innovative learning environments: On procedures, principles, and systems. In L. Schauble & R. Glaser (Eds.), *Innovations in learning: New environments for education* (pp. 289–325). Mahwah, N.J.: Erlbaum.

Dweck, C. S. (1999). *Self-theories and goals: Their role in motivation, personality, and development.* Philadalphia: Taylor & Francis/Psychology Press.

Dweck, C. S., & E. L. Leggett (1988). A social-cognitive approach to motivation and personality, *Psychological Review, 95,* 256–273.

Dweck, C. S., & L. Sorich (1999). Mastery-oriented thinking. In C. R. Snyder (Ed.), *Coping.* New York: Oxford University Press.

Ericsson, K. A., R. T. Krampe, & C. Tesch-Romer (1993). The role of deliberate practice in expert performance. *Psychological Review, 100,* 363–406.

Gruber, H. E., & D. B. Wallace (1999). The case study method and evolving systems approach for understanding unique creative people at work. In R. J. Sternberg (Ed.), *Handbook of creativity.* New York: Cambridge University Press.

Hayes, J. R. (1989). Cognitive processes in creativity. In J. Glover, R. Ronning, & C. Reynolds (Eds.), *Handbook of creativity.* New York: Plenum.

Herrnstein, R. J., & C. Murray (1994). *The bell curve: Intelligence and class structure in American life.* New York: Free Press.

Hong, Y., C. Chiu, C. S. Dweck, D. Lin, & W. Wan (1999). A test of implicit theories and self-confidence as predictors of responses to achievement challenges. *Journal of Personality and Social Psychology, 77,* 588–599.

Howe, M. J. (1999). Prodigies and creativity. In R. J. Sternberg (Ed.), *Handbook of creativity.* New York: Cambridge University Press.

Kamins, M., & C. S. Dweck (2000). Theories of intelligence, contingent self-worth, and coping. Unpublished manuscript, Columbia University.

Mueller, C. M., & C. S. Dweck (1998). Intelligence praise can undermine motivation and performance. *Journal of Personality and Social Psychology, 75,* 33–52.

Nickerson, R. S. (1999) Enhancing creativity. In R. J. Sternberg (Ed.), *Handbook of creativity.* New York: Cambridge University Press.

Perkins, D. N. (1994). Creativity: Beyond the Darwinian paradigm. In M. A. Boden (Ed.), *Dimensions of creativity.* Cambridge, MA: MIT Press.

———. (1995). *Outsmarting IQ: The emerging science of learnable intelligence.* New York: Free Press.

Policastro, E., & H. Gardner (1999). From case studies to robust generalizations: An approach to the study of creativity. In R. J. Sternberg (Ed.), *Handbook of creativity.* New York: Cambridge University Press.

Resnick, L. B. (1983). Mathematics and science learning: A new conception. *Science,* 477–478.

Rhodewalt, F. (1994). Conceptions of ability, achievement goals, and individual differences in self-handicapping behavior: On the application of implicit theories. *Journal of Personality, 62,* 67–85.

Runco, M. A., J. Nemiro, & H. J. Walberg (1998). Personal explicit theories of creativity. *Journal of Creative Behavior, 32,* 1–17.

Simonton, D. (1999). Origins of genius: Darwinian perspectives on creativity. New York: Oxford.

Sosniak, L. A. (1985). Learning to be a concert pianist. In B. S. Bloom (Ed.), *Developing talent in young people.* New York: Ballantine.

Sternberg, R. J. (1985). *Beyond IQ*. New York: Cambridge University Press.

Stone, J., & C. S. Dweck (1998). Theories of intelligence and the meaning of achievement goals. Unpublished manuscript, Columbia University.

Weisberg, R. W. (1986). *Creativity: Genius and other myths.* New York: Freeman.

——. (1999). Creativity and knowledge: A challenge to theories. In R. J. Sternberg (Ed.), *Handbook of creativity*. New York: Cambridge University Press.

RICHARD K. WAGNER

3 Smart People Doing Dumb Things

THE CASE OF MANAGERIAL INCOMPETENCE

A provost's term at a major private university was marked by unprecedented success. Eagerly sought by search committees, he accepted an offer to be president of a large state university. By all objective indicators, his success continued. During his presidency, huge increases were achieved in the university's endowment and amount of funded research. Undergraduate enrollment increased, as did the average SAT scores of admitted students. Ranking of program quality by the National Research Council indicated improvement in already high-quality programs for the most part. Yet recently this president resigned under pressure.

When I mentioned this situation to a colleague from a private university in the Midwest, he categorized it as yet another example of a successful administrator from a northern private university falling victim to the politics of a public university system in a southern state.

There may be a bit of truth in his characterization. The president's first public brush with trouble came several years ago, when he was chastised publicly by the chancellor and board of regents for working unilaterally with the state legislature to benefit his university. University presidents are supposed to work exclusively through the board of regents, which represents the entire state university system to the legislature. Although all public institutions in the state are supposed to present proposals to the board of regents, which then negotiates with the legislature, it is no secret that the top administrators of larger schools work hard to cultivate relationships with individual members of the legislature who may be inclined to be helpful. If anything, the president's early trouble arose because he was so successful in working with the legislature for the benefit of his university that he upstaged the chancellor, an individual with no small ego. He rode out the rift with the chancellor successfully, aided by politically powerful backers. Things even began to look rosy when the chancellor accepted a job elsewhere.

The president, a scholar and administrator known for his remarkable intellect, then made several apparent missteps that eventually led to his resignation. First, according to press reports, he used a pejorative term to describe an incoming chancellor in a private conversation at a holiday party for members of his administration. The remark was leaked to the press. Next, news reports indicate that two visiting deans who reviewed part of the university complained to the chancellor and school officials that the president acted like an arrogant, abusive bully in their interactions with him. Then, three weeks before agreeing to resign, the president was reported to have given substantial raises to top administrators without seeking the approval of the chancellor.

Although the specifics of this example are unique (see the note at the end of this chapter for some of the fallout from this episode), at a more general level it is representative of a common phenomenon: a previously successful individual is pressured to step aside after being accused of some surprising lapses in judgment. The purpose of this chapter is to consider alternative explanations for uncharacteristic missteps by characteristically successful individuals. The focus is on the domain of management. Managerial incompetence is a commonplace and costly phenomenon. It also is a phenomenon that most of us have had some personal experience with. The chapter is divided into three sections, each of which provides an explanation for why smart managers do dumb things. The first section addresses practical aspects of management that appear to be somewhat distinct from academic knowledge and abilities. The second section considers the honing effect of experience that leads to the development of managerial expertise. The third section is devoted to aspects of personality and temperament that may result in individuals behaving in ways that are inconsistent with their apparent abilities.

"Book Smarts" versus "Street Smarts" in the Workplace

Neisser (1976) was one of the first modern psychologists to highlight the distinction between "academic intelligence" types of tasks found in the classroom and on IQ tests, and the more practical tasks found in the everyday world. Problems found in the classroom, as well as on IQ tests, tend to:

(1) be well-defined; (2) be formulated by others; (3) come with all information required for problem solution; (4) have one correct answer; (5) have one
or at most several methods for obtaining the correct answer; and (6) be
unrelated to everyday experience (Neisser 1976; Wagner & Sternberg 1985).
In contrast, the more practical problems of everyday life, including many of
the problems encountered in diverse careers, often are: (1) ill-defined; (2)
formulated by the problem solver; (3) missing information essential to solution; (4) characterized by having multiple solutions, each associated with
liabilities and assets; (5) characterized by having multiple methods of obtaining each solution; and (6) related to everyday experience.

THE SCIENCE OF RATIONAL MANAGEMENT

The "book smarts" approach to management, known as rational or technical management, considers problems found in the workplace to be similar
to academic intelligence–type tasks. This approach is characterized by reliance on general problem solving approaches that are applied to all problems without regard to the specific context. For example, in their classic text
on rational management, Kepner and Tregoe (1965) proposed a system for
solving managerial problems that consists of five key principles:

1. *Problems are identified by comparing actual performance to an expected standard
   of performance.* The most important thing effective managers do con-
   tinuously is to compare what should be happening with what is happening. A problem is identified by a significant discrepancy between
   what is happening and what should be happening.

2. *Problems are defined as deviations from expected standards of performance.*
   Problem definition is based on an analysis of the discrepancy between
   actual and expected performance that first alerted a manager to the
   existence of a problem. For example, assume that the normal percentage of defective jeans produced in a Texas plant is 5 percent. If the
   percentage of defective jeans increases to 15 percent, the problem is
   defined as "a tripling in the percentage of defective jeans produced at
   the Texas plant."

3. *Prerequisite to identifying the cause of a problem is generating a precise and
   complete description of the problem.* Describing a problem precisely and
   completely consists of describing four things. What is happening?
   Where is it happening? When is it happening? To what extent is it happening? To provide a boundary for the problem, an effort is made to
   also describe what is not happening, that is, what is not problematical.

4. *The cause of the problem will be found by comparing situations in which the problem
   is found to similar situations in which the problem is not found.* Problems

rarely affect everything. Most problems can be isolated to a particular plant, shift, product, time, and so forth. Searching out potential causes of the problem involves identifying what differentiates the situation in which the problem is found from similar situations in which the problem is not found. For example, searching for a problem isolated to night shift workers would begin with an analysis of differences between day and night shift workers, their supervision, and the nature of their work.

5. *Problems are the result of some change that has caused an unwanted deviation from expectations.* Assuming the problem is of recent origin, something must have changed to produce it. Thus, a quality control problem might have begun when a new employee was hired on the suspect shift. Perhaps the new employee has been poorly trained or is careless.

Rational approaches to managerial problem solving such as those proposed by Kepner and Tregoe (1965) and Plunkett and Hale (1982) have a number of obvious strengths. Because they are explicit, they can readily be communicated to others. Their generality makes them applicable to virtually all problems. This generality is related to the rise of the general manager, an individual who can move from position to position and be an effective problem solver. Relying on general managers provides an organization with considerable flexibility in staffing managerial positions. Another strength of rational approaches is that they are based on principles of logic and scientific reasoning. Managers thus attempt to minimize bias and avoid jumping to conclusions prematurely. They try to generate alternative potential explanations of a problem, and they search for independent confirmation of the explanation they settle on.

Given these obvious strengths, it is perhaps surprising that rational approaches to management have been on the decline. For example, they receive little consideration in handbooks of managerial problem solving (e.g., Albert 1980; Virga 1987). What has been the downfall of rational approaches to management is a growing belief that they just do not work as effectively as alternative approaches actually employed by managers on the job. Effective problem solvers often deviate from rational approaches in significant ways. Mintzberg's (1973) influential studies of what managers actually do, as opposed to what they are supposed to do or what they say they do, showed that managers rarely if ever employed rational approaches. Rather than following a step-by-step sequence from problem definition to problem solution, managers typically groped along, with only vague impressions about the nature of the problems they were dealing with, and with little idea of what the ultimate solution would be until they had found it (Mintzberg, Raisinhani, &

Theoret 1976). Isenberg (1984) reached a similar conclusion in his analysis of how senior managers solve problems. The senior managers he studied did not follow the rational model of first defining problems, next assessing possible causes, and only then taking action to solve the problem. Instead they worked from general overriding concerns, and they worked simultaneously at a number of problems. The senior managers often took action throughout the problem-solving process. In fact, evaluating the outcomes of their preliminary actions appeared to be one of their more useful tools for problem formulation.

In addition to the fact that effective managers do not appear to use rational approaches to management, these approaches have faced growing skepticism about the power of general principles of problem solving in the absence of content knowledge of the problem-solving domain (McCall & Kaplan 1985). Proponents of rational approaches have argued that one of their major strengths is that managers can apply them without having prior knowledge of, or experience with, the problems they confront. For example, Kepner and Tregoe (1965) find it notable that a particular manager was able to solve a problem with "no special know-how or detailed technical information about this problem. He relied instead on a thorough knowledge of the process of problem analysis" (p. 130). However, content knowledge does matter. Evidence of the value of contextually bound knowledge to problem solving is considered later in this chapter.

Yet another problem for rational approaches to managerial problem solving is the recognition that biases and other limitations severely limit the ability of individuals to think completely rationally (see, e.g., Hogarth 1987; Kahneman, Slovic, & Tversky 1982; Nisbett & Ross 1980; Tversky & Kahneman 1983, 1986). Hogarth (1987) provided a catalog of common biases that affect the acquisition of information, the processing of information, and response selection. These biases have been applied to the context of managerial problem solving (Wagner 1991):

Acquisition Biases

Managers must acquire a tremendous amount of information as they attempt to understand the problems they confront. A number of biases can affect their acquisition of information:

1. *Managers overestimate the frequency of occurrence of highly salient or publicized events and underestimate the frequency of occurrence of less salient or publicized events (i.e., the availability heuristic).* Consequently, their view of events associated with the problem to be solved may be distorted.

2. *Information acquired early in the problem-solving process receives too much weight; information acquired late in the problem-solving process receives too little weight.* Managers conceptualize their problems (i.e., develop a problem-solving "set") on the basis of the initial information available to them. Subsequent information is interpreted in terms of the conceptualization that emerged from analysis of the initial information, and thus subsequent information may not receive the weight it should receive.

3. *Managers have difficulty conceptualizing problems in ways that transcend their own prior knowledge and experience.* Consequently, every problem a marketing manager is given is seen as a marketing problem, every problem that a personnel manager is given is seen as a personnel problem, and so on.

4. *Managers discover what they expect to discover.* What managers anticipate influences what they perceive. In addition, managers seek out information that is consistent with their views, and disregard or suppress information that is inconsistent with their views.

5. *When making comparisons, managers give greater weight to the total number of successes rather than to a ratio of the number of successes to the number of successes and failures.* When, for example, managers must decide whom to promote, they tend to evaluate candidates on the basis of the absolute number of previous "hits" (i.e., times when the candidate really came through on an assignment), forgetting to consider a candidate's "misses." Thus, a newer candidate who has had more hits per assignment will lose out to a candidate with a longer, yet poorer, track record.

6. *Concrete information (e.g., personal experience) is given more weight than abstract information (e.g., evaluative reports), even when the abstract information is more valid.* Managers pay more attention to things they observe firsthand, even when what they can observe firsthand presents a less representative picture than that obtainable from other sources.

Processing Biases
Once relevant information has been acquired, it must be processed. Biases that can affect processing include the following:

1. *Managers apply evaluative criteria inconsistently when they must evaluate a number of courses of action.* Because evaluative criteria shift, comparable courses of action are unlikely to be valued equally.

2. *Once an opinion has been formed, it is not likely to be changed even in the face of new information.* Managers quickly become invested in their opinions.

New information that suggests the need to revise prior opinions tends to be discounted.

3. *Managers are not able to estimate the products of nonlinear relations.* For example, a cost that increases exponentially will be underestimated.

4. *Managers are likely to continue using an alternative that has worked before even when it no longer is appropriate.* Personnel managers rely on selection tests as predictors of managerial performance. The predictive power of such tests is modest, at best, yet managers will rely on test scores when making decisions about individuals for whom criterion information is available.

5. *Managers overestimate the stability of data based on small samples.* When managers go beyond qualitative opinion and collect data relevant to solving a particular problem, they are likely to overestimate the stability of the data they have collected.

6. *Managers make predictions by adjusting expectations relative to an anchor without questioning the continued validity of the anchor.* For example, sales managers may set a goal of increasing sales by 10 percent over last quarter, without considering any special circumstances that might have affected last quarter's sales figures.

Response Biases

Managers are prone to two biases affecting their response to problems:

1. *Managers are prone to engage in wishful thinking.* As a consequence, they judge the probability of outcomes they favor to be greater than the data warrant, and the probability of outcomes they fear to be less than the data warrant.

2. *Managers succumb to the illusion of control.* The illusion of control refers to an overestimation of the potency of one's actions. By planning for the future, managers may come to believe that they have more control over future outcomes than they in fact have, and to underestimate the importance of factors such as luck and economic conditions, over which they have no control.

THE ART OF MANAGERIAL COMPETENCE

The growing awareness of the limitation of rational approaches to managerial problem solving has lead to an interest in closer study of the art of managerial problem solving, focusing on how practical competencies are manifested in the workplace. Several alternative approaches for studying the application of practical competence in the workplace are described briefly here. The first approach to be considered, that of Isenberg (1986), suggests that managers deviate from the rational model especially in terms of their propensity to act before the facts are in.

Thinking in Action

Isenberg (1986) studied how experienced managers solve problems, comparing the thinking-aloud protocols of twelve general managers and three college students who planned to pursue business careers. The individuals solved a short business case involving the Dashman company (Harvard Business School Case Services, 1947):

> Mr. Post was recently appointed vice-president of purchasing. The Dashman company has 20 plants, and in an effort to avoid shortfalls in essential raw materials required by the plants, Mr. Post decided to centralize part of the purchasing process the plants must follow. Mr. Post's experienced assistant objected to the change, but Mr. Post proceeded with the new procedures anyway. He sent a letter describing the new purchasing process to plant managers responsible for purchasing, and received supportive letters from the managers of all 20 plants. However, none of the managers complied with the new purchasing process.

The case was presented in parts on cards. The participants attempted to identify Mr. Post's problems and recommend what he should do about them. The experienced managers (1) began planning action sooner; (2) asked for less additional information; (3) made more inferences from the data; and (4) were less reflective about what they were doing and why. In many cases, managers began suggesting problem solutions after reading only half the cards containing the case, even though they were not under time pressure and additional information was available merely by turning over the remaining cards. Thus, experienced managers behaved differently from what a rational model of managerial problem solving would suggest. They were action-oriented very soon into the problem-solving process. Their analyses were cursory, rather than exhaustive, and were based on their personal experience with analogous problems rather than on more formal principles of problem solving. Consistent with Mintzberg (1973), these results suggest that managers are people of action rather than of analysis.

Isenberg (1984) has documented other ways that managers depart from traditional conceptions of managerial problem solving. The traditional view is that managers carefully choose a strategy, formulate well-specified goals, establish clear and quantifiable objectives, and determine the most effective way to reach them. Using detailed interviews and observation, Isenberg demonstrated that senior managers work from one or a small number of very general concerns or preoccupations.

Nonlinear Problem Solving

Solving managerial problems by proceeding linearly through the stages of problem recognition, analysis, and solution is the exception rather than the rule. Problem solving is recursive, with repeated delays, interruptions, revisions, and restarts (Mintzberg et al. 1976). For example, few problems are presented to managers correctly formulated (Mintzberg et al. 1976). Most problems can be formulated in ways that make reaching a solution nearly impossible. Whether a formulation is the optimal one is rarely apparent until attempts have been made at finding and implementing solutions. Thus, solving managerial problems can involve recursive cycles of problem reformulation and solution seeking. Identifying potential problem solutions also becomes a recursive operation. Managers produce solutions bit by bit, as they are guided only by a vague notion of some ideal solution.

McCall and Kaplan's (1985) extensive interviews with working managers confirm Mintzberg's observations about the nonlinear character of managerial problem solving, especially when the problems are important ones. McCall and Kaplan characterize the process as convoluted action. Convoluted action occurs over significant time periods, typically months or even years as opposed to days or weeks. Many people are involved, with different interest groups competing for their stake in the outcome. Convoluted action appears to meet organizational needs in that problems often are caused by— and affect—a web of interrelated groups and individuals in an organization. Solutions to such problems must involve the cooperative efforts of many parties if they are to succeed. Convoluted action provides the opportunity for all interested parties to attempt to influence the process. A disadvantage of convoluted action is the frequency with which the process breaks down before a solution is identified and implemented. Because so many individuals are involved, and because each has the opportunity to derail or at least delay the process, it is not an unusual outcome for a solution to be put on the shelf rather than be implemented, if the process even makes it to the point of solution implementation. Problems are much more likely to be solved through convoluted action if they have a "champion" who refuses to let the problem-solving process derail.

Reflection-in-Action

Schon (1983) proposed that because problems are complex and interconnected and environments are turbulent, rational analytic methods will not suffice. What is required is a manager who can imagine a more desirable future, and invent ways of reaching it. Managerial competence cannot be described easily. Rather it appears as action that is nearly spontaneous, and based more on intuition than on rationality. When asked to explain their behavior, managers either are at a loss for words or will make up an explanation that may be fictitious, perhaps not intentionally, but only in the spirit of trying to satisfy the questioner. According to Schon, "Our knowing is ordinarily tacit, implicit in our patterns of action and in our feel for the stuff with which we are dealing. It seems right to say that our knowing is *in* our action" (p. 49).

Although managers typically are not able to describe accurately how they do what they do, many do occasionally attempt to reflect on their actions as they perform them. These *reflections-in-action* are on-the-spot examination and testing of a manager's intuitive understanding of a situation, often in the form of a reflective "conversation" with the situation (Schon 1983). These reflections are the cornerstones of Schon's analyses. For example, a manager might ask herself why she feels uneasy about a decision she is about to make, or whether she might come up with a new way of framing an intractable problem. Although the practice of reflection-in-action is widespread among managers, they rarely if ever reflect on their reflection-in-action.

Tacit Knowledge

Because the practical problems we face on the job and in everyday life are ill-defined, lacking in essential information, and have no single correct answer, it would seem that they would be nearly impossible to solve. Yet, ordinary people often do quite well at solving practical problems. What appears key is having everyday experience to draw upon. Individuals often have a great deal of specific knowledge they can apply to practical problems, and, as has become clear from countless studies of problem solving, domain-specific knowledge is extraordinarily powerful for successful problem solving. In a series of studies, Wagner, Sternberg, and colleagues have studied practical know-how in the form of *tacit knowledge* (Sternberg & Horvath 1999; Sternberg et al. 1995; Wagner 1987; Wagner & Sternberg 1985). Tacit knowledge refers to practical know-how that rarely is described formally or taught directly (Wagner 1987).

Tacit knowledge has been measured by presenting individuals with scenarios depicting real-world situations and then having them rate the quality of various courses of action. The scenarios were based on interviews with successful managers who were asked to describe important yet characteristic tasks they faced and possible responses to them, as well as some theoretical notions about the nature of practical know-how. An example of a tacit knowledge scenario is presented in Table 3.1. Scoring is done by comparing an individual's responses to an expert key. Studies of tacit knowledge have

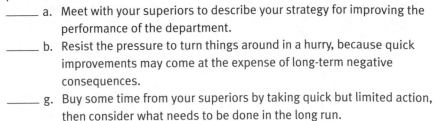

TABLE 3.1. A Scenario Used to Measure Managerial Tacit Knowledge

You have just been promoted to head of an important department in your organization. The previous head has been transferred to an equivalent position in a less
important department. Your understanding of the reason for the move is that the
performance of the department as a whole has been mediocre. There have not
been any glaring deficiencies, just a perception of the department as so-so rather
than very good. Your charge is to shape up the department. Results are expected
quickly. Rate the quality of the following strategies for succeeding in your new
position.

_____ a. Meet with your superiors to describe your strategy for improving the
          performance of the department.
_____ b. Resist the pressure to turn things around in a hurry, because quick
          improvements may come at the expense of long-term negative
          consequences.
_____ g. Buy some time from your superiors by taking quick but limited action,
          then consider what needs to be done in the long run.

been carried out in diverse domains ranging from business management,
sales, academic psychology, and schooling. A number of consistent findings
have emerged from these studies:

1. *Managerial tacit knowledge differentiates experts from novices.* Wagner and
   Sternberg (1985) gave a measure of managerial tacit knowledge to a
   sample of 127 participants that included experienced managers, students in Masters of Business Administration programs, and undergraduate students. Performance on the tacit knowledge measure reliably differentiated the three groups of participants. Wagner (1987)
   administered a different measure of managerial tacit knowledge to a
   similar sample of 159 participants. Again, the three groups of participants differed reliably in managerial tacit knowledge.
2. *Managerial tacit knowledge predicts managerial performance.* Wagner and
   Sternberg (1985) reported correlations between tacit knowledge
   scores and various criterion measures of managerial performance.
   Significant correlations were found between tacit knowledge scores
   and criterion measures including salary, whether one's organization
   was at the top of the Fortune 500 list, annual percentage of salary
   increase (based on merit), and success in generating new business.
   Wagner and Sternberg (1990) found tacit knowledge to be the strongest predictor ($r = 0.61$, $p < 0.001$) of rated performance in managerial simulation exercises for a group of managers who were partici-

pants in a leadership development program at the Center for Creative Leadership.

3. *Managerial tacit knowledge predicts real-world performance independently of IQ and personality measures.*   Scores on measures of tacit knowledge rarely correlate significantly with IQ. For example, Wagner and Sternberg (1985) reported nonsignificant correlations between tacit knowledge and the Verbal Reasoning subtest of the Differential Aptitude Tests of 0.16 and 0.12 for samples of twenty-two and sixty undergraduates, respectively. The correlation between tacit knowledge and IQ for the sample of managers who participated in a leadership development program at the Center for Creative Leadership in Greensboro, North Carolina, was 0.14.

One limitation of these studies involving students or business managers is that such samples are characterized by a limited range of IQ relative to the general population, and perhaps even a limited range in tacit knowledge as well. A limited range of IQ might limit the size of the correlation between IQ and tacit knowledge. However, near zero correlations between IQ and tacit knowledge have been reported even for more general samples. Eddy (1988) obtained scores on a tacit knowledge inventory for business management and on the Armed Services Vocational Aptitude Battery (ASVAB) for a sample of 631 Air Force recruits. The ASVAB is a multiple-aptitude battery used by the armed services to select recruits for all branches of the United States Armed Forces. Prior studies of the ASVAB have shown that it is a typical measure of cognitive ability. Correlations between the ASVAB and other cognitive ability tests are about 0.7, and factor analytic studies show that the ASVAB measures the same verbal, quantitative, and mechanical abilities measured by the Differential Aptitude Tests, and the same verbal and mathematical abilities measured by the California Achievement Tests.

The median correlation between tacit knowledge and the ASVAB subtests was 0.07, with a range of -0.06 to 0.15. Of the ten correlations examined, only two were significantly different from 0 despite the power provided by a sample size of over 600 individuals. Factor analysis of these data yielded the usual ASVAB factors and a separate tacit knowledge factor. The loading of the tacit knowledge measure was 0.99 on the tacit knowledge factor, whereas the maximum loading of the tacit knowledge measure on the ASVAB factors was only 0.06. The use of oblique rotation of factors permitted estimates of the correlations among the ASVAB and tacit knowledge factors. The ASVAB factors were moderately correlated among themselves, as would be expected, but the correlations between the tacit knowledge factor and the four ASVAB factors were minimal (0.075, 0.003, 0.096, and 0.082).

Turning to relations between tacit knowledge and personality, participants in the Center for Creative Leadership study mentioned above completed a battery of personality and interest inventories. These included the California Psychological Inventory, the Myers-Briggs Type Indicator, the Fundamental Interpersonal Relations Orientation—Behavior, and the Kirton Adaptation Innovation Inventory, among others.

Hierarchical multiple regression was used to determine whether the relation between tacit knowledge and managerial performance was independent of relations between personality variables and managerial performance. This was done by adding tacit knowledge last to various batteries of predictors that represented combinations of the various personality variables, interest variables, and IQ that were available. Regardless of which predictors already were in the model, tacit knowledge added significant and substantial predictive power. These results indicate that relations between tacit knowledge and career performance are not subsumed by personality constructs, at least when measured by common personality inventories.

4. *Tacit knowledge appears to be relatively general both within and across career domains, despite its being relatively unrelated to general cognitive ability.* Wagner (1987) used confirmatory factor analysis to test alternative models of relations between tacit knowledge scenarios that measured practical know-how important for managing others, oneself, and one's tasks. The results supported a single general factor. This suggests that people who have a lot of tacit knowledge about one aspect of domain performance, such as knowing how to manage others effectively, also tend to have a lot of tacit knowledge about other aspects of domain performance, such as knowing how to maximize their own productivity and knowing how to perform tasks that are important to doing their jobs well. When undergraduates were given tacit knowledge measures for different domains (e.g., business management and academic psychology), correlations of scores across domains were in the 0.5 to 0.6 range. Thus, individuals who scored well on a tacit knowledge measure for one domain tended to score well on a tacit knowledge measure for another domain. This should not be taken to suggest that all tacit knowledge is general rather than specific. The scenarios used in the tacit knowledge studies that have been described were brief descriptions of common problems with few details provided. It is

entirely possible that detailed scenarios that richly described situations in a particular organization would elicit quite specific tacit knowledge from members of that organization.

The Honing Effect of the Development of Expertise

The research just described suggests that an ability to do well when presented with academic problems is not always accompanied by an ability to do well when confronted by more practical ones. The topic of this section covers a different dimension that further limits the range of domains in which an individual can be highly competent. The research on the development of expertise considered here suggests that experience leading to the development of expertise hones broader abilities into sharper but narrower ones.

Most of us appreciate the range of ordinary levels of performance in a domain enough to recognize and admire extraordinary levels of performance when we see them. Thus, weekend hackers are drawn to the television when a PGA tournament is broadcast. This admiration extends to intellectual accomplishments as well, as when a chess master competes against an entire roomful of skilled chess players simultaneously.

Quantifying just how high a level of performance an individual has achieved on an intellectual task is difficult to do meaningfully. We know that a perfect score (1600) on the Scholastic Aptitude Test (SAT) is a rare event, but exactly how much better is that level of performance compared to a score of 1400? It may be easier to appreciate the incredible range of performance that is possible by turning to simpler intellectual tasks such as digit span. The digit span task is simply to repeat a random series of single digits that one listens to. The digits are presented at a pace—say, 1 per second—that precludes complex rehearsal strategies for most individuals. This task is common to individually administered IQ tests. The typical span for digits is under 10. Yet after rigorous training, exceptionally skilled individuals have attained a digit span in excess of 100 digits (Chase & Ericsson 1981). If we assume a mean of 7 and a standard deviation of 2 for digit span, a span of 100 digits would correspond to an IQ of approximately 800, or an SAT score of roughly 5300!

Digit span involves recall of random sequences of digits presented orally. What would be the maximum possible number of digits recalled if the task were to memorize a single string of digits written down and available to be studied repeatedly? The case of *pi* provides an answer. As you may remember from elementary geometry, *pi* is a constant that most of us know as 3.1416. However, *pi* actually is a nonrepeating string of digits that continues indefinitely. A recent graduate student in our psychology program had memorized *pi* to over 30,000 places, and the current world record approaches 100,000 places!

HOW EXPERTISE IS ACQUIRED

What accounts for the development of extraordinary levels of performance? A complete answer to this question remains well beyond existing knowledge, but some important things are known.

Something that does not accurately predict degree of attainment of advanced levels of performance in a domain is individual differences in initial levels of performance. Hulin, Henry, and Noon (1900) carried out a meta-analysis of predictive validity studies. A meta-analysis is a method for quantitatively combining the results of a large number of studies into a representative composite result. Predictive validity studies are studies in which performance on some predictor, such as performance on the SAT, is used to predict performance on some criterion of interest, such as first-year college grades. The predictors included in the studies ranged from IQ test scores to measures of physical coordination. The criterion measures ranged from grades in college and graduate school, quantitative measures of athletic performance, and rated job performance. The key result was that the validity of predictors of initial levels of performance dropped an average of 0.6 (a huge decrement) for advanced levels of performance. In other words, IQ test scores and other predictors of initial levels of performance are less predictive of later levels of performance.

The development of expertise appears to involve a more intense and sustained application of the same training and acquisition mechanisms that result in more ordinary levels of attainment for the rest of us (Ericsson 1996; Ericsson & Charness 1994; Wagner & Oliver 1996; Wagner & Stanovich 1996). Historically, cognitive abilities such as those measured by IQ tests and expertise have been treated as separate phenomena. Sternberg (1998) has provided an important theoretical framework that encompasses both phenomena in which abilities are viewed as forms of developing expertise. Key characteristics of the acquisition of expertise include the following (Ericsson et al. 1993):

1. Despite folk accounts to the contrary, even the most eminent individuals in science, in sports, or in the arts require a decade or more of intense training prior to achieving world-class levels of performance.
2. All practice and training is not equally profitable. A key appears to be

deliberate practice, which is an effortful and intense regime of training activities designed for the single purpose of improving current levels of performance.

3. Expertise is not acquired cheaply. It requires intense effort, sustained motivation, and sufficient resources, all applied for a decade or more.

In the world of work, very few individuals receive frequent feedback and participate in training activities designed to improve their performance. Most of us receive only yearly performance reviews, the majority of which are exceedingly general. Learning that results in improved performance usually happens informally in the form of learning from one's own experience (Wagner 1991).

THE NATURE OF EXPERTISE

Cognitive studies of expert performance have provided important insights into the nature of expertise. Beginning with de Groot's (1965) seminal studies of chess masters, studies of expert performance expanded to include a wide variety of domains (for reviews see Chi et al. 1988; Ericsson 1996; Ericsson & Smith 1991; Hoffman 1996). Major findings of particular relevance to problem solving include the following (Patel, Arocha, & Kaufman 1999):

1. Experts spend proportionally more time assessing the problem and less time solving it, compared to novices who do just the opposite.
2. Experts recognize and categorize problems on the basis of deeper principles, whereas novices recognize and categorize problems on the basis of surface features.
3. Experts are able to perceive large patterns of information quickly.
4. Experts have superior memory, both short- and long-term, for problem-relevant information.

For present purposes, the most important characteristic of the nature of expertise is that the superior assessment, categorization, perceptual, and memory abilities just mentioned *are restricted to the expert's specific domain of expertise*. Thus, chess masters show superior memory for chess pieces when deployed in game configurations but not for chess pieces deployed randomly.

In summary, the phenomenon of uneven levels of performance for an individual across different contexts—described in the previous section for academic and practical contexts—is exacerbated by the development of expertise. The development of expertise is a process whereby broader abilities are honed to sharper ones in which extremely high levels of performance are manifested in extremely narrow domains.

The topic of this final section is aspects of personality and temperament that compound the problem of uneven performance by leading individuals to behave in ways that are inconsistent even with their uneven abilities. In keeping with the theme of this chapter, the specific focus is managerial incompetence.

In the area of management, studies and surveys carried out over the past three decades provide some data as to the estimated prevalence of individuals who ostensibly are smart yet whose managerial practices are perceived to be wanting in the eyes of their employees. Hertzberg (1966, 1968) reported large-scale studies that indicate between 60 and 75 percent of workers identify their immediate supervisor as the worst or most stressful aspect of their jobs. Based on an evaluation of surveys carried out in a recent six-year period, Hogan, Raskin, and Fazzini (1990) estimated that "between six and seven out of every ten managers in corporate America are not very good as managers" (p. 347).

In a groundbreaking study of managerial failure at Sears and Roebuck, Bentz (1967) reported emotional instability and insensitivity to the needs and expectations of subordinates and co-workers as the most common causes of managerial failure. Insensitivity to the needs and expectations of subordinates is not limited to management at Sears. A Harris poll of 150 top executives and 1,031 office workers documented gaps between the groups in their opinions about what employees value (*New York Times,* June 14, 1988, cited in Hogan et al. 1990). For example, whereas 77 percent of office workers indicated that having a "lot of freedom to decide how they do their own work" was very important, only 37 percent of executives thought this was an important issue for their employees. Honesty was a key issue for office workers, as indicated by the fact that 89 percent of them rated as very important the statement that management be "honest, upright, and ethical in its dealings with employees and the community." However, only 41 percent of the office workers reported that this was actually true of their employers.

What differentiates successful from failed managers was the topic of a study by Lombardo, Ruderman, and McCauley (1988). They studied 169 middle- and upper-level managers, of whom about half (83) were terminated and the other half (86) were performing satisfactorally. All managers were rated by their superiors on 61 items related to managerial performance for the purpose of identifying factors that differentiate successful and failed managers. The characteristics of failed managers that differentiated them from successful managers are displayed in Table 3.2. Of interest is that, with

TABLE 3.2. Characteristics of Failed Managers

1. Unable to build a cohesive team
2. Over- or undermanages
3. Overly ambitious
4. Not supportive, and demanding of subordinates
5. Overly emotional
6. Insensitive, cold, and arrogant
7. Maintains poor relations with staff
8. Has overriding personality defects

Source: Adapted from Lombardo, Ruderman, & McCauley.

the exception of the characteristic of being overly ambitious, all items concerned perceived inadequacies in interpersonal relations with others in the workplace.

Hogan and colleagues (1990) describe three idealized types of individuals who typically rise in organizations before failing, often with catastrophic results to the organization. The *high-likability floater* has a profile on personality inventories of high scores on likability, low to average scores on ambition, and normal scores on other dimensions. High-likability floaters are congenial and charming. They make great dinner companions and entertainers. They are supportive of the organization and others, and never complain or argue. They rise in organizations because they are so well liked. However, they have no real point of view or vision, no agenda, and they do not take a stand on important issues. They accomplish little with the exception of maintaining morale. Eventually, they rise to the point of being in charge of a unit that matters, and their incompetence becomes obvious. However, getting rid of them is very difficult because they are so well liked.

The second type of managerial failure, called *hommes de ressentiment*, refers to individuals who appear on the surface to be composed, socially skilled, and even charming. However, they are motivated by an underlying deep strain of resentment, hostility, and desire for revenge. Such individuals who attain managerial positions tend to be cautious and to make minimal self-disclosures, thereby concealing their underlying resentment. Eventually they get caught in some act that seems totally out of character and unbelievable, but actually it is consistent with their underlying anger.

The third type of managerial failure is the *narcissist*. Narcissism is a well-studied personality disorder that represents a combination of attitudes including feelings of entitlement, exhibitionism, expectations of special privileges, exemptions from social demands, feelings of omnipotence in controlling others, intolerance of criticism, and a tendency to focus on one's own mental products, including viewing contributions of others as extensions of oneself. What makes this type of managerial failure interesting is that narcissists share many of the positive characteristics that are attributed to aggressive managers, athletic coaches, military commanders, and political leaders. Narcissistic individuals tend to be described as appearing self-confident, highly energetic, competitive, achievement-oriented, aggressive, outgoing, and leader-like. By comparison, a twenty-year study of Army brigadier generals yielded comparable attributes including dominant, competitive, action-oriented, and aggressively adventurous (Campbell 1987). However, narcissistic individuals also tend to be egotistical, manipulative, self-seeking, and exploitative. Narcissists do not accept suggestions from others. Doing so might make them appear weak, which conflicts with their need for self-enhancement. Some narcissists have such an inflated self-confidence that they don't believe that others have anything useful to say to them. They also take more credit than they deserve, often at the expense of taking credit for the contributions of co-workers and subordinates. Conversely, they avoid taking responsibility for shortcomings and failures. Narcissistic individuals often are influential in group settings because they have such conviction in the worth of their ideas that others tend to believe them and follow. They also tend to self-nominate, thereby filling leadership gaps that open above them. Narcissistic managers survive as long as they do by currying favor with their superiors. Eventually, they slip and behave in an egotistical way with an important superior or fall in a revolt carried out by exploited subordinates who seize an opportunity.

The importance of these results for the issue of why smart managers behave stupidly is that they add yet another source of disparate performance. Because of characteristics involving personality and temperament, managers may behave in uncharacteristically ineffective ways in some situations.

In conclusion, when one combines the evidence that (1) academic and practical intelligence are not highly correlated, (2) the development of expertise sharpens abilities by simultaneously increasing and narrowing them, and (3) aspects of personality and temperament result in irrational, uncharacteristic behavior, an answer to the question of why smart managers do dumb things emerges: it is virtually impossible for them to do otherwise. Uneven patterns of ability across academic and practical domains are common. Experience leading to the development of expertise hones some abilities to sharp points of superior performance. Finally, on top of this very uneven landscape of ability, nonintellectual factors result in behavior that is uncharacteristic of the individual's competencies.

NOTE

The published account of the former university president suggests a classic case of a downfall that results from somewhat narcissistic tendencies. That an ugly remark about an incoming chancellor made in private was leaked to the press suggests the presence of subordinates who took advantage of an opportunity to damage the former president. In a telling story that followed the announcement that the president would resign, the provost of a neighboring university began by describing to a reporter the many accomplishments of the former president. But interestingly, he went on to recount his first-ever meeting with the former president. At a legislative session, the president came over to the provost and introduced himself by stating, "You're an idiot," apparently a response to anger related to information shared by the provost with the legislature. That the provost would volunteer this story suggests a bit of retaliation for perhaps a perceived mistreatment by the former president, which again is consistent with responses elicited by colleagues of narcissistic leaders. Of course, it is important to point out that this assessment could be completely off the mark. It is based solely on a subjective and cursory analysis of press reports, which rarely provide a complete and fair story. The value of the example of the former president is only to provide an apparent illustration of a common pattern of managerial failure, the validity of which in the present example is unknown.

REFERENCES

Albert, K. J. (Ed.) (1980). *Handbook of business problem solving*. New York: McGraw-Hill.

Bentz, V. J. (1967). The Sears experience in the investigation, description, and prediction of executive behavior. In F. R. Wickert & D. E. McFarland (Eds.), *Measuring executive effectiveness* (pp. 147–206). New York: Appleton-Century-Crofts.

Campbell, D. (1987). The psychological test profiles of brigadier generals: Warmongers or decisive warriors? Address presented to Division 14 of the American Psychological Association Annual Meeting, New York, August.

Chase, W. G., & K. A. Ericsson (1981). Skilled memory. In J. R. Anderson (Ed.), *Cognitive skills and their acquisition* (pp. 141–189). Mahwah, N.J.: Erlbaum.

Chi, M. T. H., R. Glaser, & M. J. Farr (1988). *The nature of expertise*. Mahwah, N.J.: Erlbaum.

de Groot, A. D. (1965). *Thought and choice in chess*. The Hague: Mouton.

Eddy, A. S. (1988). *The relationship between the Tacit Knowledge Inventory for Managers and the Armed Services Vocational Aptitude Battery*. Unpublished master's thesis, St. Mary's University, San Antonio, Texas.

Ericsson, K. A. (Ed.) (1996). *The road to excellence: The acquisition of expert performance in the arts and sciences, sports and games*. Mahwah, N.J.: Erlbaum.

Ericsson, K. A., & N. Charness (1994). Expert performance: Its structure and acquisition. *American Psychologist, 49,* 725–747.

Ericsson, K. A., R. T. Krampe, & C. Tesch-Romer (1993). The role of deliberate practice in the acquisition of expert performance. *Psychological Review, 100,* 363–406.

Ericsson, K. A., & J. Smith (Eds.) (1991). *Toward a general theory of expertise: Prospects and limits*. New York: Cambridge University Press.

Hertzberg, F. (1966). *Working and the nature of man*. New York: Crowell.

———. (1968). One more time: How do you motivate employees? *Harvard Business Review, 46,* 53–62.

Hoffman, R. R. (Ed.) (1996). *The psychology of expertise: Cognitive research and empirical AI*. Mahwah, N.J.: Erlbaum.

Hogan, R., R. Raskin, & D. Fazzini (1990). The dark side of charisma. In K. E. Clark & M. B. Clark (Eds.), *Measures of leadership* (pp. 343–354). Greensboro, N.C.: Center for Creative Leadership.

Hogarth, R. M. (1987). *Judgment and choice.* New York: Wiley.

Hulin, C. L., R. A. Henry, & S. L. Noon (1990). Adding a dimension: Time as a factor in the generalizability of predictive relationships. *Psychological Bulletin, 107,* 328–340.

Isenberg, D. J. (1984). How senior managers think. *Harvard Business Review, 62,* 81–90.

—— (1986). Thinking and managing: A verbal protocol analysis of managerial problem solving. *Academy of Management Journal, 4,* 75–78.

Kahneman, D., P. Slovic, & A. Tversky (Eds.) (1982). *Judgment under uncertainty: Heuristics and biases.* New York: Cambridge University Press.

Kepner, C. H., & B. B. Tregoe (1965). *The rational manager: A systematic approach to problem solving and decision making.* New York: McGraw-Hill.

Lombardo, M. M., M. N. Ruderman, & C. D. McCauley (1988). Explanations of success and derailment in upper-level management positions. *Journal of Business and Psychology, 2,* 199–216.

McCall, M. W., & R. E. Kaplan (1985). *Whatever it takes: Decision-makers at work.* Englewood Cliffs, N.J.: Prentice-Hall.

Mintzberg, H. (1973). *The nature of managerial work.* New York: Harper & Row.

Mintzberg, H., D. Raisinhani, & A. Theoret (1976). The structure of "unstructured" decision processes. *Administration Science Quarterly, 21,* 246–275.

Neisser, U. (1976). General, academic, and artificial intelligence. In L. Resnick (Ed.), *Human intelligence: Perspectives on its theory and measurement* (pp. 179–189). Norwood, N.J.: Ablex.

Nisbett, R. E., & L. Ross (1980). *Human inference: Strategies and shortcomings of social judgment.* Englewood Cliffs, N.J.: Prentice-Hall.

Patel, V. L., J. F. Arocha, & D. R. Kaufman (1999). Expertise and tacit knowledge in medicine. In R. J. Sternberg & J. A. Horvath (Eds.), *Tacit knowledge in professional practice: Researcher and practitioner perspectives* (pp. 75–99). Mahwah, N.J.: Erlbaum.

Plunkett, L. C., & G. A. Hale (1982). *The proactive manager.* New York: Wiley.

Schon, D. A. (1983). *The reflective practitioner.* New York: Basic Books.

Sternberg, R. J. (1998). Abilities are forms of developing expertise. *Educational Researcher, 27,* 11–20.

Sternberg, R. J., & J. A. Horvath (Eds.) (1999). *Tacit knowledge in professional practice: Researcher and practitioner perspectives.* Mahwah, N.J.: Erlbaum.

Sternberg, R. J., R. K. Wagner, W. M. Williams, & J. A. Horvath (1995). Testing common sense. *American Psychologist, 50,* 912–927.

Tversky, A., & D. Kahneman (1983). Extensional versus intuitive reasoning: The conjunctive fallacy in probability judgment. *Psychological Review, 90,* 293–315.

——. (1986). Rational choice and the framing of decisions. *Journal of Business, 59,* 251–278.

Virga, P. H. (Ed.) (1987). *The National Management Association handbook for managers.* Englewood Cliffs, N.J.: Prentice Hall.

Wagner, R. K. (1987). Tacit knowledge in everyday intelligent behavior. *Journal of Personality and Social Psychology, 52,* 1236–1247.

——. (1991). Managerial problem-solving. In R. J. Sternberg & P. Frensch (Eds.), *Complex problem solving: Principles and mechanisms* (pp. 159–183). Hillsdale, N.J.: Erlbaum.

Wagner, R. K., & W. L. Oliver (1996). How to get to Carnegie Hall: Implications of exceptional performance for understanding environmental influences on intelligence. In D. K. Detterman (Ed.), *Current topics in human intelligence* (Vol. 5) (pp. 87–102). Norwood, N.J.: Ablex.

Wagner, R. K., & K. E. Stanovich (1996). Expertise in reading. In K. A. Ericsson (Ed.), *The road to excellence: The acquisition of expert performance in the arts and sciences, sports and games* (pp. 189–226). Mahwah, N.J.: Erlbaum.

Wagner, R. K., & R. J. Sternberg (1985). Practical intelligence in real-world pursuits: The role of tacit knowledge. *Journal of Personality and Social Psychology, 49,* 436–458.

——. (1990). Street smarts. In K. Clark & M. Clark (Eds.), *Measures of Leadership* (pp. 493–504). Greensboro, N.C.: Center for Creative Leadership.

DAVID N. PERKINS

4 The Engine of Folly

Making a Wreck of Things

On a night in mid-March 1999, a truck driver carrying a load of heavy steel bars from a nearby steel plant trundled through the small town of Bourbonnais, Illinois, toward a railroad crossing. At the same time, a train approached the crossing and the gates came down. Apparently the truck driver tried to beat the train by swerving around the closed gates—various reports indicate this, although the driver contested it. Unfortunately, he didn't make it. The train collided with the body of the truck, injuring over one hundred passengers and crew. Some fifty were hospitalized, and eleven were killed. Investigation revealed that he had been driving on a provisional license resulting from a record of speeding offenses.

If events transpired as they appeared to, the driver did something very foolish. He took a chance that put him and others at unnecessary risk, with disastrous consequences. Moreover, his record suggests that such risk-taking was not an isolated incident but part of a pattern of folly.

We should not be surprised. Folly is very much a part of the human condition. Our minds might turn to our own foibles, to those of friends and neighbors and colleagues, or look upward to such high offices as the presidency of the United States without failing to find folly. Lives are not usually at stake, but from time to time they are.

While we should not be surprised, we should be puzzled. How is it that sometimes people who are not particularly foolish do foolish things? Of course, there are regrettable but uninteresting explanations. The person may lack relevant knowledge. Or the person may face a risky situation for the first time and fail to recognize the implications even though perhaps capable in principle of doing so. Although such circumstances arise, arguably they fall short of true folly because the person may not be in a position to do better.

64

In contrast, one might say that folly in a strong sense involves *recurrent foolishness that seems in principle within the intellectual reach of the person to discern.*

Such a characterization drives a wedge between narrower and broader conceptions of intelligence. We would commonly say that the truck driver did something stupid. But this is not so much a comment on the truck driver's IQ as on the general adaptiveness of his thinking and behavior. Some models of intelligence, including the classic conception of IQ, focus on analytical capabilities and efficiency of information processing (e.g., Jensen 1980; Herrnstein & Murray 1994). Other conceptions of intelligence look to a broader range of mechanisms involved in intelligent behavior. For instance, dispositional perspectives foreground not just how well people deal with problems that are given them but their sensitivity to problematic situations and their motivation to engage them thoughtfully (Baron 1985; Perkins 1995; Stanovich 1999). The Triarchic theory of Sternberg looks not only to analytical capabilities but also to creative and practical intelligence, the latter including the good management of one's thinking and behavior in various practical contexts (Sternberg 1985). Perspectives such as these would count the truck driver's conduct as stupid—in the sense of an unnecessary failure to anticipate negative consequences and adjust one's behavior—no matter how he would score on an intelligence test or a test of critical thinking.

Within this conception of folly, it's worth distinguishing two varieties: blind folly and plain folly. *Blind folly* occurs when a capable person appears oblivious to it. This seems to involve deep self-deception. One need not look to clinical circumstances to locate such situations. Writing about organizational behavior, Argyris and Schön (1996) find blindness commonplace. They draw a distinction between *espoused* theories and *theories in use.* They note that people often espouse, for instance, a democratic management style for themselves and others and perceive themselves to be walking their talk, yet they behave in ways that others see as autocratic. Such paradoxes can be accounted for in terms of mental models that drive perceptual filtering to sustain a kind of illusory reality.

Although blind folly is discouraging, even more so is *plain folly.* This occurs when we are not really blind. We can, and perhaps from time to time do, recognize a pattern of behavior as unwise, but we nonetheless persist in it. Such commonplace patterns as procrastination, smoking, ready loss of temper, and so on come to mind. Even the truck driver might fit. Under conditions that did not foster defensiveness, he might admit to himself that racing trains to the crossing is a risky business. Sooner or later the odds might catch up with him.

So blind folly aside, let us focus on the even more puzzling plain folly—

henceforth referred to simply as "folly." What, then, are we to make of this phenomenon of recurrent foolishness with a measure of self-awareness?

It's natural to look for explanations in the particulars of individual character. Some people are weak-willed, one might say. It's natural to look at the emotional side of human nature. Emotions can overwhelm rational judgment. Such considerations certainly help us to understand folly at the level of folk psychology. However, the aim of this article is to critique folk-psychological accounts and suggest an explanation at quite a different level: an engine of folly deeply embedded in the technicalities of how behavior is activated. Here is a preview.

Behavior, the argument goes, is controlled in large part by a relatively simple bottom-up activity switching mechanism. An activity increases in urgency, gradually or rapidly, until it captures control. For example, as thirst increases, water-seeking activities become increasingly likely to secure control of the organism. This mechanism can be called *emergent activity switching*. The dynamics of emergent activity switching are a special case of a general systems phenomenon called *self-organizing criticality*. In this phenomenon, drivers in a system increase in intensity, eventually reaching a tipping point that reorganizes the system into another pattern of activity (Gell-Mann 1994; Waldrop 1992).

Emergent activity switching as a behavioral control mechanism is a simple and serviceable way of guiding behavior in most circumstances. However, in some situations it generates recurrent foolish episodes of behavior that are difficult to change. These include such familiar patterns as impulsiveness, neglect, procrastination, vacillation, backsliding, indulgence, and overdoing something. Although various particular factors contribute to such patterns of behavior, at a general level of analysis they reflect three common shortfalls associated with emergent activity switching:

- *Mistuning,* in which key parameters of the switching process such as buildup time are not well tuned to generate adaptive behavior.
- *Entrenchment,* where a counterproductive pattern of emergent activity switching paradoxically becomes more persistent through a variety of mechanisms.
- *Undermanagement* of the switching process in the moment and in the long term, so that the only mechanisms of control and change are relatively low-level conditioning processes.

There is considerable hope that better self-management can help to avoid folly. However, it's important to ground such management practices in an understanding of the mechanisms involved. Although the term "rational" suits them, appropriate management practices are rather different from what is ordinarily meant by critical or reflective thinking. Rather than focus on matters of alternative hypotheses and supporting evidence, they focus on regulating the distinctive challenges of emergent activity switching. Although such practices bear some relation to folk-psychological concepts like weakness of will, folk-psychological remedies—for instance, trying to exercise more will power—typically lack the practical leverage needed and may even exacerbate the problems.

Self-Organizing Criticality

A piece of chalk squeaks on a blackboard. San Francisco dwellers experience yet another earthquake. A single saucer placed carelessly on the stack of dishes in the sink causes the whole pile to tumble down. At a relatively abstract level of analysis, such vastly different phenomena share a mechanism called *self-organizing criticality* (Gell-Mann 1994; Waldrop 1992).

Consider, for example, the dishes in the sink. As yet another dish goes onto the pile, the forces destabilizing the pile increase. Eventually, they reach a critical point and the pile topples. The criticality is "self-organizing" in the sense that the system converges on the tipping point automatically, as part of the way it works, in contrast with, for instance, a cat knocking the pile of dishes over.

Squeaky chalk and earthquakes work in the same way. A piece of chalk squeaks on the blackboard because the chalk sticks slightly on the surface of the board. As the pressure from the hand holding the chalk builds up over a fraction of a second, the chalk slips, relieving the pressure. Then the force starts to build up again. The same thing happens with earthquakes, as the motion of tectonic plates gradually builds pressures that are eventually released in a quake.

Processes that display the pattern of self-organizing criticality are commonplace in material phenomena. They play a role in the organization of human behavior too, a theme revisited in the next section. It's useful, therefore, to recognize certain broad phases and features within self-organizing criticality (see Figure 4.1):

1. *Buildup.* Drivers build up over time toward reorganization into a new pattern of activity. The drivers can be physical forces or, in the human case, primary drives, motives, even an accumulation of reasons and evidence.
2. *Critical phase.* A period arrives when the system is on the brink of toppling into the new pattern of activity.

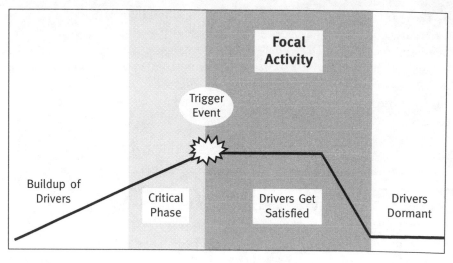

FIGURE 4.1

3. *Reorganization.* At some moment the system reorganizes into the new pattern of activity—for instance, the dishes start to topple. This typically reflects a *trigger event,* one that takes the system past what is sometimes called the *tipping point.* The event can be internal, such as putting that last saucer on the pile of dishes, or it can be external, such as a shout that triggers an avalanche. The same event, internal or external, would have no notable effect were the system not in the critical phase.

4. *Focal activity.* The reorganization initiates a period of activity, such as the pile of dishes tumbling down. This period of activity has a momentum all its own. It's difficult to interrupt and redirect substantially. Imagine trying to stop the dishes from toppling once they have started.

5. *Dormancy.* The activity ends, and for a period all is calm.

While these five features mark the basic pattern of self-organizing criticality, variations can occur. The buildup may be slow or rapid. The critical phase may be long, waiting for the right trigger event, or there may be hardly any critical phase, the system reorganizing into the activity as soon as a threshold is reached. The focal activity can be rapid or prolonged. Buildup may start immediately after the activity phase, as happens with earthquakes or the case of the squeaky chalk. Or there may be a dormancy phase—no more dishes piled on until the next meal.

Patterns of self-organizing criticality also appear in human and animal behavior. Thirst offers a convenient example. As we proceed about our affairs without drinking, the need for water builds. Eventually, the need becomes pressing: We have entered a critical phase where our behavior can easily reorganize into the activity of seeking water and drinking. An external trigger event such as encountering a convenient water cooler may initiate the activity. Lacking such an external trigger, thirst will continue to build until it eventually initiates active seeking of water. Then we find water, we slake our thirst amply, and the need for water enters a dormant state reflecting the surplus of water now in our system.

It is easy to see this pattern of emergent activity switching at work in such animal basics as hunger, thirst, and elimination of wastes. However, the pattern also figures prominently in loftier activities. Consider, for example, preparing for an upcoming interview. For a while, you don't worry about it at all. As the time approaches, it's more and more on your mind. Eventually, you worry enough about it so that you sit down and begin to prepare. The period of preparation continues until you feel secure. Having rendered the worry dormant, you switch out of the preparation behavior, proceeding with other activities until the interview. Or, alternatively, worry may begin to build again as you think of real or imagined shortfalls in your initial preparation.

As this example suggests, emergent activity switching should not be considered an unconscious process. Indeed, it can play out unconsciously or consciously depending on the circumstances, even in the case of a primary drive like thirst. At the unconscious end, one may find oneself heading for a drinking fountain when one sees it, without any particular prior awareness of thirst or conscious intent to drink. At the conscious end, one may be acutely aware of thirst and adopt a range of strategies to suppress the drive until it's convenient to drink.

MECHANISMS THAT CONTRIBUTE TO
EMERGENT ACTIVITY SWITCHING

The general phenomenon of emergent activity switching can occur through the operation of many different mechanisms. Consider again the behavior of seeking a drink of water. The driver might be the buildup of thirst. It also might be increasing awareness that one is about to set off on a hike: best to drink up, even if one isn't thirsty. It also might be the repeated prompts of a parent to "Take a drink before we set off on this hike." The ramp up to the critical phase can take any number of forms.

Buildup basically consists in priming the focal activity or, equivalently, establishing a response set for the focal activity. Primary drives such as thirst can accomplish this. So can deliberate intentions. So can unconscious associations that generate expectancies for a particular behavior (Kirsch & Lynn 1999). The critical phase constitutes a state of high priming for the focal activity. Under such conditions, the focal activity is easily triggered or released. Triggering can occur through pattern recognition of an opportunity for the focal activity, or simply through one or another association that boosts the priming yet more and finally tips the system toward engagement in the activity.

The focal activity, once engaged, continues until the mission is complete or the person gives up or another activity pulls the person away. Completing a mission may be a matter of reaching satiation of a primary drive—the thirst example again. It may be a matter of accomplishing a particular physical or cognitive task—weeding the garden or working out a math problem. The "Zeigarnik effect," introduced by German psychologist Bluma Zeigarnik (1927), avers that an unfinished cognitive task tends to linger near the top of the problem solver's memory until it is resolved. Interruptions take the form of other rounds of emergent activity switching that pull one away from the activity at hand. For instance, the phone rings, very quickly reorganizing most people's behavior into phone answering. An activity may be abandoned because disagreeable aspects of it negatively reinforce efforts to persist, or because we reach the cognitive conclusion that it's not worth doing or that we are not able to do it.

Thus, mechanisms such as drives, intentions, priming, pattern recognition, and satiation in various combinations fill out the details for particular episodes of emergent activity switching. At a more general level, emergent activity switching relates to various models of thought and action that posit a stimulus-response structure in a cognitive context. These include, for instance, production systems (Anderson 1983; Newell 1990), test-operate-test-exit (TOTE) hierarchies (Miller, Galanter, & Pribram 1960), and cognitive agents and agencies (Minsky 1986). All these models posit ample machinery of the mind to allow for multiple driving factors, threshold effects, and the other phenomena of emergent activity switching discussed here.

EMERGENT ACTIVITY SWITCHING
AND RATIONAL MANAGEMENT

To acknowledge the bottom-up character of emergent switching is not to deny the importance of rational management of it. In the case of ordinary thirst, we do not abandon whatever we are doing at the first hint of thirst to search for water. We recognize our thirst approaching the critical phase and try to manage the transition more or less gracefully. We wait for a good moment—when it's appropriate to excuse ourselves or when we're between meetings. The same occurs with preparation for the interview.

Nonetheless, we should not take too much credit for the rational ordering of our lives. Most of the time, we are merely managing the "when" and "how" of a transition driven by an emergent switching process that inevitably plays out its course one way or another. We are not managing the "whether" and sometimes overriding the impulse. However, plainly managing the "whether" is important. Indeed, there are situations where even the impulse to drink needs to be overridden for a long time, as when the only water available is seawater.

But why should things work this way, with buildups that lead to somewhat managed transitions? Emergent activity switching appears to be a highly adaptive way of resolving what behaviors to execute when. Forget for a moment that we like to think of ourselves as intelligent organisms capable of managing our behavior in global, planful top-down ways. Perhaps I am not so mindful this week, or sleepy today; or perhaps I am a dog or a cat instead of a human being. Emergent activity switching keeps me drinking when I need to drink, without reliance on self-knowledge and panoramic planning.

The convenience and efficiency of emergent activity switching is hard to gainsay. I don't have to monitor deliberately whether I'm thirsty. My body tells me. I usually don't even have to make a rational master plan for the various events upcoming on my calendar. I can "trust my worry" to prompt me to get moving on each of them with enough lead time, so long as I don't forget about them altogether. Finally, it is important to recall Herbert Simon's (1957) and others' arguments for the limited rationality of human beings. According to this perspective, we lack the central processing capacity and cognitive architecture to optimize our affairs. We must "satisfice," getting along well enough. Emergent activity switching, especially *managed* emergent activity switching, is a good way to satisfice.

Emergent Folly

While generally effective, emergent activity switching is also from time to time an engine of folly. Indeed, it is not difficult to tell the story of the truck driver and the train wreck from the perspective of self-organizing criticality. The driver approaches the crossing, perhaps slowing down as he sees the gates lower. But he's eager to get on with his job. Here's that train delaying him. Well, the train is a good way off yet. The impulse builds. What the heck. His behavior reorganizes into a swerve-around-the-barriers-and-beat-the-train activity. Only he doesn't beat the train.

What went wrong with emergent activity switching in this case? The urge to beat the train built up rapidly and strongly. Perhaps, if the driver had had a day full of other delays, he was already in a critical phase of impatience. In any case, the rapid buildup allowed little time for self-management. Moreover, given the driver's previous record, management of emergent activity switching may not have been his strength.

The truck driver example suggests that one can analyze various kinds of folly in terms of shortfalls in emergent activity switching. Several familiar shortfalls follow, each with a brief analysis in these terms.

IMPULSIVENESS

The truck driver's behavior falls into this category. Other typical examples of impulsiveness include inappropriate loss of temper, misplaced spontaneous remarks that hurt people or reveal confidential information, hasty purchases, and the like. Impulsiveness reflects a rapid and strong buildup of drivers, with minimal management. Besides rapid buildup, impulsiveness also can occur when a person is already in a critical phase, for instance, when a rough day has brought someone to the point of ready anger. The buildup has already happened, and all that's needed is a trigger event.

NEGLECT

Typical examples of neglect include not studying for exams, not attending to health needs, not having a will made, and the like. Whereas impulsiveness involves acting too hastily, neglect involves acting too late or not at all. Neglect reflects buildup that is too slow and that perhaps never reaches the critical phase. Often a lack of motivating stimuli in the environment figures in this—the "leaky roof" syndrome, where you don't want to fix the roof while it's raining, and when it's not raining the leaky roof doesn't bother you.

PROCRASTINATION

Typical examples of procrastination involve active avoidance of study, of breaking up a relationship, or of having a medical symptom checked. Like neglect, procrastination involves not getting to something. Unlike neglect, procrastination entails not simply ignoring but actively avoiding the matter in question. Accordingly, procrastination depends on a suppressed buildup of drivers. For instance, one rationalizes a medical symptom, saying, "It's probably just a cold. I'll go to the clinic the week after next if it doesn't go away." Suppression is itself emergent, triggered by a buildup of fears that launch defensive rationalizations.

VACILLATION

Vacillation involves dithering to excess over a decision—to invest or not, marry someone or not, buy that car or not, take that stance or not. Sometimes you're feeling "yes," sometimes you're feeling "no," but you can't seem to settle for long on one path. Vacillation can involve overtly changing paths—for instance, rearranging the living room furniture endlessly to try to hit on the "right" configuration—or it can involve decisions made mentally but not yet acted upon.

From the perspective of emergent activity switching, vacillation resembles the chalk squeaking on the blackboard, but with two competing activities in play. Drivers build up recommending path A, so I choose A (in actuality or in a mental try-it-on-for-size way). But choosing A satisfies the drivers to some extent, allowing other competing B drivers to become salient and build up, perhaps switching my allegiance to B, and so on.

BACKSLIDING

Backsliding occurs when we adopt a new practice—of health, work, human relations, or whatever nature—and then after a period of success lapse back into the old practice. Structurally, backsliding resembles vacillation. If I commit myself to a new path and advance along it for a while, I have satisfied some of the drivers. So other drivers (including simply "force of habit") from the original pattern can recapture my behavior. Meanwhile, the drivers that originally initiated the new behavior may no longer be present. This commonly happens in professional development programs, where consultants and advisors at first provide frequent reminders but later disappear from the scene.

INDULGENCE

Indulgence implies a pattern of excess, as in snacking or watching TV too much. Substance addictions can be viewed as extreme physiologically driven cases of indulgence. Characteristically, indulgence involves a frequent and overly strong buildup that initiates the focal activity more often than would be desirable; drivers are hard to satisfy fully, so the activity continues longer than would be desirable. Thus, for instance, one eats too often and too much. Patterns of indulgence often gain even more of a grip because of escapism: the drivers include not only the pleasure of the activity but respite from troubles, including respite from worry about the indulgence itself.

Indulgence throws into relief the limits of typical management of emergent activity switching. Common experience teaches that it's not easy to manage patterns of indulgence. Despite the best intentions, the drivers build up to a critical phase and tip behavior into the problematic activity. In general, self-management is more successful in creating reasonably well-timed and organized transitions (you don't interrupt a meeting to eat chocolate cake) than it is in contravening an impulse altogether (you end up eating the cake after the meeting).

OVERDOING

Sometimes people overdo an activity—say, working to excess on a paper or the preparation for a presentation or an interview. Overdoing is like indulgence except that the activity is seen as effortful rather than pleasurable. The drivers are harder to satisfy than they ought to be. The person feels compulsively driven to do more. For instance, a person may be unduly anxious about the difficulty or importance of an interview, recognize this, and nonetheless overprepare.

WALKING THE EDGE

In this pattern of behavior, a person tries to avoid a problematic behavior but skirts the edge of it frequently and sometimes tips into trouble. An example would be chronically filling one's time with commitments. Most of the time you get away with it, but every now and then you have to rescind a commitment despite the awkwardness this entails. Much of the time you feel too rushed. From the perspective of emergent activity switching, walking the edge involves a laudable try at self-management: holding one's behavior just short of a critical phase. But folly lurks behind this gesture of self-management. Walking the edge almost inevitably leads to falling over from time to time. Of course, this is not necessarily folly if "falling over" is an infrequent and low-cost event, a price worth paying, so to speak. But often this is not the case.

Faults in the Engine of Folly and How to Repair Them

Impulsiveness, neglect, procrastination, and the rest differ from one another in our experience of them and in exactly what goes wrong. But they share the feature of an emergent activity switching process that has gone wrong in one way or another. Generalizing from the examples, three sources of folly can be identified. *Mistuning* concerns maladaptive rates and intensities of buildup and persistence. *Entrenchment* concerns ways in which a particular switching pattern, even though counterproductive, becomes more potent over time. *Undermanagement* concerns the relative absence of supervisory management of the switching process. For each of these three, there are strategies that might reduce folly.

MISTUNING

Whether folly or reasonably adaptive behavior occurs depends on relatively automatic matters of timing and intensity in buildup toward the critical phase and in persistence of the focal activity. Consider anger, for instance. If aggravating circumstances prime displays of anger too quickly and strongly, the resulting hair-trigger outbursts may do great harm. People will be asking, "Why doesn't so-and-so learn to keep the cork in?" However, just as inappropriate anger can constitute folly, so can inappropriate calm. In some situations, displays of anger are apt, for instance, blatant cruelty or violation of human rights. If such circumstances leave a person perpetually unmoved, this is a quiet kind of folly.

Many factors influence the pace and magnitude of buildup: the stimuli in play, the history of conditioning, automatization, inhibitions, and more. Likewise, underpersistence and overpersistence in a focal activity have various causes. For example, underpersistence may reflect a misjudgment about "how much is enough" or premature quitting because of the self-attributions of an "entity learner," who codes difficulty as a reflection of possessing inadequate intelligence (Dweck 1975; Dweck & Bempechat 1980). Overpersistence may reflect anxiety about performance or physiological delays in registering satiation of a drive like hunger.

Experience tunes better the parameters of most episodes of emergent activity switching. However, tuning can take a long time. Many of us know people who "had a short fuse" or "tried too hard" but have mellowed with the years. If only they had mellowed sooner!

One can accelerate the process. Problems of mistuning can benefit from direct attention through changing the environment and deliberate conditioning strategies. For one example, medical researchers conducted a study addressing risk factors for people likely to develop heart disease (Barth 1999). Half the participants carried in their wallets an ultrasound image of one of their major arteries and placed a copy of the picture on their refrigerator doors. The presence of these reminders led those participants to quit smoking, lose weight, and start exercising more than the participants without the pictures. One can easily interpret this result in terms of emergent activity switching. By shifting the saliency of cues in the environment, the intervention changed the level of activation of competing drivers and thus altered behavior.

Another effective way to retune likely patterns of response in advance is to develop *implementation intentions*. These are specific plans for following through on a general goal. For instance, a person having difficulty facing up to the need to make a will might make specific plans for when and how to go about it. Research shows that the formation of implementation intentions greatly increases the likelihood of follow-through on general goals (Gollwitzer 1999).

ENTRENCHMENT

As if mistuning did not pose enough problems, a counterproductive pattern of emergent activity switching can become more persistent. For various reasons, experience over time sometimes entrenches maladaptive patterns rather than eliminating them. Several factors contribute to entrenchment.

- Retuning in response to the negative reinforcement provided by unfortunate outcomes has to battle with the tendency to automatize the particular pattern of switching itself. Every time the pattern occurs, it becomes more fluent.
- Some activities lead to powerful positive reinforcement even when "our better selves" see them as undesirable—for example, smoking.
- Some behaviors are reinforced by affording escape from anxieties about those very behaviors, as alcoholics or food or drug addicts indulge in part to forget their worries over their addictions.
- A history of failures to manage the folly can yield "learned helplessness" regarding the activity: one decides one cannot manage it and gives up (Seligman, Maier, & Solomon 1971).
- One can try too hard to suppress an undesired activity. Research has shown that in certain cases, efforts to suppress a behavior actually prime it further, making its activation more likely (Kirsch & Lynn 1999).

As with mistuning, recognizing the challenges of entrenchment leads to ways to reduce it. Clinical psychologists list a number of relevant strategies (Kirsch & Lynn 1999). These include, for example, avoiding extreme efforts to control troublesome behaviors, which may backfire by priming them; setting expectations for incremental gains so that small steps are seen positively rather than negatively; using "paradoxical injunctions" that allow either progress or backsliding to be framed as positive gains in control; and deconditioning stubborn responses through relaxation techniques.

The discussions of mistuning and entrenchment emphasized that neither need be left to its natural course. Both can be managed through techniques such as changing the environment and deconditioning. Failure to do so constitutes one kind of undermanagement.

Besides long-term management of emergent activity switching, it's also possible to manage the moment—or fail to do so. When we feel ourselves becoming irritable, we can try to step out of the situation, metaphorically or sometimes literally. When we feel an outburst in the making, we can engage in the classic strategy of counting to ten. When we discover that we're about to give up on an important task, we can try to motivate ourselves with a pep talk.

Unfortunately, managing the moment is not easy. People may be too absorbed in the situation itself. They only recognize later that they might have tried to take themselves in hand, or they recognize this fleetingly but cannot summon enough focus to try. Even when they do try, they may not be successful in overriding the momentum of emergent activity switching.

However, people can strive to invest more in managing the moment and be smarter about it. One can cultivate alertness to typical situations, such as the strong and rapid buildup of drivers. Once alert to undesirable scenarios, one can do any number of things. Many tactics of this sort are familiar. The classic "count to ten" method for controlling anger generalizes to introducing any sort of delay that might sidetrack the behavior that's about to tip into action. In the same spirit, one may lure oneself away from an activity by substituting another, or may restrict the activity by establishing time or resource limits. One can encourage engagement in a hard-to-start activity by taking a couple of initial steps or promising oneself a reward.

The idea of management of emergent activity switching may seem paradoxical. Does it posit some kind of executive homunculus with a mechanism of activation that's different from emergent activity switching? In fact, there is no need for such a homuncular executive. Management of emergent activity switching can occur through additional episodes of switching that accompany the main episode. To return once more to the example of anger, a buildup of anger can institute buildup toward another behavior: suppression of anger. If we have our timing right, suppression routines kick in before the anger blasts off. All this aligns with contemporary views that treat self-regulation as a process that can be as automatic as the processes that get regulated externally (Kirsch & Lynn 1999).

The Folk Psychology of Folly

One hardly need turn to ideas like self-organizing criticality and emergent activity switching to find an account of folly. Ordinary folk psychology—the psychology of everyday intentions, will, motives, and so on (e.g., Dennet 1984)—has a good deal to say about folly. For example, it's commonplace to attribute folly to weakness of will, overwhelming emotions, mindlessness, or irresponsibility.

These folk-psychological explanations for folly raise several questions. How well do they explain folly? What practical leverage do they afford? What does emergent activity switching add to our understanding, beyond technical jargon? And finally, are there ways in which folk psychological explanations actually exacerbate folly?

WEAKNESS OF WILL

Weakness of will is one of a folk-psychological cluster of concepts that foreground psychological forces of one sort or another—will, force of habit, and motives that push and pull us, that we resist or to which we submit (Lipson & Perkins 1990). Moreover, this is a folk-psychological concept with an ancient pedigree. Plato held that to truly understand the good is to enact it. However, Aristotle posited a gap between understanding and action: one can understand the good and not muster one's energies to follow through because of *acrasia*—roughly, weakness of will. Likewise, when people fail to control impulses or when they procrastinate or indulge, we often diagnose a weak will.

Even in its own terms, weak will offers an incomplete account of folly. We suspect weakness of will when someone cannot resist doing something bad or cannot persist in doing something good, but not usually when the person persists in doing something that would be good were it not overdone. For instance, when a person overprepares for an interview, an author fiddles endlessly with a manuscript, or a parent hovers anxiously over a child, we do not normally attribute these follies to weakness of will. When a person persists in advancing his or her agenda at the expense of others, we sometimes view this as a form of folly and speak of the person as strong-willed or willful.

Besides offering an incomplete account of folly, will is a problematic construct in any case. The will involved in a potential action might be interpreted as the strength of the intention to carry it out. According to a review by Gollwitzer (1999), strength of intention correlates with actual behavior but accounts for only 20 to 30 percent of the variance in following through. Moreover, conscious intentions arguably do not cause behavior

directly at all. Various studies suggest that conscious intentions to act immediately do not initiate the action but rather reflect a process already set in
motion at a nonconscious level. Conscious intentions about future actions
can create a response set, making the occurrence of the action more likely,
but again they do not directly cause actions.

However puzzling the will may be, it invokes the general idea of self-
regulation. Self-regulation is a more viable concept, not subject to concerns
about intentions causing actions, and leaving ample room for unconscious
and automatized self-regulative mechanisms as well as conscious and deliberate ones. Management of emergent activity switching is a case in point.

Heuristically, weakness of will appears to be a concept that does more
harm than good. As a self-attribution, it is likely to create expectancies
against successful self-regulation that function like self-fulfilling prophecies.
In this spirit, Lipson and Perkins (1990) argue that it's less effective to think
in terms of strength of will than of "strategic use of the will"—instead
of trying to overpower a troublesome tendency, try to configure the environment and your expectations and practices in order to undermine the
tendency.

OVERWHELMING EMOTIONS

Folk psychology also attributes folly to overwhelming emotions. Thus
one may be seduced by temptation, driven by ambition, lured by a promise,
compelled by fear, and so on. Such language reinforces the force motif
alluded to earlier—the psychological pushes and pulls that one submits to
or resists.

Conceptually, it certainly makes sense to speak of emotions as stronger or
weaker. Indeed, emergent activity switching allows for drivers that bring a
focal activity to the critical phase more or less quickly, as well as factors that
promote or undermine the persistence of the activity once engaged.

Even so, like the idea of the weak will, the notion of overwhelming
emotions lacks generality in explaining folly. While some kinds of folly
conspicuously involve strong emotions, others do not. The driver of acute
thirst can lead to the folly of drinking seawater, yet one does not normally
call such a driver an emotion. Moreover, another familiar aspect of the force
theory of folk psychology—force of habit—plays a common role in folly.
When Americans driving in England find themselves dangerously slipping
into the right-hand lane, it's not because they feel some passionate attrac-
tion. It's a conditioned reflex.

Like the idea of the weak will, heuristically the concept of overwhelming
emotions appears to do more harm than good. In fact, it leads one back into
the vexing area of the will. If you are at risk of falling into temptation, is this

because your will is too weak or the emotion too strong? Moreover, if you opt for "emotion too strong," then what? We usually view emotions as absolutes: one feels what one feels. So it seems that the only recourse is to muster an even stronger will.

MINDLESSNESS

Yet another folk-psychological attribution looks for the causes of folly in a failure of attention. We speak of overlooking the obvious, getting distracted, going along in a cloud, being out of touch, muddling through, and express in other ways the idea that people often are not dealing with the world as alertly as they might, and paying the costs thereof.

Ellen Langer's and others' development of the concepts of mindfulness and mindlessness offers a formalized version of such ideas (Langer 1989; Salomon 1983). According to Langer, mindfulness is a state of mind that features readiness to draw novel distinctions, explore new perspectives, and display sensitivity to context. In contrast, mindlessness involves fixed mindsets formed prematurely, ready overgeneralization, automaticity, and actions that reflect a single perspective. Studies by Langer and her colleagues make a case for the reality of such states of mind.

Mindfulness and mindlessness show a clear connection to emergent activity switching. The more mindful one is, the more one is in a position to manage the process rather than just let it happen. In the mindless state, behavior is more likely be governed by the native parameters of drivers cued by a particular situation.

From a heuristic standpoint, certainly some folly can be blamed on mindlessness, and cultivating mindfulness seems like a good idea in many situations. However, mindfulness also has its drawbacks. First, mindfulness is difficult to sustain. It's the nature of the organism to automatize in order to reduce cognitive load, and it's generally adaptive to do so. It is easy to be mindful for a moment, especially a critical moment, but trying to sustain mindfulness is a formidable challenge, like trying to remain vigilant for extended periods of time. With this caveat in mind, the way to subdue recurrent folly may often be to mindfully introduce responses that defeat the threat and strive to make them automatic.

Second, as with weak will and overwhelming emotions, the notion of mindfulness does not encompass the scope of folly. Much folly occurs not because one lacks awareness of what's going on but because factors lure and nudge and tip one into unwise activity despite knowing what's going on. Although mindlessness leads people to respond automatically and mindfulness encourages them to manage their behavior, that isn't necessarily enough to explain why folly occurs.

Still another folk-psychological explanation for folly accuses the perpetrator of irresponsibility. Such an attribution characterizes the person as not sufficiently invested in something for which he or she should take responsibility.

One problem with the concept of irresponsibility is that it has several variants. The truck driver, for example, certainly could be said to have acted irresponsibly. This might mean that the truck driver did not care about other people's well-being sufficiently to watch out for them. It might mean that the truck driver did not try to override his own impulsiveness, a concern that correlates with the "weak will" and "overwhelming emotions" categories. It might mean that the truck driver did not pay enough attention to his actions and their likely consequences, a problem of "mindlessness." It might mean all these things.

In other words, "irresponsibility" is a vague diagnosis, at great remove from mechanism. While alluding to an insufficient investment, it leaves unspecified just where the critical investment should have been made.

In summary, folk psychology offers several ways of interpreting folly. These perspectives allow some degree of operationalization, although often with crucial changes. Nonetheless, folk psychology's prescriptions for coping with folly tend to do more harm than good. Apart from technical problems with their underlying concepts, they are limited in scope. They also often lead to self-attributions and attempted practices that are vague and even counterproductive, establishing expectancies that may aggravate rather than reduce the problem and involving strategies that may be difficult to sustain.

Social Folly

Social folly addresses folly on a social scale, from families to organizations to cultures and nations. It is certainly reasonable to expect folly, as analyzed here, to occur on a social scale. Individual folly is grounded in systems-level phenomena such as buildups, critical phases, and trigger events. While the particular drivers, critical phases, and triggers are different on a social scale, much the same dynamic is in operation.

Emergent activity switching is indeed apparent on a social scale, and in many adaptive ways. For instance, the early signs of an epidemic constitute drivers that rapidly activate a number of counteroffensive coping mechanisms modern societies have developed. The assertive actions of environmentalists over past decades, for example, have prompted a range of shifts in laws, policies, and practices in the United States and some other countries. Within a corporation, increased competition from a rival firm may provoke a chain of adaptations around efficiency, advertising, and diversification. To be sure, sometimes such shifts in activity occur through the decision making of a chief executive or decision making body such as a legislature, but many changes occur in a rather distributed way. Even when a chief executive or small decision making body is involved, that entity rarely acts unilaterally but in response to a range of drivers within the local culture.

If emergent activity switching is in play at all, naturally it will go wrong from time to time. One compendium of folly in this context appears in historian Barbara Tuchman's (1984) book *The March of Folly*. According to Tuchman's definition, historical folly involves decisions that do not represent a single voice, with at least one voice foreseeing the dire consequences. Among the follies she discusses are the involvement of the United States in the Vietnam war and the British monarchy's handling of the American colonists in ways that led predictably to a revolution Britain could not quell in the long term.

The Watts riots of 1965 and those in 1992 provoked by the acquittal of police accused of brutalizing Rodney King can also be considered examples of impulsiveness on the social scale. Similar to individual impulsiveness, they involved a rapid buildup through strong drivers, with minimal mechanisms of management. They differ from calculated social protest in their blindly destructive character, which injured the very communities where the rioters resided.

Although the dynamic pattern of impulsiveness applies to these episodes, the term "impulsiveness" arguably does not. In its particularities, impulsiveness concerns individual human beings and their self-regulation or lack thereof. In discussing analogs of common types of individual folly at the social level, it's not implied that the usual labels apply in a seamless way, only that the underlying dynamics are the same at a structural level.

In this spirit, and despite the progress environmentalists have made, problems of the impact of human population increase and industrialization can be viewed as a long-term case of procrastination. Recall that individual procrastination involves deferred action despite drivers that prompt action resulting from various suppression and displacement mechanisms. Likewise, on the scale of national environmental policies, while some scientists and environmentalists argue for long-term risks and advocate strong self-management by society, other interests marshal defensive forces that question whether there is a problem at all, how serious it is, whether stringent remedies are truly needed, and so on, thereby preventing societies from shifting into a fully responsible pattern of managing environmental concerns. To be sure, one cannot predict how badly this will turn out and, consequently, how great a folly this could be, but at least one can say that it is a candidate for about as big a folly as one could imagine.

The 1986 *Challenger* disaster provides a case of what is called "walking the edge," with some elements of procrastination. The space shuttle *Challenger* exploded about a minute after launch, killing its crew. The explosion reflected the failure of an "O-ring" designed to provide a critical seal. The O-ring proved fragile in the cold 36-degree ambient temperature at launch. As analyzed by Starbuck and Milliken (1988), this disaster was preventable. Engineers from Morton Thiokol, the company responsible for the solid rocket boosters, had raised concerns for some time about the adequacy of O-rings under conditions of low temperature. This concern was investigated to some extent, without decisive results and in an unreceptive atmosphere: Morton Thiokol management naturally wanted their product to look good, and NASA felt political pressure to proceed with their launch program. In a crucial teleconference the day before the tragic launch, Morton Thiokol management and NASA representatives discussed the danger. Initially, and reluctantly, both Morton Thiokol and NASA participants agreed that the flight had to be delayed. But possible alternative interpretations of the warning signs were brought forward. Eventually, the Morton Thiokol management overrode their engineers' concerns and recommended proceeding. After all, the O-rings had performed adequately on previous launches, even in cold weather. Unfortunately, they were walking too close to the edge.

With such examples at hand, it also makes sense to ask whether the three basic mechanisms of folly—mistuning, entrenchment, and undermanagement—also have their social analogs. Again, the answer appears to be yes. Mistuning seems apparent in the abrupt and destructive race riots, the limited attention to environmental concerns, and the underreaction to engineers' cautions about the O-rings. Entrenchment seems most pertinent to the environmental and *Challenger* examples. Around environmental concerns, it is easy to become complacent in the face of a seemingly endless debate, but such complacency contributes to the status quo. Regarding the *Challenger* disaster, Starbuck and Milliken (1988) note how a history of getting away with small risks created an inappropriate confidence that things would be all right. Undermanagement appears throughout these examples in the absence of a regulatory mechanism with the insight and power to stand back, recognize the dynamic in play, and make deliberate adjustments.

With folly clearly positioned as a general systems phenomenon, it should come as no surprise that the engine of folly has other manifestations besides shifts in individual and social patterns of action. Folly as conceived here—blind folly or plain folly—occurs whenever an adaptive system, which normally relies in part on emergent activity switching as an effective mechanism, suffers in particular cases of switching too early, too late, persisting too long, and so on. An entire class of examples can be found among the so-called autoimmune diseases, including, for example, pernicious anemia and some types of hepatitis and arthritis. The diseases are caused by overreactions of the immune system, which ends up attacking healthy elements of the body. Other examples appear in ecologies, which may, for instance, underreact to an invasive organism from another part of the world.

Over time, through evolution and other adjustments, such systems are likely to become better tuned. However, they are born blind. They lack the kind of highly developed regulatory mechanism that can stand back, anticipate the problem, and deal with it. The immune system is incapable of saying to itself, "Wait a minute; I'm attacking my own cell-brothers. Let me manage things differently." Elm forests have no way of noticing Dutch elm disease and concluding, "We better work harder on this one."

Sometimes it seems that human beings do little better than elm trees. The engine of folly has its way with trees and people alike. Although we are not born blind to folly, we can easily become blind. In cases of plain folly, we try to do better, but often we are not wise enough about how emergent activity switching works. Instead, we think of our difficulties in terms of weakness of will, overwhelming emotions, mindlessness, and similar constructs that, although pertinent in limited ways, miss the crux of the phenomenon. Thus folk psychology erects a barrier to more effective self-regulation in much the same way that people's naïve conceptions of phenomena in physics erect barriers to understanding scientific theories (e.g., Gardner 1991; Gentner & Stevens 1983; Perkins & Simmons 1988).

Erratic though the track record is, managing the engine of folly at individual and collective levels is a much more promising enterprise for human beings than for trees. We can learn to do better by managing moments of switching and through longer-term efforts to retune and avoid entrenchment. We have the cognitive equipment to make serious and far-reaching efforts to regulate emergent activity switching at individual and social levels, with insight and finesse. The better the underlying dynamics of the process are understood, the better a position we will be in to make the necessary regulations.

REFERENCES

Anderson, J. R. (1983). *The architecture of cognition*. Cambridge, Mass.: Harvard University Press.

Argyris, C., & D. A. Schön (1996). *Organizational learning II: Theory, method, and practice.* New York: Addison-Wesley.

Baron, J. (1985). *Rationality and intelligence.* New York: Cambridge University Press.

Barth, J. D. (1999). Research presented on April 29, 1999, at the American Heart Association meeting in Boston, MA, as reported in *Science News, 155*(19), 302.

Dennett, D. C. (1984). *Elbow room: The varieties of free will worth wanting.* Cambridge, Mass.: MIT Press.

Dweck, C. S. (1975). The role of expectations and attributions in the alleviation of learned helplessness. *Journal of Personality and Social Psychology, 31,* 674–685.

Dweck, C. S., & J. Bempechat (1980). Children's theories of intelligence: Consequences for learning. In S. G. Paris, G. M. Olson, & H. W. Stevenson (Eds.), *Learning and motivation in the classroom* (pp. 239–256). Hillsdale, N.J.: Erlbaum.

Gardner, H. (1991). *The unschooled mind: How children think and how schools should teach.* New York: Basic Books.

Gell-Mann, M. (1994). *The quark and the jaguar: Adventures in the simple and the complex.* New York: Freeman.

Gentner, D., & A. L. Stevens (Eds.). (1983). *Mental models.* Hillsdale, N.J.: Erlbaum.

Gollwitzer, P. M. (1999). Implementation intentions: Strong effects of simple plans. *American Psychologist, 54,* 493–503.

Herrnstein, R. J., & C. Murray (1994). *The bell curve: Intelligence and class structure in American life.* New York: Free Press.

Jensen, A. R. (1980). *Bias in mental testing.* New York: Free Press.

Kirsch, I., & S. J. Lynn (1999). Automaticity in clinical psychology. *American Psychologist, 54,* 504–515.

Langer, E. J. (1989). *Mindfulness.* Menlo Park, Calif.: Addison-Wesley.

Lipson, A., & D. N. Perkins (1990). *Block: Getting out of your own way.* New York: Lyle Stuart.

Miller, G. A., E. Galanter, & K. H. Pribram (1960). *Plans and the structure of behavior.* New York: Holt, Rinehart, and Winston.

Minsky, M. (1986). *The society of mind.* New York: Simon & Schuster.

Newell, A. (1990). *Theories of cognition.* Cambridge, Mass.: Harvard University Press.

Perkins, D. N. (1995). *Outsmarting IQ: The emerging science of learnable intelligence.* New York: Free Press.

Perkins, D. N., & R. Simmons (1988). Patterns of misunderstanding: An integrative model of misconceptions in science, mathematics, and programming. *Review of Educational Research, 58*(3), 303–326.

Salomon, G. (1983). The differential investment of mental effort in learning from different sources. *Educational Psychologist, 18,* 42–50.

Seligman, M. E. P., S. F. Maier, & R. L. Solomon (1971). Unpredictable and uncontrollable aversive events. In F. R. Brush (Ed.), *Aversive conditioning and learning.* New York: Academic Press.

Simon, H. A. (1957). *Models of man: Social and rational.* New York: Wiley.

Stanovich, K. E. (1999). *Who is rational? Studies of individual differences in reasoning.* Mahwah, N.J.: Erlbaum.

Starbuck, W. H., & Milliken, F. J. (1988). Challenger: Fine-tuning the odds until something breaks. *Journal of Management Studies, 25,* 319–340.

Sternberg, R. J. (1985). *Beyond IQ: A triarchic theory of human intelligence.* New York: Cambridge University Press.

Tuchman, B. (1984). *The march of folly.* New York: Knopf.

Waldrop, M. M. (1992). *Complexity: The emerging science at the edge of order and chaos.* New York: Simon & Schuster.

Zeigarnik, B. (1927). Uber das Behalten von Erledigten und Unerledigten. *Handlungen Psychologisches Forschung, 9,* 1–85.

OZLEM AYDUK & WALTER MISCHEL

5 When Smart People Behave Stupidly

RECONCILING INCONSISTENCIES IN SOCIAL-EMOTIONAL INTELLIGENCE

A curious discrepancy exists between everyday experience and the widespread belief that intelligence is a broad, generalized attribute that characterizes a person consistently. The latter suggests that a smart person should generally be smart; the former makes it clear that smart people often behave in remarkably stupid ways. Recent documentation comes in the painful details of President Clinton's sojourn to impeachment (Marrow 1999). Even more surprising, if less publicized, was the fall of Sol Wachtler, chief judge of the State of New York and the court of appeals, to incarceration as a felon in federal prison. Judge Wachtler was well known for advocating laws to make marital rape a punishable crime, and he was deeply respected for his landmark decisions on free speech, civil rights, and right-to-die issues. After his mistress left him for another man, however, Judge Wachtler spent thirteen months writing obscene letters, making lewd phone calls, and threatening to kidnap her daughter. His descent from the court's bench as the model of jurisprudence and moral wisdom to federal prison testifies that smart people are not necessarily consistently so across different areas of their lives: as novelists (even if not all social scientists) have long known, smart lives are not without their stupid episodes. Although stupidity on the part of generally competent people can take endless forms and produce all sorts of unfortunate outcomes, in this chapter we focus on those "stupid behaviors" in which people undermine the pursuit and achievement of valued long-term goals by failing to control or forgo immediate temptations and impulses—as when the tobacco addict, coughing with emphysema, lights another cigarette after having solemnly resolved to never do so again.

Multiple Determinants of Stupid Behavior

As with any behavior, when smart people behave in stupid ways, there are usually many contributing factors, including the construals, expectations, beliefs, and values relevant to the choices and temptations these individuals confront and create (Mischel & Shoda 1995). For example, both the president and the judge may have been guided by a sense of self-entitlement—of being special and therefore immune from the consequences of their behavior. They may have not expected to be found out. Speculation aside, Clinton repeatedly told the public that he saw his affair as part of his private life, believing that it had neither moral nor legal implications for the presidency. Likewise, after his verdict, Judge Wachtler complained that his punishment was incommensurate to his crime, resenting the attorney who sought incarceration for him rather than psychological treatment (Wachtler 1997). Apparently, he had seen his behavior as minor threats of revenge with no real intention to harm. In his view, they were petty crimes of a person who needed psychological help at worst. Given such construals and beliefs, strenuous self-control may not have seemed necessary either to Clinton or to Wachtler.

Hillary Clinton's preferred explanation for her husband's infidelity, however, was that it was "a sin of weakness": an inability to control himself despite his best intentions (Blitzer 1999). Similarly, Wachtler attributed his own behavior to his problems with an uncontrollable romantic obsession (Caher 1998). Such explanations illustrate yet another reason why smart people can engage in self-defeating behavior: the failure to exert self-control or "willpower" despite knowing and wanting to do "the right thing."

Demystifying Willpower

Like Hillary Clinton, the ancient Greeks attributed failures in self-control to a character trait: *akrasia,* or "deficiency of the will." Although the notion of willpower as a character trait persists in contemporary lay accounts and psychological theories, it is no more informative now than it was 2,500 years ago. While trait accounts describe failures of control, they do not explain them and they fail to address the processes involved in exerting (or failing to exert) willpower. The major concern in this chapter is to shed light on how people can transcend the temptations of the here and now, exert control in the service of long-term goals, and outsmart their own tendencies to behave stupidly just when they need to be particularly smart.

How does the dieter prevent himself from succumbing to the steaming slice of pizza in front of him, the AA member resist taking up the bottle again, or the teenager pause in the heat of the moment to put on a condom? Initial insights to these critical questions came from a series of studies involving four-year-olds, edible treats, and a bell.

In this procedure, known as the delay of gratification paradigm (e.g., Mischel & Ebbesen 1970; Mischel, Shoda, & Rodriguez 1989), a young child is shown some consumable that he or she desires, for example marshmallows or pretzel sticks. A dilemma is presented: wait until the experimenter returns and receive two of the desired treats or, alternatively, ring a bell and the experimenter will come back immediately—but then only one treat will be obtained. Most children prefer the larger outcome, and commit to wait for it. As the children actually begin to wait for the experimenter to return to the room, however, the delay becomes increasingly difficult because of the growing frustration and temptation to ring the bell and take the immediately available treat.

For the young child, this type of conflict, when it is carefully structured in age-appropriate ways, is utterly real and involving and has yielded a route to examine the underlying processes systematically. Although this method is simple in its structure, it has been found to tap the types of skills and self-regulatory strategies crucial for impulse control and for persisting with willpower or "strength" in the face of temptation.

Studies of the delay situation have shown large individual differences in children's willingness and ability to delay. In follow-up studies continuing into participants' early thirties, these differences in the number of seconds children were able to wait for the preferred but delayed treats turned out to be remarkably indicative of important social and cognitive outcomes in later life. For example, these studies revealed that the longer a preschooler waited for the delayed treats, the higher his or her SAT scores tended to be a dozen years later, and the more he or she exhibited effective, planful, goal-oriented behavior as well as personal and cognitive efficacy both in adolescence and in adulthood (e.g., Ayduk et al. 2000; Mischel, Shoda, & Peake 1988; Shoda, Mischel, & Peake 1990).

Given that behavior in this situation has much diagnostic value, the question becomes: What is happening psychologically that makes some children ring the bell quickly and others wait for what seems forever?

Pictures in the Head:
The Role of Goal-Related Mental Representations in Delay

Understanding the transition from the young infant, who has virtually no impulse control and delay ability, to the adult who must have at least some self-control to survive, is one of the greatest challenges for students of human development. When the caretaker ceases to be constantly available and responsive, the young child's need to delay gratification soon becomes indispensable. Freud (1911/1959) was one of the first to try to understand what enables delay of gratification to become manageable in the course of development. He theorized that when delay is externally imposed, the young infant forms realistic "hallucinationary" images of the physically absent objects of desire and cathects energy onto them; these images provide some time of temporary gratification that allows "time binding" and are the first steps toward making delay bearable. In a similar vein, but in a very different language, learning theories suggest that both animal and human organisms reinforce their own delay behavior by anticipating the delayed reward they expect to receive in the form of "fractional anticipatory goal responses." Thus, both the psychodynamic and learning approaches imply that internal or mental representations of the desirable features of the delayed outcomes mediate progress along the route to a delayed goal (see Mischel 1974, 1996).

Despite much theorizing, however, the effects of mental representations in making delay of gratification manageable were never experimentally tested in either tradition (see Mischel 1996). This is understandable given the difficulty of measuring and testing such internal representations objectively. In an attempt to examine whether mental representations of the delayed rewards mediate the ability to delay gratification, a delay experiment was conducted with young children at age four—the point in development at which delay of gratification is assumed to develop. In this experiment both the delayed and the immediate rewards were either exposed and available for attention or covered and thus unavailable for attention (Mischel & Ebbesen 1970). In two other conditions, either the delayed or the immediate reward was exposed while the other was covered. It was reasoned that children would be more likely to form a mental representation of the rewards if the rewards were exposed during the delay period than if they were covered. The results showed that, contrary to the predictions of psychodynamic and learning approaches, children who were exposed to the rewards (whether they were the delayed ones, the immediate ones, or both) were able to wait only for a few minutes. In contrast, they waited over eleven minutes on average when both the delayed and the immediate rewards were obscured from view.

To get a possibly closer approximation of internal representations or "mental images" (in a sense, "pictures in the head"), in the next phase of the research the delay procedure was repeated but with an important difference. Instead of waiting while facing the actual rewards, children were shown pictures of the reward objects they were waiting for on a slide projector (Mischel & Moore 1973). These slides depicted realistic, life-sized pictures of the reward objects. In this situation, then, the image of the rewards was present for attention even though the rewards themselves were physically absent. The results with these images were the opposite of those found with the actual objects: whereas exposure to the actual rewards made it difficult for children to delay, exposure to the pictures or the images of the delayed objects made the waiting task easier for them.

To further explore this reversal, another study investigated the effect of pictorial mental representations of rewards on delay (Moore, Mischel, & Zeiss 1976). In one condition, the experimenters presented children with the actual rewards but asked them to "put a frame around them." In another, they showed the children pictures of the rewards but asked them to imagine that they were real. The findings indicated that regardless of whether the children were looking at the real rewards or at the pictures, thinking about them as real made it harder to delay whereas thinking about them as pictures made it easier to wait.

Why did representing the rewards as pictures make it easier for children to wait? Drawing on the distinction between the motivational (consummatory, arousal, action-oriented) function and informational (cognitive cue) functions of a stimulus (Berlyne 1960; Estes 1972), it was reasoned that the actual rewards or their mental representations by the child as real may have made the arousing, consummatory features of the delayed outcomes more salient, increasing the conflict between their opposing desires to wait for the larger reward and to take the immediately available treat. The heightened difficulty of the delay task under such circumstances may have eventually led to a failure of the regulatory system. In contrast, the pictures of the rewards or their mental representations as pictures may have emphasized the cognitive, informational features of the rewards rather than their consummatory features. After all, as one child noted, "You can't eat the picture." Focusing on the nonarousing aspects of the rewards may have reduced the conflict between wanting to wait and wanting to ring the bell, decreasing the frustration of the delay situation and making it easier for children to wait.

Hot/Cool System Analysis of Delay of Gratification

Drawing on diverse areas of research on self-regulation, and consistent with the reasoning and the findings presented, two systems have been proposed to account for self-regulatory behavior: an emotional "hot" system and a cognitive "cool" system (Metcalfe & Mischel 1999). The hot system is an emotional "go" system, specialized for quick reactions to strong, emotion-provoking stimuli that trigger pleasure and pain. It is fully developed at birth, and in current neural models its processing has been associated with the amygdala (Gray 1987; LeDoux 1996; Metcalfe & Jacobs 1996, 1998). Once activated, hot system processing calls for instantaneous action: rapid hot reactions to appetitive and sexual stimuli, and the automatic enactment of defensive reactions when faced with threat. Similar to what Freud (1911/1959) referred to as the "id," the unconscious structure of the mind that responds to sexual and aggressive impulses and seeks immediate gratification or tension reduction, the hot system is under stimulus control (e.g., the steaming pizza for the dieter, the cocaine for the drug addict). Put another way, it responds to consummatory aspects of the stimulus, and motivates individuals for the ultimate goal response (e.g., ringing the bell and eating the pretzels).

The cool system, on the other hand, is an emotionally neutral "know" system—cognitive, complex, and contemplative—that develops with age. It is attuned to the informational, cognitive, and spatial aspects of stimuli and generates rational, reflective and strategic behavior. This system is thought to be associated with hippocampal and frontal lobe processing, two structures of the brain that, like delay ability, begin to develop around the age of four (Metcalfe & Mischel 1999).

The hot/cool system analysis makes the specific prediction that focusing attention on the consummatory features of the delayed rewards should activate hot system processing and hinder delay, whereas focusing on its informational, abstract, cool features should activate the cool system and enhance delay. Data that support the predicted effects of "hot" and "cool" representations on delay come from a study in which some children were cued to think about the exposed rewards in one of two ways. Some children were instructed to think about the cool, abstract qualities of the rewards— for example, by thinking about the marshmallows they were waiting for as puffy, round clouds. Other children were told to think about how sweet and chewy the marshmallows would be in their mouth, thus activating a hot representation of the rewards. As expected, when children thought about the rewards in hot terms, they were able to wait only for five minutes, whereas when they thought about them in cool terms, delay time increased to thirteen minutes (Mischel & Baker 1975).

Overall, the evidence reviewed so far shows that regardless of the objective situation (i.e., whether one's temptations are present or absent from view), people can activate either hot or cool system processing through the ways in which they construe and mentally represent events. Despite inherent difficulties and frustration in certain self-regulatory tasks, then, people have the power to create the mental conditions that can help them resist temptation and cope with adversity.

The Role of Purposeful Self-Distraction in "Cooling" Operations

An alternative control strategy to cooling representations of "hot" temptations may be to avoid thinking about them altogether. Such purposeful self-distraction should prevent hot system activation and make self-control efforts more manageable. Indeed, compared to focusing on the cool aspects of temptations, purposeful self-distraction may be a more efficient self-control strategy because cool and hot representations are mentally connected (Metcalfe & Mischel 1999) and cool thoughts themselves may unintentionally prime hot, arousing thoughts.

The role of distraction in enhancing delay ability was examined in an experiment (Mischel, Ebbesen & Zeiss 1972) in which some children were cued to think about fun thoughts ("If you want to, while you're waiting, you can think about Mommy pushing you on a swing") and some others to think about the rewards ("If you want to, while you're waiting, you can think about the cookies"). When children were prompted to think about the rewards, delay time was low, regardless of whether the rewards were exposed or covered. However, when they were led to think about pleasant, distracting thoughts, delay time was long, again regardless of whether the rewards were covered or exposed. In other experiments (Mischel et al. 1972), instead of cueing children to "Think fun thoughts," the experimenters led children to distract through overt activity by leaving a toy with them in the waiting room and telling them that they could play with it as long as they wanted. Similar to prompting children directly with distracting thoughts during the delay period, providing them with distracting activities helped them take their minds off the rewards and enhanced their ability to delay.

Not Everything Is a Good Distracter

In the experiments described above, the kinds of thoughts and activities that helped children delay longer were fun and pleasant in nature. Can aversive, negative thoughts (e.g., "Last time you fell off the swing and really hurt your knee") facilitate delay ability equally well? To address this question, children were also cued to think about sad thoughts (e.g., "Think about the last time you fell off the swing") when the rewards were exposed to them (Mischel et al. 1972). The results showed that thinking sad thoughts had the same effect on delay time as thinking about the rewards themselves and led to lower waiting times than did thinking fun thoughts.

Negative thoughts may have had an adverse effect on delay time because the very aversiveness of such thoughts increases stress and frustration, and motivates people to avoid thinking them. In the delay situation, one way to avoid thinking unpleasant thoughts is to think pleasant thoughts, such as the yummy and chewy rewards themselves. Ironically, then, instead of focusing on the negative distracters to decrease the aversiveness of the delay situation, children may have preferred to focus on reward-related thoughts to attenuate the effects of negative distracters, giving in to temptation more readily in the delay task.

The Role of Planning in the Pursuit of Long-Term Goals

In contrast to the childhood delay of gratification paradigm in which children needed to "just" wait to pursue long-term goals, many real-life control situations require one to work (as well as wait) to gain desired outcomes. A life goal like getting a college degree, for example, requires more than just waiting four years; it calls for studying, taking and passing courses, and resisting the diverse distractions and temptations along the route (Cantor & Fleeson 1991; Gollwitzer 1993; Mischel & Patterson 1978). Current self-regulatory analyses of goal attainment point to the importance of *implementation plans* in the actualization of the objectives one has set for oneself (Gollwitzer 1999). Implementation plans specify where, when, and how to pursue a goal intention by linking a specific situation to a specific response (e.g., I will read the textbook for my course from 5 to 8 p.m. everyday) (Gollwitzer 1993, 1999; Gollwitzer & Schall 1998). Implementation intentions, when properly planned, structured, and rehearsed, help self-control because goal-directed action is initiated automatically when the relevant situational cues present themselves (e.g., when the clock hits 5 p.m.) (Gollwitzer 1993, 1999). For instance, they facilitate action initiation (e.g., I will start writing the paper the day after Christmas) (Gollwitzer & Brand-stätter 1997), inhibition of unwanted habitual responses (e.g., when the dessert menu is served, I will not order the chocolate cake), as well as resistance to temptation (e.g., whenever the distraction arises, I will ignore it) (Schall & Gollwitzer 1999).

These adult studies were based on earlier research that investigated the role of similar self-instructional implementation plans in goal attainment among young children. In a resistance-to-temptation paradigm, preschool children were told that they could play with attractive, desirable toys, but only if they completed a boring, repetitive task of placing pegs in a pegboard. During the work period, however, children were periodically distracted by "Mr. Clown Box," a mechanical clown that talked to the children by means of a tape recording and produced noises and flashing lights to engage their attention. In one study (Patterson & Mischel 1975) the experimenter suggested to the children ways to resist distraction when Mr. Clown Box attempted to get their attention. For example, children were told that when Mr. Clown Box said "Hey, look," they could say "No I can't, I'm working." Those who were given such strategies resisted distraction and kept on working for longer than those who were not given strategies. In other studies (Mischel & Patterson 1976; Patterson & Mischel 1976), children were provided with either task-facilitating plans (e.g., "I am going to look at my work"), temptation-inhibiting plans (e.g., "I am not going to look at Mr. Clown Box"), or reward-oriented plans (e.g., "I want to play with Mr. Clown Box and the toys later") in the face of distraction. The results showed that the temptation-inhibiting and the reward-oriented implementation plans facilitated self-control better than the task-facilitating plans.

Note that although attention to rewards hinders self-control in the delay of gratification paradigm (depending on just how the rewards are represented cognitively), reward-oriented plans assist self-control in resisting distraction. Thus, whether a reward focus will improve or impair efforts toward self-control may depend upon whether goal pursuit requires individuals to perform active, instrumental behaviors or to wait passively. In the former scenario, reward-related thoughts may motivate action toward goal attainment by reminding people of the positive consequences of completing the instrumental task (i.e., "the light at the end of the tunnel"), enhancing resistance to distraction. During passive waiting, however, delay is facilitated only if the reward-related thoughts focus on the cool, informational aspects of the rewards.

Delay Ability as a Protective Factor against Dispositional Vulnerabilities

The cognitive-attentional strategies necessary for exertion of willpower and impulse control discussed so far may also help protect people against their personal vulnerabilities. Consider the disposition to anxiously anticipate and severely react to personal rejection, referred to as rejection sensitivity. A cognitive-affective vulnerability characterized by heightened fears and expectations of rejection, rejection sensitivity is believed to stem from experiences of neglect and rejection in early life (Downey & Feldman 1996; Feldman & Downey 1994). When people high in rejection sensitivity encounter behaviors that could be interpreted as rejection (e.g., one's partner talking to somebody else at a party), they tend to construe them as intentionally hurtful. Perceptions of intentional rejection trigger strong negative emotions such as anger, resentment, or jealousy, and activate maladaptive, automatic behavioral scripts. For example, rejection-sensitive men who seek and value intimacy are more physically violent toward their partners than are men who are low in rejection sensitivity (Downey, Feldman, & Ayduk 2000). Similarly, highly rejection-sensitive women express more hostility during conflicts, and withdraw support and start fights when they feel rejected (Ayduk et al. 1999). Not surprisingly, the relationships of highly rejection-sensitive people end sooner than those of low rejection-sensitive people (Downey et al. 1998). In sum, when people who are sensitive to rejection feel that they have been rebuffed, "hot" responses occur without the mediation and benefit of more complex, "cool" cognitive processes that enable reflection and rational problem solving (Metcalfe & Mischel 1999).

Not all people who fear and expect rejection, however, end up in a jealous rage or lash out at their partners at the slightest sign of inattentiveness. Some highly rejection-sensitive people may be able to cope better than others with situations likely to elicit impulsive, potentially relation destructive reactions. The self-regulatory task for the rejection-sensitive person may be similar to that of the four-year-old waiting for the marshmallows: the former must deal with the sense of threat and stress elicited by signs of rejection, while the latter must attenuate the frustration and aversiveness of the waiting period. In both cases the regulatory task is to inhibit reflexive, hot system reactions by accessing cool system processing. Thus, theoretically, there is reason to believe that the attentional processes that enable people to delay gratification and inhibit impulsive reactions in the face of temptation may also help protect them from their own tendencies to react maladaptively in situations that activate their rejection concerns (Metcalfe & Mischel 1999; Mischel, Cantor, & Feldman 1996; Lang, Bradley & Cuthbert 1990).

Therefore, we examined whether delay of gratification ability protects people high in rejection sensitivity against negative outcomes in terms of both their personal well-being (self-esteem, depression) and their relationships with others (aggression) (Ayduk et al., 2000). Preschoolers who had participated in the original delay experiments were followed up when they were around the age of twenty-seven, more than twenty years after the initial assessment of their delay ability. The results from this study showed that rejection-sensitive people who had low ability to delay gratification as preschoolers reported lower self-esteem, self-worth, and general coping ability as adults compared to those low in rejection sensitivity in young adulthood. By contrast, highly rejection-sensitive adults who had high delay ability as preschoolers were not distinguishable from low rejection-sensitive individuals. They were also perceived by their parents as having higher self-esteem and being more able to deal with stress than were rejection-sensitive people with low delay ability. This general pattern was replicated in a preadolescent, at-risk sample. Highly rejection-sensitive middle schoolers who had shown low delay of gratification ability in kindergarten were more susceptible to low self-worth, to heightened physical aggression against peers, and to being shunned by their peers than were their similarly rejection-sensitive peers who had been able to wait longer in the delay situation.

Role of Cognitive-Attentional Strategies in Coping with Rejection Sensitivity

To more directly address the role of cognitive-attentional strategies in protecting rejection-sensitive individuals from their own maladaptive tendencies, a self-control strategies measure for college students was developed, and its interactions with rejection sensitivity were explored (Ayduk 1999). The measure asks participants to imagine they are on a diet and have the intention of not eating a slice of hot, steaming pizza in front of them. Thus, the measure activates the basic conflict inherent in the childhood delay situation of wanting to consume an immediate reward after having committed to not eating it. The scenario is followed by a series of potential cognitive-attentional strategies, some of which are theoretically ineffective (e.g., thinking about how yummy the pizza is) and some effective (e.g., thinking about how unhealthful fat and grease are) in exerting willpower. Strategic self-control is indexed by the use of effective strategies and the avoidance of ineffective strategies.

In a study that examined hostility in relationship conflict using this measure (Ayduk 1999), people high in rejection sensitivity reported higher levels of verbal aggression (e.g., yelling, insulting, cursing) toward their partners than people low in rejection sensitivity only if they also had lower levels of strategic self-control. Those highly rejection-sensitive people with high strategic self-control, however, reported lower levels of hostility and were similar to people low in rejection sensitivity.

Taken together with the previous findings reviewed, these results suggest that attention deployment and cognitive reconstrual may play a role in regulating the interpersonal self. In interpersonal situations, for example, highly rejection-sensitive individuals who cannot deploy attention strategically may have an attentional bias to focus on rejection cues as well as their own internal emotional states. This may make it difficult for them to encode contextual information that could provide alternative explanations for others' behaviors (Dodge 1980; Downey & Feldman 1996), leading them to readily perceive intentional rejection in a perpetrator's behavior. Conversely, rejection-sensitive individuals with high self-regulatory ability may strategically and purposefully avoid focusing on negative behaviors of others or the sense of foreboding that they typically feel when facing potential rejection. Such cooling strategies should enable them to instead attend to situational information, and generate alternative explanations to others' behavior. By making finer distinctions between intentional rejection and ambiguous behavior that may be benignly intended, they may be less susceptible to false alarms and a rapid generation of the fight-or-flight response.

Rejection-sensitive people high in delay of gratification ability also may be better in attenuating the threat they perceive in rejection cues through cognitive reappraisal (Kelley 1955; Mischel 1974). Rather than taking an argument with a romantic partner as indicative of the end of their relationship, they may reconstrue it as simply a difference of opinion, restrict the event's negativity to a single occasion, and prevent themselves from overemphasizing its significance. Likewise, a partner's currently negative behavior can be understood as transitory and situationally induced (e.g., owing to stress), and its importance or centrality for the person's long-term goals can be attenuated by placing such behavior in a broader context.

Summarizing the Cognitive-Attentional Strategies of Social-Emotional Intelligence

Adaptive and intelligent functioning requires one to voluntarily postpone immediate gratification in the pursuit of preferred but delayed goals and outcomes. The frustration and conflict involved in such delay is particularly challenging when the immediate situation includes "hot" cues that activate a biologically hardwired automatic response system. Different things are "hot" for different people—for one person, the possibility of rejection may test his or her self-regulatory strength, while for another, chocolate cake may be the ultimate test. Ironically, it is particularly in these situations that self-regulatory strength is needed to inhibit tendencies to react reflexively and to act adaptively and purposefully.

This chapter has outlined some of the principles of willpower based on findings from three decades of research on preschool delay of gratification. Self-regulatory success or failure seems to be contingent on the attentional deployment strategies people use and the way they cognitively transform temptations and obstacles (Baumeister, Heatherton, & Tice 1994; Carver & Scheier 1981; Mischel et al. 1996). Strategies that involve diverting attention away from the tempting stimulus generally involve self-distraction, and lead to effective self-control because they facilitate a shift away from its hot, "here and now" features and their compelling pull.

The effectiveness of strategies that involve attention to the desired objects, on the other hand, depends on the features attended to by the individual. For example, if attention is focused on the taste of a slice of pizza, self-control failure is likely despite the dieter's best intentions because the conflict-arousing qualities of the stimulus are intensified (see Mischel et al. 1989). This intensification, in turn, makes one's short-term goals (e.g., the satisfaction one would get from eating the pizza) more salient, making it harder to exert willpower in delaying gratification. In contrast, focusing on the grease and sodium content of the slice of pizza can change the meaning of the stimulus (Lazarus, Averill, & Opton 1970; Mischel 1973, 1974) and the nature of the behavioral tendencies associated with it. Focusing on grease may activate avoidance instead of approach tendencies, making it easier for the individual to go beyond the immediate environment and focus instead on more distal, abstract, but ultimately desirable outcomes (e.g., good health).

It would be a mistake, however, to think that a strategy that is effective in one situation will lead to more intelligent social behavior across all contexts. Rather, being sensitive to the demands of different situations and adjusting one's behavior flexibly in accordance with the situational constraints may lie at the heart of adaptive social and emotional behavior (Cantor & Kihlstrom 1987; Chiu et al. 1995; Shoda, Mischel, & Wright 1993). The connection between social competence and sensitivity to situational demands in behavior is evident in children as young as six years old. Shoda, Mischel, and Wright (1993) have shown that cognitive social competence predicted the extent to which children (ages six to twelve) in a summer camp varied their pro-social behavior in relation to particular situations in a consistent and predictable manner (e.g., pro-social when warned by counselors but aggressive when teased by peers). In a similar vein, the literature on stress and coping indicates that people who are high in social competence show a discriminative, adaptive pattern in how they seek information about potential stressors. Socially competent adults tend to monitor (seek) information during threatening, controllable events because information in this situation helps them gain control but avoid information (blunt) during uncontrollable events because information cannot be used in a way to alleviate distress (Chiu et al. 1995).

As these findings imply, effective self-control requires one to be strategic in knowing when to "cool" and when to "warm," taking into account characteristics of each situation. Indeed, self-distraction, when employed across all contexts, may actually lead to mental disengagement and wishful thinking, resulting in further emotional distress (e.g., Bolger 1990).

Other Mediators of Strategic Self-Regulation in Adulthood

In addition to the cognitive-attentional strategies that have been explored in the preschool delay of gratification experiments, effective self-control and adaptive behavior has many other psychological mediators. For instance, people high in self-regulation may be more motivated to attain their long-term goals than people low in self-regulation (Cantor & Blanton 1996). Higher levels of motivation to attain one's long-term goals may help transcend the often overwhelming salience of one's short-term goals under emotional arousal or threat. The transcendence of a here-and-now motivational state, in turn, reduces the likelihood of reflexive responses and helps ensure that individuals behave in more thoughtful and strategic ways (Baumeister & Heatherton 1996; Mischel 1996).

The ability to access and utilize self-regulation strategies may also critically depend on perceived control and self-efficacy beliefs (Bandura 1977; Thompson 1981). If people approach difficult tasks with the belief that the outcomes are under their control, they may actually try harder to access attentional, motivational, and emotional control strategies that facilitate effective self-regulation. These beliefs may also serve as protective factors against adversity directly by promoting an active coping style, and indirectly by maintaining optimism even in the face of obstacles (Taylor & Aspinwall 1996; Scheier & Carver 1987).

Conclusions: Reconciling Smart Lives and Stupid Behaviors

This chapter began with the seemingly paradoxical question of how "smart" people like Bill Clinton and Judge Wachtler could have behaved in such self-defeating, nearsighted ways. Historically, psychologists have dealt with such inconsistencies in behavior by trying to differentiate between the "surface" person and the deeper, "real" person, assuming there could be only a single, genuine self (Mischel 1968). Over the past decade, however, a growing body of research has begun to recognize that people's behavior varies stably and predictably across situations (e.g., if situation A then he does X, but if situation B then he does Y), and that such variability reflects the core of personality and provides a window through which to glimpse the underlying goals and motivations of the person (Mischel & Shoda 1995; Shoda & Mischel 1998; Shoda, Mischel, & Wright 1993, 1994).

To illustrate, consider the example of Jack, who is a generally calm, sociable person. Every time his girlfriend attempts to do something with others that does not involve him, however, he becomes hostile and lashes out. Now imagine James, who is also a calm and sociable person. He does not mind so much if his girlfriend wants to do things without him. Instead, he gets very angry and spiteful when his girlfriend tells him what to do. Whereas both Jack and James are calm and friendly in general, each gets predictably angry and hostile in certain situations: Jake when his significant others try to establish independence from him, and James when they try to control him. Thus, being both gentle and hostile—like being smart and stupid—may be equally genuine facets that can coexist in the same, "real" person.

As noted at the beginning of the chapter, behavior has multiple determinants. The relationship between situational features and behaviors generated is determined by the individual's construals, goals, affects, beliefs, and self-regulatory competencies that are relevant to and get activated in those circumstances (Mischel & Shoda 1995, 1998). Sometimes stupid behavior in smart people may arise from faulty expectations, erroneous beliefs, or merely a lack of motivation to enact control strategies even when one has them. But sometimes it is an inability to regulate one's affective states and the behavioral tendencies associated with them that leads to stupid and self-defeating behavior.

In situations that contain "hot" features and activate automatic response tendencies, the power of the hot system may make it difficult for even the smartest people to exert self-control. As Clinton recently remarked, "Presidents are people too" (CNN 1999). Hot reflexive reactions may be part of the overall arousal state that mobilizes the body's resources efficiently in response to sudden danger. The accentuation of the hot system may have survival value in evolutionary terms, preventing humans from wasting time thinking and contemplating, and instead allowing them to fight, run from danger, or seize the moment for an appetizing meal or an opportunity for procreation. On the other hand, such an emergency system can become destructive if it governs reactions in situations that require patience and reflective, strategic behavior (LeDoux 1996).

Unlike lower animals on the evolutionary ladder, however, human beings have the capacity to eventually take control with high-level brain centers (e.g., involving the frontal lobe and hippocampus areas) and to start thinking and planning their way through the problem that the amygdala had already begun to respond to automatically and emotionally—although not necessarily wisely. As the delay of gratification experiments show, rather than being slaves to our impulses and automatic response tendencies, humans have the ability to change the ways they construe and represent the objects and events around them. Through such transformations, reconstruals, and attention deployment strategies, people can exert volitional control even in situations that might otherwise be dominated by hot system processing. For example, those highly rejection-sensitive people who can access and utilize cooling strategies in interpersonal interactions do not experience the negative outcomes that are typically associated with this vulnerability.

Final Remarks

The individual's "self-regulatory system" includes a number of interconnected components, all relevant to how complex, relatively long-term patterns of goal-directed behavior are planned, generated, and maintained even when the environment offers weak supports, diverse impediments, and frustrating and conflicting elements. To a considerable degree, individuals direct and control their own behaviors toward delayed (i.e., future) outcomes and goals. They influence the quality of their performance by self-imposed goals and standards—by self-monitoring, self-evaluations, and self-produced consequences as they generate and pursue their plans and projects (e.g., Bandura 1986; Cantor & Kihlstrom 1987). Even in the absence of external constraints, people set goals for themselves, monitor their own behavior, and encourage or demoralize their own efforts through their own ideation as they progress toward subgoals.

William James (1890/1981) differentiated between *wishing* and actively *willing* in the opening to his chapter on the will over one hundred years ago: "Desire, wish, will, are states of mind which everyone knows and which no definition can make plainer. If with the desire there goes a sense that attainment is not possible we simply wish; but if we believe the end is in our power, we will that desired feeling, having, or doing shall be real . . . and real it presently becomes, either immediately upon the willing or after certain preliminaries have been fulfilled" (p. 486). As James insightfully noted, to go from wishing something to actually willing it, not only must one believe that attainment of the goal is under potential control but one must also fulfill a set of "preliminary" conditions. Research in the past three decades has shown that although expectancies, beliefs, and goals are all essential preliminaries for even attempting to exert effortful control, the success of those efforts depends critically on the self-control skills and strategic competencies that are employed to pursue them—and that are so often forgotten when they are most urgently needed.

NOTES

This research was supported by a grant from the National Institute of Mental Health (MH39349).

We would like to thank Rodolfo Mendoza-Denton for his extremely constructive comments on several drafts of this chapter.

Correspondence concerning this chapter should be addressed to Walter Mischel or Ozlem Ayduk, Columbia University, Department of Psychology, 1190 Amsterdam Avenue, Mail Code 5501, New York, NY 10025. Electronic mail may be sent to wm@psych.columbia.edu or to ozlem@psych.columbia.edu.

REFERENCES

Ayduk, O. (1999). Impact of self-control strategies on the link between rejection sensitivity and hostility: Risk negotiation through strategic control. Unpublished doctoral dissertation, Columbia University, New York.

Ayduk, O., G. Downey, A. Testa, Y. Yen, & Y. Shoda (1999). Does rejection elicit hostility in high rejection sensitive women? *Social Cognition, 17,* 245–271.

Ayduk, O., R. Mendoza-Denton, W. Mischel, G. Downey, P. Peake, & M. Rodriguez (2000). Regulating the interpersonal self: Strategic self-regulation for coping with rejection sensitivity. *Journal of Personality and Social Psychology, 79,* 776–792.

Bandura, A. (1977). Self-efficacy: Toward a unifying theory of behavioral change. *Psychological Review, 84,* 191–215.

———. (1986). *Social foundations of thought and action: A social cognitive theory.* Englewood Cliffs, N.J.: Prentice-Hall.

Baumeister, R. F., & T. F. Heatherton (1996). Self-regulation failure: An overview. *Psychological Inquiry, 7,* 1–15.

Baumeister, R. F., T. F. Heatherton, & D. M. Tice (1994). *Losing control: How and why people fail at self-regulation.* New York: Academic Press.

Berlyne, D. (1960). *Conflict, arousal, and curiosity.* New York: McGraw-Hill.

Blitzer, W. (1999). Hillary Clinton: President's infidelities were "weakness" caused by childhood abuse. http://cnn.com/all politics/stories/1999/08/01/first .lady.interview.02

Bolger, N. (1990). Coping as a personality process: A prospective study. *Journal of Personality and Social Psychology, 59,* 525–537.

Caher, J. M. (1998). *King of the mountain: The rise, fall, and redemption of Chief Judge Sol Wachtler.* New York: Prometheus.

Cantor, N., & H. Blanton (1996). Effortful pursuit of personal goals in daily life. In P. M. Gollwitzer & J. A. Bargh (Eds.), *The psychology of action: Linking cognition and motivation to behavior* (pp. 338–359). New York: Guilford Press.

Cantor, N. , & W. Fleeson (1991). Life tasks and self-regulatory processes. In M. Maehr & P. Pintrich (Eds.), *Advances in motivation and achievement,* Vol. 7 (pp. 327–369). Greenwich, Conn.: JAI.

Cantor, N. , & J. F. Kihlstrom (1987). *Personality and social intelligence.* Englewood Cliffs, N.J.: Prentice-Hall.

Carver, C. S., & M. F. Scheier (1981). Self-consciousness and reactance. *Journal of Research in Personality, 15,* 16–29.

Chiu, C., Y. Hong, W. Mischel, & Y. Shoda (1995). Discriminative facility in social competence: Conditional versus dispositional encoding and monitoring-blunting of information. *Social Cognition, 13,* 49–70.

CNN (1999). *Clinton says "Presidents are people, too": First lady would be a 'fabulous senator,' he declares.* http://cnn.com/allpolitics /stories/1999/02/19/clinton.presser/

Dodge, K. (1980). Social cognition and children's aggressive behavior. *Child Development, 51,* 162–170.

Downey, G., & S. Feldman (1996). Implications of rejection sensitivity for intimate relationships. *Journal of Personality and Social Psychology, 70,* 1327–43.

Downey, G., S. Feldman, & O. Ayduk (2000). Rejection sensitivity and male violence in romantic relationships. *Personal Relationships, 7,* 45–61.

Downey, G., A. L. Freitas, B. Michealis, & H. Khouri (1998). The self-fulfilling prophecy in close relationships: Do rejection sensitive women get rejected by romantic partners? *Journal of Personality and Social Psychology, 75,* 545–560.

Estes, W. K. (1972). Reinforcement in human behavior. *American Scientist, 60,* 723–729.

Feldman, S., & G. Downey (1994). Rejection sensitivity as a mediator of the impact of childhood exposure to family violence on adult attachment behavior. *Development and Psychopathology, 6,* 231–247.

Freud, S. (1911/1959). Formulations regarding the two principles of mental functioning. *Collected Papers,* Vol. 4. New York: Basic Books.

Gollwitzer, P. M. (1993). Goal achievement: The role of intentions. In W. Stroebe & M. Hewstone (Eds.), *European review of social psychology,* Vol. 4 (pp. 141–185). London: Wiley.

——. (1999). Implementation intentions: Strong effects of simple plans. *American Psychologist, 54,* 493–503.

Gollwitzer, P. M., & V. Brandstätter (1997). Implementation intentions and effective goal pursuit. *Journal of Personality and Social Psychology, 73,* 186–199.

Gollwitzer, P. M., & B. Schall (1998). Metacognition in action: The importance of implementation intentions. *Personality & Social Psychology Review, 2,* 124–136.

Gray, J. A. (1987). *The psychology of fear and stress* (second edition). New York: McGraw-Hill.

James, W. (1890/1981). *The principles of psychology.* Vol. 2. Cambridge, Mass.: Harvard University Press.

Kelley, G. A. (1955). *A theory of personality: The psychology of personal constructs.* New York: Norton.

Lang, P. J., M. M. Bradley, & B. N. Cuthbert (1990). Emotion, attention, and the startle reflex. *Psychological Review, 97,* 377–395.

Lazarus, R. S., J. R. Averill, & E. M. Opton, Jr. (1970). Towards a cognitive theory of emotion. In M. Arnol (Ed.), *Third International Symposium on Feelings and Emotions* (pp. 207–232). New York: Academic Press.

LeDoux, J. (1996). *The emotional brain.* New York: Touchstone.

Marrow, L. (1999). The reckless and the stupid: A character of a President eventually determines his destiny, *Time.*

Metcalfe, J. & W. J. Jacobs (1998). Emotional memory: The effects of stress on "cool" and "hot" memory systems. In D. L. Medin (Ed.), *The psychology of learning and motivations.* Vol. 38. *Advances in research and theory.* San Diego: Academic Press.

——. (1996). A "hot-system/cool-system" view of memory under stress. *PTSD Research Quarterly*, 7, 1–6.

Metcalfe, J., & W. Mischel (1999). A hot/cool system analysis of delay of gratification: Dynamics of willpower. *Psychological Review*, 106, 3–19.

Mischel, W. (1968). *Personality and assessment*. New York: Wiley.

——. (1973). Toward a cognitive social learning reconceptualization of personality. *Psychological Review*, 80, 252–283.

——. (1974). Cognitive appraisals and transformations in self-control. In B. Weiner (Ed.), *Cognitive views of human motivation* (pp. 33–49). New York: Academic Press.

——. (1996). From good intentions to willpower. In P. M. Gollwitzer and J. A. Bargh (Eds.), *The psychology of action: Linking cognition and motivation to behavior* (pp. 197–218). New York: Guilford Press.

Mischel, W., & N. Baker (1975). Cognitive appraisals and transformations in delay behavior. *Journal of Personality and Social Psychology*, 31, 254–261.

Mischel, W., N. Cantor, & S. Feldman (1996). Principles of self-regulation: The nature of willpower and self-control. In E. T. Higgins and A. W. Kruglanski (Eds.), *Social psychology: Handbook of basic principles* (pp. 329–360). New York: Guilford Press.

Mischel, W., & E. B. Ebbesen (1970). Attention in delay of gratification. *Journal of Personality and Social Psychology*, 16, 29–337.

Mischel, W., E. B. Ebbesen, & A. Zeiss (1972). Cognitive and attentional mechanisms in delay of gratification. *Journal of Personality and Social Psychology*, 21, 204–218.

Mischel, W., & B. Moore (1973). Effects of attention to symbolically presented rewards on self-control. *Journal of Personality and Social Psychology*, 28, 172–179.

Mischel, W., & C. J. Patterson (1976).

Substantive and structural elements of effective plans for self-control. *Journal of Personality and Social Psychology*, 34, 942–950.

——. (1978). Effective plans for self-control in children. In W. A. Collins (Ed.), *Minnesota Symposium on Child Psychology* (Vol. 11) (pp. 199–230). Hillsdale, N.J.: Erlbaum.

Mischel, W., & Y. Shoda (1995). A cognitive-affective system theory of personality: Reconceptualizing situations, dispositions, dynamics and invariance in personality structure. *Psychological Review*, 102, 246–268.

——. (1998). Reconciling processing dynamics and personality dispositions. *Annual Review of Psychology*, 49, 229–258.

Mischel, W., Y. Shoda, & P. Peake (1988). The nature of adolescent competencies predicted by preschool delay of gratification. *Journal of Personality and Social Psychology*, 54, 687–696.

Mischel, W., Y. Shoda, & M. L. Rodriguez (1989). Delay of gratification in children. *Science*, 244, 933–938.

Moore, B., W. Mischel, & A. Zeiss (1976). Comparative effects of the reward stimulus and its cognitive representation in voluntary delay. *Journal of Personality and Social Psychology*, 34, 419–424.

Patterson, C. J., & W. Mischel (1975). Plans to resist distraction. *Developmental Psychology*, 11, 369–378.

——. (1976). Effects of temptation-inhibiting and task-facilitating plans on self-control. *Journal of Personality and Social Psychology*, 33, 209–217.

Schall, B., & P. M. Gollwitzer (1999). Implementation intentions and resistance to temptations. Manuscript submitted for publication.

Scheier, M. F., & Carver, C. S. (1987). Dispositional optimism and well-being: The influence of generalized outcome expectancies on health. [Special Issue: personality and physical health]. *Journal of Personality*, 55, 169–210.

Shoda, Y., & W. Mischel (1998). Personality as a stable cognitive-affective activation network: Characteristic patterns of behavior variation emerge from a stable personality structure. In S. Read & L. C. Miller (Eds.), *Connectionist models of social reasoning* (pp. 175–208). Mahwah, N.J.: Erlbaum.

Shoda, Y., W. Mischel, & P. Peake (1990). Predicting adolescent cognitive and self-regulatory competencies from preschool delay of gratification: Identifying diagnostic conditions. *Developmental Psychology, 26,* 978–986.

Shoda, Y., W. Mischel, & J. C. Wright (1993). The role of situational demands and cognitive competencies in behavior organization and personality coherence. *Journal of Personality and Social Psychology, 65,* 1023–1035.

——. (1994). Intra-individual stability in the organization and patterning of behavior: Incorporating psychological situations into the idiographic analysis of personality. *Journal of Personality and Social Psychology, 67,* 674–687.

Taylor S. E., & L. G. Aspinwall (1996). Mediating and moderating processes in psychosocial stress: Appraisal, coping, resistance, and vulnerability. In H. B. Kaplan (Ed.), *Psychosocial stress: Perspectives on structure, theory, life-course, and methods* (pp. 71–110). San Diego: Academic Press.

Thompson, S. C. (1981). Will it hurt less if I can control it? A complex answer to a simple question. *Psychological Bulletin, 90,* 89–101.

Wachtler, S. (1997). *After the madness: A judge's own prison memoir.* New York: Random House.

DIANE F. HALPERN

6 Sex, Lies, and Audiotapes

THE CLINTON-LEWINSKY SCANDAL

It is always risky to use political events as examples of cognitive or social phenomena because the political leanings of the writer and the audience figure prominently in how the event is interpreted and how the critique of the event is received. In politics, as in many other arenas, judgments about the degree to which an action is smart or stupid are in the eyes of the beholder. Often, the "beholders" of political events view the world through the corrective lens of their political party, with each lens creating its own unique distortion. As a prime example of the way existing beliefs influence evaluative judgments, consider the U.S. Congress, where members usually vote "along party lines," often unable to recognize any merits in proposals originating on the other side of the aisle or any demerits in ones coming from their own side. Like Congress, the American public is also divided in multiple ways in its evaluation of political events, with each party and interest group vying for opportunities to sway public opinion in its direction. To ensure that no one engages in the risky business of thinking for him- or herself, every political event is accompanied by a bevy of "spin doctors," who tell the public how to interpret the event in a way that is most favorable to the preferred party or candidate.

Current events quickly turn into history, where they are judged with the smug certainty of hindsight. Consider, for example, the break-in at the Democratic headquarters at the Watergate complex (and its subsequent cover-up) and the attempted rescue of Americans held captive in Iran, respectively known as Nixon's and Carter's fiascoes. Media pundits roundly criticized both of these disasters as the inevitable outcomes of poor decisions, a view that was reinforced by Nixon's and Carter's political adversaries. These two examples represent very different political decisions in terms of the goals they were trying to achieve and the reasoning that went into the decision processes. Most significantly, there are fundamental moral differences between Nixon's attempt to conceal his participation in illegal activities and Carter's attempt to rescue innocent Americans being held hostage. For the purposes of this discussion, readers are asked to ignore the moral issues and other ways in which these two ill-fated decisions differed, and focus on the likelihood that the decisions made by Nixon and Carter would have achieved their desired goal. Of course, if they had succeeded, both former presidents would have celebrated their careful planning and astute assessments of risk (with Nixon's celebration held privately because he would have succeeded at concealing a crime). But, when we consider the decisions that led to these disastrous actions, many years after the fact and with full knowledge of their outcomes, it seems clear that any rational person should have recognized that these were bad decisions at the time the decisions were made.

Although there is usually much that can be disputed in judging the quality of past actions by political leaders, there does seem to be at least one example where most people can agree that a seemingly smart person made some really dumb mistakes—the Bill Clinton–Monica Lewinsky scandal. There is still considerable disagreement over whether the mistakes were egregious enough to impeach the president or whether he should have been removed from office. Not surprisingly, the votes to impeach Clinton, with only a few exceptions, were cast along party lines.

Many Americans cannot view any aspect of the Clinton-Lewinsky affair apart from the moral issues of sexual infidelity and "misleading" (or lying to, depending on one's point of view) the public and grand jury. For them, these actions can be described only in negative terms—there is no need to consider alternative interpretations. But it is possible to assess the intelligence or stupidity of Clinton's behavior apart from the questions of morality or honesty. In this chapter, I consider moral issues as relevant only insofar as they determine the reactions of those involved—the media, public, and Clinton's family—and thus influence whether or not the president achieved his desired goal of engaging in sexual relations with Lewinsky while avoiding negative consequences. I focus on a cognitive analysis of Clinton's behaviors as a way of inferring his decision making process because I do not have direct access to his thinking at the time. One question that was asked repeatedly by many people around the world during the nonstop media blitz was, "How could Clinton have been so dumb?"

Who Is Smart?

It is not surprising when someone we believe to be stupid does stupid things, but how can we explain the same actions when they are committed by someone we believe to be intelligent? In general, we recognize people as intelligent if they have some combination of these achievements: (1) good grades in school; (2) a high level of education; (3) a responsible, complex job, or (4) some other recognition of being intelligent, such as winning prestigious awards or earning a large salary. Other common indicators of high intelligence include (5) the ability to read complex text with good comprehension or (6) solve difficult and novel problems.

Despite the fact that many psychologists spend their professional lives designing and interpreting measures of intelligence that can be used to classify people along an intelligence dimension, these tests are meaningless to the general public, which generally distrusts intelligence tests and has little understanding of them. Individuals who take intelligence tests receive an IQ score. IQ stands for "intelligence quotient," a term that was derived from the original method for computing these scores. High IQ scores, without any of the other indicators of intelligence, do not confer an advantage in real life. Low IQ scores for individuals who have achieved these ecologically valid markers of intelligence (for western industrialized societies) can only be used as evidence that these tests are flawed because they fail to identify individuals who perform intelligently in American society. Most people have never taken an intelligence test and know very little about the IQ scores of other people. (There are a few exceptions, which include people who want to join MENSA, a group that restricts membership to people with high IQ scores, and children who are being placed in special education classes for the retarded or gifted.) For most purposes, formal measures of intelligence have little impact on how the general public thinks about intelligence.

By all the commonly accepted criteria, Bill Clinton is an intelligent man. His grades in college were high enough to get him into Yale law school; he won a Rhodes scholarship to study in England; he was a governor of a small state and president of a powerful country. He is also a man whose life is conducted in the public domain. As president, he was always accompanied by secret service agents; every visitor to the White House was checked in and out; his secretary and others kept a detailed schedule for him; and the media and political friends and enemies kept close tabs on him. Did he really believe that he could have multiple sexual encounters with a young woman at the White House without experiencing any consequences? It seems that he did. How can we explain this seemingly stupid behavior by an otherwise intelligent man?

One way to understand the motives and actions of another person is to try to assume his or her perspective or worldview (Fisher, Ury, & Patton 1991). The colloquial expression for this cognitive exercise is "putting yourself in the other person's shoes." It is important that when assuming the perspective of another person, you remain mindful of what was known and not known by that person at the time the decisions were made and judge the quality of the thinking by the actor's own objectives and goals. Following the Lewinsky scandal, Clinton publicly apologized for his sexual affair and for misleading the American public, and Hillary Clinton talked publicly about Bill Clinton's remorse. It is reasonable to conclude that he would not have become involved with Lewinsky if he had known that it would result in his impeachment and public humiliation.

Clinton certainly was capable of intelligent, reflective decision making. When he was president of the United States, Clinton was (arguably) the most powerful individual in the world. As such, there were numerous times when he had to consider the consequences of his decisions, many of which literally meant the difference between life and death for many Americans and other people around the world. For example, Clinton's decision to send troops to Kosovo altered the course of history in that troubled region. When he made the Kosovo decision, there were too many unknowns to ensure a favorable outcome. At the time the decision was made, Clinton clearly articulated the risks and benefits of this and countless other possible alternatives, showing that he was capable of linking future actions with their long-term consequences and assessing the associated risks. Yet he seemed to abandon these principles of critical thinking when he arranged for a few brief sexual encounters with Lewinsky. There are two important differences between the decisions that involved public policies and those that pertained to his sexual liaisons. First, the decision making process regarding Kosovo (and similar events) was public, whereas we can only deduce the thinking process that led to his handling of the Lewinsky affair because of its private nature. Second, Clinton had multiple, knowledgeable advisors giving him their honest assessments to assist him with the Kosovo decisions. It seems likely that even those who were aware of his extramarital sexual affairs either failed to advise him in this area or did so in a gentle way, minimizing the probability that he would respond in a negative way to unwanted advice.

In Hillary Clinton's explanation of her husband's marital infidelities, she attributed his behavior to the "abuse" he suffered as a young child when his mother and grandmother clashed over his mother's decision to remarry (Miller 1999). But there is no need to appeal to psychodynamic concepts like early psychological trauma to explain his sexual affairs. Cognitive principles more directly related to his behaviors can help us understand why he did not adequately assess the likelihood of detection and the consequences of his affair with a young intern at the White House.

PRIOR LEARNING

There is considerable evidence that for many years prior to his encounters with Lewinsky, Clinton had had sexual liaisons with different partners, even during his term as governor of Arkansas when state troopers were assigned to accompany him everywhere he went. In sworn testimony, Gennifer Flowers, an Arkansas state employee and part-time nightclub singer, declared that she had had sexual relations with Clinton many times over a twelve-year period that included his gubernatorial term. In 1992, during his successful presidential campaign, Clinton denied having had sex with Flowers. It was Paula Jones's contention that Clinton had committed lewd acts when he was governor of Arkansas that led to Lewinsky's subpoena to appear before a grand jury. In Clinton's deposition in the Paula Jones lawsuit, he reversed his earlier denial of sexual relations with Gennifer Flowers. In addition, a state trooper told newspaper reporters that when he had been assigned to Clinton as a security aide, he had accompanied Clinton on other sexual encounters. Thus, prior to his affair with Lewinsky, Clinton had apparently engaged in sexual acts with many different women (throughout his marriage and during his many pre-presidential years in other highly visible elected offices), he publicly denied having had these relations, and he experienced no negative consequences as a result of those behaviors.

A frequently repeated aphorism in psychology is that the best predictor of future behavior is past behavior. Based on this premise, Clinton's sexual encounters with Lewinsky could have been predicted by examining his prior behavior. Learning theorists would note that sexual satisfaction (perhaps enhanced by the risk of being caught) served to increase the probability that Clinton would enter into repeated sexual relations. Prior to the Lewinsky scandal, there were few or no negative consequences (in the jargon of psychology, "punishers") of this behavior—consequences that would have served to decrease the probability of his repeating it. Thus, when viewed in the context of his life experiences, Clinton's affair with Lewinsky is not only understandable, it epitomizes at least one aspect of the definition of intelligence that was provided by a task force of psychologists assembled by the American Psychological Association. They defined intelligence as the "ability to understand complex ideas, to adapt effectively to the environment, to learn from experience, to engage in various forms of reasoning, and to overcome obstacles by taking thought" (Neisser et al. 1996, p. 77).

Clinton had learned from his past experience. Standard learning principles of reward and punishment can be used to explain his apparently stupid behavior. When viewed in context, his actions seem less stupid than they did at first glance. In a review article about what constitutes poor judgment and decision making, the authors ask, "Are the person's beliefs grossly out of kilter with available evidence?" (Meller, Schwartz, & Cooke 1998, p. 449). The answer for Clinton in regard to his affair with Lewinsky would have to be "No." Many readers will balk at this conclusion because Clinton's relations with Lewinsky had all the trappings of a "sleazy affair," and the outcome was quite negative.

THE MACHISMO OF THE U.S. PRESIDENCY

Bill Clinton's seemingly stupid liaisons with Monica Lewinsky can also be understood by examining them within a societal context. Many men in visible public offices have acknowledged extramarital sexual affairs with few or no negative consequences. In fact, these extramarital affairs have sometimes been seen as a benefit. In a discussion of contemporary attitudes toward extramarital affairs, Norment (1998) wrote: "The cheating man has long been the subject of boasts, jokes, novels, and movies" (p. 34). The double standard for female and male behavior is alive and well in American culture and many other parts of the world. When males brag about having many sexual partners, they are often described as "sowing their wild oats," and such behavior is often excused (with expressions like "Boys will be boys" or "He's a regular Don Juan"). The willingness to engage in frequent sex with a variety of women is part of a machismo mentality that is openly encouraged in many Latin societies and discretely supported by at least a segment of the population in American society. The job of U.S. president is almost too big for any single person. A macho president is, in some sense, communicating that he is man enough to handle it—and more.

History has shown that Americans have been very tolerant of our presidents' sexual infidelities. Many historical accounts chronicle Franklin Roosevelt's love affair with his wife's social secretary, Lucy Page Mercer, including the well-documented fact that Mercer was with Roosevelt at the time of his death but quickly left before Eleanor arrived at the death scene. Kay Summersby wrote a book in which she described in intimate detail her extramarital love affair with Dwight Eisenhower. John Kennedy's reputation as a womanizer came from his sexual affairs with many famous Hollywood stars and anonymous aides. The news media also carried stories about extramarital affairs between Lyndon Johnson and female guests at his Texas ranch. Public awareness of presidential dalliances dates back to over a century ago when Grover Cleveland's bid for the presidency was rocked with the news that he had been paying child support for a child born out of wedlock years before he had become a presidential candidate. Despite public taunts about the out-of-wedlock birth and missing fathers, Cleveland was elected president of the United States.

In fact, a sizable proportion of the American public expects sexual infidelity from their elected officials. In a poll conducted for Time/Cable Network News in December 1998, 1,031 adult Americans were asked, "Compared with the average married man, do you think members of Congress are more likely to engage in adultery?" Their responses were probably shaped, in part, by the news about President Clinton's affairs, but they also help us understand how Clinton could have believed he was invulnerable in this area of his life: 52 percent responded "no difference"; 37 percent responded "more likely"; and 7 responded "less likely" (Lacayo & Branegan 1998).

The history of sex scandals involving U.S. presidents should have provided Clinton with ample evidence to conclude that his extramarital affairs, even if discovered, would be tolerated by the public. If we were to conclude that Clinton was stupid because he had extramarital affairs, then similar labeling would apply to these other presidents as well. We would end up concluding that many presidents in the past century behaved stupidly because they engaged in sexual relations outside of marriage. Furthermore, the fact that sexual affairs were so common among past presidents and so nonchalantly received by the public suggested that these affairs were generally acknowledged as the moral norm for persons in public office. According to social learning theorists, most learning occurs by observing models, with particular attention to the rewards and punishments they receive. In general, models are effective in shaping behavior when the learner perceives a similarity between her- or himself and the model (Bandura 1977). It seems natural that any current president would study the lives of past presidents as a way of learning about the presidential role. The lessons learned are not always explicit, but if Clinton were motivated to seek sexual partners outside of marriage, he did not have to look beyond earlier inhabitants of his White House bedroom to find examples where that behavior was condoned.

Social Mores

The divorce rate at the start of the twentieth century was in the low single digits, and a divorced woman in the early decades of the twentieth century (more so than a divorced man) was shamed by her failed marriage. By the sixth and seventh decade, divorce was a common occurrence in North America and many other parts of the world. Along with the dramatic rise in the rate of divorce, people openly speculated on the reasons for so many divorces. Frequently, blame for the high rate of failed marriages was attributed to an unfaithful partner (more usually the male).

When Alfred Kinsey began his famous surveys of human sexual behavior in the 1940s, very little was known about the sexual practices and preferences of average adults. It was surprising to Kinsey and the rest of society to learn that many sexual activities that had been assumed to be unusual were, in fact, quite common. Perhaps the most surprising was the large number of married individuals who engaged in extramarital affairs. Kinsey (with his co-authors, Martin and Pomeroy, 1948) estimated that half of all married men and a third of all married women would, at some point in their lives, engage in extramarital sex. Later surveys, most with biased samples of volunteer subjects, gave even higher estimates (e.g., Hite 1987). Some evidence suggests that these figures are too high; a recent reanalysis of a National Opinion Poll puts the figures at 23 percent for men and 12 percent for women (Wiederman 1999). Regardless of the "true" population figures, there is a sizable percentage of married adults who are engaging in sexual relations outside of marriage.

Thus, if President Clinton had been looking for predictors that his sexual affairs while in the White House would be condoned as "normative" behavior, he could take refuge in the data on this topic that were commonly reported in the popular press. Besides, with so many people having extramarital sex, wouldn't it be difficult for them to criticize Clinton for the same behavior?

What Went Wrong?

Personal learning experiences based on successful affairs while in the governor's mansion and later in the White House, the sexual legacy of many prior presidents, and the survey data from large random samples of married adults all taught Clinton the same simple lessons. The probability that his affairs would be disclosed to the general public was low, and even if they were, there would be no negative repercussions. While Clinton was deciding how to respond to news media reports about his sexual encounters, François Mitterand, his counterpart in France, was making news with his own extramarital relations. The reaction of most French citizens ranged from mild condemnation to amusement, support, and even encouragement, providing another example that may have emboldened Clinton to take even more risks. How else can we understand why he would have phoned Lewinsky at her home, given her gifts, and also (allegedly) made unwelcome sexual advances toward Kathleen Willey, an acquaintance of the Clintons', when she visited him at the White House? What went wrong? Clinton failed to notice a critical factor that rendered his earlier lessons invalid. In the words of a popular song from the 1960s, he failed to recognize that "The times, they are achangin'."

Public Office in the Post-Watergate Era

Sexual scandals are not the only improprieties associated with former presidents. American history was altered when a break-in at the Democratic National Committee headquarters in Washington's Watergate complex turned into a tale of espionage that brought down an American president. Richard Nixon resigned as president of the United States when a laundry list of illegal activities in which he had participated became public knowledge. The attitude of the American public and the media changed radically after Watergate. The sanctity of the office of the president had been breached, and any respect for privacy that had previously been accorded to presidents and their families was destroyed. If there was wrongdoing at the White House, sexual or otherwise, the press was determined to ferret it out and report it. Clinton's critical mistake in his handling of the Lewinsky scandal was his failure to recognize this change. Thus, although his affair with his intern seems intelligent when we look at lessons learned from prior experience, his handling of events as news of the affair became public does not.

When news of the Clinton-Lewinsky scandal first broke, it seemed that the attitudes of the American public also had changed in ways that were not predictable from their responses to past presidential indiscretions. Numerous indicators show that Americans are increasingly concerned with morals and values. Perhaps the new millennium was a natural time for people to reflect on the "state of the state," and perhaps it was a cumulative effect from the post-Watergate era and the rash of extramarital affairs for several Democrats and Republicans that came to light during Clinton's impeachment. It might even be a simple correction from a large swing in the liberal direction. Myers (2000) has summarized the results of several studies in which 67 percent of Americans agreed that "Values and moral beliefs . . . have gotten pretty seriously off on the wrong track"; 78 percent rated "the state of moral values in the country today" as "somewhat weak" or "very weak"; and 53 percent said that they are more concerned with moral problems than with economic problems. Perhaps the strongest indicator of the shift in public opinion against sexual affairs by those in public office can be seen in Vice

President Al Gore's comments about Clinton's sexual activities: "What he did was inexcusable, and particularly as a father, I felt it was terribly wrong, obviously" (quoted in Seelye 1999, p. 19). Gore's comment is not indicative of the laissez-faire attitude that Clinton might have expected.

There are many reasons why Clinton failed to notice that the behaviors he "got away with" earlier would not be ignored this time. Wishful thinking can be a powerful influence on what we attend to and how we interpret cues from the environment. In general, people estimate the probabilities of desired events to be higher than the probability of undesired events, even when the probabilities are objectively equal. (See Halpern, 1996, for a review.) Without the power of wishful thinking, how can we explain the huge popularity of lotteries, which grows as the amount to be won increases (ironically, the probability of winning is then reduced because more people are purchasing tickets, thus reducing the expected value).

Clinton should have been more sensitive to the changing attitudes of the public because the questions "Did the president commit an impeachable crime?" and "If so, was the crime serious enough to remove him from office?" are resolved by applying societal standards. Clinton certainly must have been aware of Gerald Ford's remarks on this question, presented to Congress in 1970: "The only honest answer is that an impeachable offense is whatever a majority of the House of Representatives considers [it] to be at a given moment in history" (p. 11913). No absolute criteria can be relied upon to set these standards. Clinton was impeached for lying under oath (denying his sexual relationship with Lewinsky—he maintained that although he had misled the American public, he didn't lie) and for obstructing justice (pressuring others to lie and to conceal the exchange of gifts). Society decides when standards have been breached. Criminal behavior, like mental illness, pornography, and addiction, is a matter of definition. The real question is who has the power to make the definitions. Unfortunately for Clinton, the power of definition belonged to the Republican majority in Congress. Definitions also drift over time. One of Clinton's biggest mistakes was his apparent failure to recognize this drift and to change his behavior based on contemporary standards.

The Changing Nature of Evidence

Another important change that sets the Clinton affairs apart from those that occurred earlier in the twentieth century is the widespread use of electronic devices, specifically recording machines. In an earlier time, a president's paramour may have confided in indiscrete friends, but these confessions could later be denied and left to circulate as unsubstantiated rumors. In Clinton's case, Linda Tripp, Monica Lewinsky's confidante, captured Lewinsky's version of the affair secretly on tape, making a permanent copy available for further scrutiny and preventing Lewinsky from denying the allegations. This is reminiscent of the most immediate cause for Nixon's resignation from the office of president—the discovery of audiotapes, which prevented him from denying his involvement in the Watergate scandal.

Other advances have transformed "he said, she said" exchanges into provable claims based on physical evidence. The semen stain on the infamous blue dress was Clinton's final undoing. It is unlikely that the president knew Lewinsky had not had the dress cleaned. DNA testing showed conclusively that Clinton had had an inappropriate relationship with "that woman, Miss Lewinsky," despite his televised denials. Unlike other types of evidence, DNA does not leave open many alternative interpretations.

Clinton's Failure to Adapt to a Changing Environment

If intelligence is defined as the ability to learn from one's experiences, then Clinton's sexual involvement with Lewinsky is consistent with this definition. It is safe to assume that he put little or no conscious thought into the decision to become sexually involved with her—the opportunity presented itself to him. If Lewinsky's account of the affair is accurate, she approached him and signaled her willingness by showing him her bikini underwear. Langer (1989) has provided many useful examples of the "mindlessness" of many decisions like this one.

Clinton's crucial error was his continued reliance on behaviors that had worked in the past when there was clear evidence that they would no longer work. The definition of intelligence proposed by the Task Force on Intelligence includes the general idea that an intelligent person should be able to adapt to the surrounding environment (Neisser et al. 1996). Our environment changes constantly, which can mean that behaviors and expectations that are valid in one context may not be valid in another. An intelligent person recognizes critical changes and adapts to them. One reason for seemingly stupid behavior is reliance on old habits or expectations that do not work in the changed environment.

The literature on critical thinking is filled with examples where even experts fail to consider evidence that would disconfirm a preferred hypothesis (Mynatt, Doherty, & Tweney 1978). Psychologists know a great deal about errors and biases in the thought process (Halpern 1996). The tendency to seek only confirming evidence is robust and probably operates in many settings where it goes unrecognized (Nickerson 1998). Often, people cannot think of any reason why the preferred hypothesis might be wrong. Based on the timeline of events that Monica Lewinsky presented as part of her grand jury testimony, Clinton continued his liaisons with her while the Supreme Court was deciding whether or not he should be immune to civil law suits. By that time, he should have realized that this behavior was far too risky—there was too much to lose. Even if we were to assume that he has a preference for high risk, it is difficult to imagine that these sexual encounters were worth that level of risk.

The Psychology of Explaining

Krull and Anderson (1997) show how explanations of events are often stored in memory, much like other well-learned responses, instead of being constructed based on the facts at hand. When a pattern of events triggers the need to understand what is happening, people retrieve an explanation in a highly automatic manner. The stored explanation is applied to the present situation without considering possible differences between the event we are trying to explain and those that led to the memory of the explanation. The idea of stored mental models to explain events can be hypothesized as contributing to Clinton's failure to change behaviors as the situation changed. As it became more obvious that his sexual liaisons with Lewinsky were not going to present the same set of low-risk problems that prior liaisons had presented, Clinton was slow to abandon responses that had worked in the past. He continued his attempts to cover up the affair and to deny it long after there was considerable evidence that he would not succeed with these strategies.

In a study of the way leaders respond to foreign policy situations, Houghton (1996) found that analogical reasoning is the most frequently used process for dealing with novel problems. Leaders first attempt to identify an appropriate analogy to the current situation, even when none is readily apparent. They then look for information that will increase the similarity between the earlier situation and present one. The ubiquitous confirmation bias—that is, the tendency to seek information that confirms what one believes to be true—is manifest in attempts to make the prior problem more similar to the new one than it actually is. It is easy to imagine how Clinton might have used the same strategy, possibly without any awareness that he was doing so.

Sex in the workplace has become a political and legal hot potato. Twenty years ago, sexual harassment claims were often treated as a joke. By contrast, approximately 15,000 sexual harassment complaints are now filed every year with the Equal Employment Opportunity Commission (*U.S. News & World Report* 1998). The jeers have stopped. In recent judgments, Mitsubishi paid $34 million to more than 500 female employees, and Astra, Inc., paid more than $10 million to 120 female employees (Stephen 1996). As an increasing number of women bump their heads against the glass ceiling, laws are being passed to protect their right to a harassment-free workplace. "Sexual relations" in the workplace has been redefined as an abuse of power because the lower-status worker (usually the woman) is not in a position to make a consensual decision about engaging in sexual relations, especially when the other party has power over job security, advancement, or salary. In the past two decades, most large employers have developed and posted policies that discourage sexual liaisons in the workplace, especially between individuals of unequal power. It is the disparity in power, not the willingness of the individuals, that emerges as the critical determinant of what constitutes sexual harassment. The president of the United States and a young intern with few job qualifications is an extreme example of the power differential that harassment laws are designed to prohibit. Lewinsky both got and lost a job because of her sexual relationship with the president. For most people, this constitutes sexual harassment, despite Lewinsky's willingness to engage in the offending behavior.

It did not help that Clinton is generally perceived as a "pro-feminist" president. He ran on a platform of "women's issues"—issues like equal pay, the need for high-quality child care at an affordable price, and the right to a harassment-free workplace. When Clinton won the election in 1996, he won with an eleven-point "gender gap." This was the largest gap in the voting patterns of men and women in the history of the United States (Kiefer 1999). The strength of his support from women voters was critical to his election and to his generally high approval ratings by the public. Thus, as the tawdry details of his sexual activities with a young, powerless woman (by most accounts) became public knowledge, his large cadre of feminist supporters were particularly distressed. He simultaneously violated several core values of these women and men—he cheated on his wife, a much-admired figure among feminist voters, and, at a minimum, he violated the spirit of laws designed to prevent sexual relations in the workplace.

Clinton's sexual liaisons illustrate the adage "Politics makes strange bedfellows." There are probably none stranger than the ideological shifts and alliances that formed as a result of the Jones harassment suit against Clinton. Conservative groups that had previously scoffed at the need for laws to prevent sexual harassment in the workplace suddenly championed the cause. The conservative Rutherford Institute, which had been concerned primarily with religious issues in the past, supported Paula Jones's sexual harassment suit against Clinton (Young 1998). Clinton's feminist backers responded in kind by increasing their strong support of the president, even at the cost of apparently abandoning antiharassment laws. He could not have anticipated the loyalty of the pro-feminists, who cared more about equal pay, child care and custody issues, equal access to education, and related matters than they cared about his harassment suit. The loyalty of Clinton's feminist supporters may have made the critical difference that allowed him to stay in office.

Two More Critical Errors

Clinton made many mistakes during the investigation of the Lewinsky mess. He apparently underestimated the public's growing intolerance for immoral acts; he was either careless about or unaware of the physical evidence of his sexual activities; and he did not see the parallels between his relationship with Lewinsky and the strong anti–sexual harassment laws he had championed. Despite these "errors," it is likely that there would have been no negative consequence of his behavior with Lewinsky if he had not made two additional mistakes.

THE STARR SPOTLIGHT

Politics is an inherently antagonistic enterprise, with one winning party and many losers at each election and on each issue. The economical and psychological investments in politics are large, so it is not surprising that many wealthy people were eager to spend large sums of money to convince the world that President Clinton had committed egregious crimes—infidelity, lying under oath, obstructing justice, and misuse of power. Those opposed to Clinton had a major advantage that earlier adversaries of cheating presidents did not have—independent counsel Kenneth Starr, who had broad powers and a bottomless pit of money to investigate the president.

Clinton could have stopped the grand jury investigation before news of his involvement with Lewinsky became known by quickly by settling the lawsuit with Jones. Initially, all Jones wanted was a public apology. Clinton refused this early settlement, obviously believing that he could win the case and that he had too much to lose by admitting guilt. Unfortunately for him, Clinton was only half-right. He was correct with regard to the lawsuit—as it was dismissed—but his unwillingness to put a quick end to the Jones suit gave Starr a large amount of time to investigate a wide range of Clinton's behaviors. Clinton's affair with Lewinsky, the alleged sexual advances toward Willey, and the anonymous Jane Does who came forward to testify against the president would never have been discovered if he had settled with Jones early on. Clinton knew that he had much to hide, yet he gave Starr considerable time to uncover additional information that was used against him. It can only be surmised that Clinton underestimated Starr's tenacity. This seems like a severe case of wishful thinking, in which Clinton failed to recognize the (almost) unlimited powers accorded to the independent counsel.

LIES AND DAMN LIES

Clinton's second major error was his use of a "technically correct" definition of sexual relations as a way of denying that he'd had an affair with Lewinsky. His denial was based on a definition that restricted sexual relations to intercourse. Much like Nixon's now infamous remark "I am not a crook," Clinton's denial worked against him. One principle of psycholinguistics (the psychology of language usage) is that a denial means that whatever is being denied is plausible. The purpose of this "legally accurate" definition was to mislead the public. It opened the way for prosecutors to charge Clinton with lying under oath. At the time, he had other alternatives, which included saying nothing, telling the truth, telling a bald-faced lie (for which there would be no possible defense), and issuing a "legally accurate" but pragmatically false denial. Research has shown that the ability to successfully discern lies consistently is restricted to a small minority of specially trained people (only secret service agents can discern lies at a rate that is higher than chance) (Ekman & O'Sullivan 1991).

Unfortunately for Clinton, the Republicans in Congress perceived his use of a "technically correct definition" that was intended to "mislead" as a lie, which led to his impeachment for perjury. In a discussion of the psychology of lying, Saxe (1991) warns that "The line between a lie and the truth is just not ... clear cut" (p. 412). Given the ambiguity in this situation, the Republican majority heard Clinton lie, whereas the Democratic minority did not. Once the charge of perjury was decided, the charge that he had abused the power of his office was endorsed along (virtually) the same party lines.

At the time of Clinton's televised denial and taped testimony for the grand jury, too much was already known for the president's wished-for outcome to occur. The unwillingness to abandon strategies that had been successful in earlier times proved to be Clinton's biggest mistake. Thus, it is his behavior once the investigation began that appears stupid. In considering this interpretation of one smart man's stupid behavior, readers are urged to keep in mind Fischhoff's (1975 / 1994) caveat about hindsight bias: "Those who know how things turned out have trouble believing others didn't see what was coming" (p. 410).

So Dumb, After All?

Compare the historian's job to that of a forecaster. Everyone can assess a situation with more confidence after it has occurred. It's like watching the movie *The Titanic* or *Saving Private Ryan,* in which you already know that the ship sinks or the Nazis lose the war. There are no surprise endings with history. Clinton was impeached, he was publicly humiliated by, among other revelations, the pornographic posting of his sexual escapades on the internet, and he caused great pain for his wife and daughter. Lewinsky and her family have also suffered and will live in the shadow of the scandal their entire lives. But assuming the analysis presented here is correct, even in some small part, then how dumb, really, was President Clinton?

Many readers will not be able to consider the quality of Clinton's thinking apart from its morality, but moral issues are not in question here. For many Americans, sexual infidelity in a marriage, lying to or misleading the public, and asking employees who are in a less powerful position to assist with a cover-up are unquestionably negative acts. Yet an article in a weekly news magazine made this observation: "What interests me most is not how much trouble President Clinton is in, but how little trouble he is in" (Adler & McCormick 1998, p. 66). The public rejected attempts to make Clinton the first president in the history of the United States to be removed from the Oval Office. The U.S. economy had enjoyed a boom in the final years of his presidency, and it seemed that the economic prosperity over which he had presided was far more important than the sordid sexual affairs he ultimately acknowledged. Clinton's job performance ratings improved after Lewinsky's testimony was publicized and the tasteless jokes about cigars and stained dresses made their final rounds on e-mail lists.

Perhaps future presidents can learn some lessons about the American perspective on extramarital sex, honesty, and the office of the presidency. Of course, there would have been no scandal, no huge cost to American taxpayers, and no expenditure of valuable congressional time if Clinton had not engaged in extramarital affairs or had simply admitted the truth early in the investigations. Fidelity and honesty would have been the best policy. But for those future politicians whose inclinations lie elsewhere, I offer these caveats: be aware of changing tides in public opinion and societal standards if you want to avoid detection and punishment. If you are caught in a "compromising situation," honesty may be far less painful than the legal and social consequences of compounding "bad" behavior with lies. Whatever the issue, a more negative outcome can be expected if one's own party is not in the majority. But it is more important to recognize that other performance indicators—like the economy and education—are important to a majority of Americans, who ultimately prevented Clinton's removal from office. When Clinton's behavior is seen from his perspective, it is easy see that mistakes were made, but the long-term view shows that the Clinton-Lewinsky scandal was not a critical determinant of Clinton's place in American history.

REFERENCES

Adler, J., & J. McCormick (1998, Nov. 12). Voices from the culture. *Rolling Stone Magazine, 799,* 66–78.

Bandura, A. (1977). *Social learning theory.* Englewood Cliffs, N.J.: Prentice-Hall.

Ekman, P., & M. O'Sullivan (1991). Who can catch a liar? *American Psychologist, 46,* 913–920.

Fischhoff, B. (1975/April 1994). Kidding yourself with hindsight. Reprinted in *The Best of Psychology Today.* New York: McGraw-Hill Primus, Inc.

Fisher, R., W. Ury, & G. Patton (1991). *Getting to yes* (second edition). New York: Penguin.

Ford, G. R. (1970, Apr. 15). Remarks in Congress. *Congressional Record, 116,* 11913.

Halpern, D. F. (1996). *Thought and knowledge: An introduction to critical thinking* (third edition). Mahwah, N.J.: Erlbaum.

Hite, S. (1987). *The Hite Report: Women and love; a cultural revolution in progress.* New York: Knopf.

Houghton, D. P. (1996). The role of analogical reasoning in novel foreign-policy situations. *British Journal of Political Science, 26,* 523–552.

Kiefer, F. (1999). Clinton stands for women's issues. *Christian Science Monitor, 91*(133), 2.

Kinsey, A. C., C. E. Martin, & W. B. Pomeroy (1948). *Sexual behavior in the human male.* Philadelphia: Saunders.

Krull, D. S., & C. A. Anderson (1997). The process of explanation. *Current Directions in Psychological Science, 6,* 1–5.

Lacayo. R., & J. Branegan (1998). Washington burning. *Time, 152*(26), 60–67.

Langer, E. J. (1989). *Mindfulness.* Reading, Mass.: Addison-Wesley.

Meller, B. A., A. Schwartz, & A. D. J. Cooke (1998). Judgment and decision making. *Annual Review of Psychology, 49,* 447–477.

Miller. A. C. (1999, Aug. 2). Hillary Clinton explains why she stayed. *Los Angeles Times,* pp. A1/A11.

Myers, D. (2000). *The American paradox.* New Haven: Yale University Press.

Mynatt, C.R., M. E. Doherty, & R. D. Tweney (1978). Consequences of confirmation and disconfirmation in a simulated research environment. *Quarterly Journal of Experimental Psychology, 30,* 395–406.

Neisser, U., G. Boodoo, T. J. Bouchard, Jr., A. W. Boykin, N. Brody, S. J. Ceci, D. F. Halpern, J. C. Loehlin, R. Perloff, R. J. Sternberg, & S. Urbina (1996). Intelligence: Knowns and unknowns. *American Psychologist, 51,* 77–101.

Nickerson, R. S. (1998). Confirmation bias: A ubiquitous phenomenon in many guises. *Review of General Psychology, 2,*175–220.

Norment, L. (1998, Dec. 7). Why women cheat. *Newsweek, 132*(23), 34.

Saxe, L. (1991). Lying: Thoughts of an applied social psychologist. *American Psychologist, 46,* 409–415.

Seelye, K. Q. (1999, June 6). Gore terms Clinton affair inexcusable. *New York Times, 148*(51555), p. A26.

Stephen, A. (1996, June 14). Fondle a woman; pay $250,000 (sexual lawsuits result in gargantuan damages). *New Statesman, 128*(4440), 20.

U.S. News & World Report. (1998, Dec. 14). Cupid's cubicles (growing industry preventing workplace sexual harassment lawsuits—Industry overview).

Wiederman, M. W. (1999, July). Life in America. *USA Today Magazine, 128,* 74–76.

Young, C. (1998, Nov. 9). The scandal III: Harassment hypocrites. *National Review,* 1.

KEITH E. STANOVICH

7 Rationality, Intelligence, and Levels of Analysis in Cognitive Science

IS DYSRATIONALIA POSSIBLE?

In a 1994 article in the journal *Cognition,* Eldar Shafir describes a very straightforward rule from decision theory. The rule, termed the sure-thing principle by Savage (1954), says the following. Imagine you are choosing between two possible outcomes, A and B, and event X is an event that may or may not occur in the future. If you prefer prospect A to prospect B if X happens and also you prefer prospect A to prospect B if X does not happen, then you definitely prefer A to B, and that preference is in no way changed by knowledge of event X—so you should prefer A to B whether you know anything about event X or not. Shafir calls the sure-thing principle "one of the simplest and least controversial principles of rational behavior" (p. 404). Indeed, it is so simple and obvious that it hardly seems worth stating. Yet in his article, Shafir reviews a host of studies that have demonstrated that people do indeed violate the sure-thing principle.

For example, Tversky and Shafir (1992) created a scenario where subjects were asked to imagine that they were at the end of the term, tired and run down, and awaiting the grade in a course they might fail and be forced to retake. They were to imagine that they had just been given the opportunity to purchase an extremely attractive vacation package to Hawaii at a very low price. More than half of a group of students who were informed that they had passed the exam chose to buy the vacation package, and an even larger proportion of a group who had been told that they had failed the exam chose to buy the vacation package. However, only one-third of a group who did not know whether they had passed or failed the exam chose to purchase the vacation. What these results collectively mean is that, by inference, at least some subjects were saying "I'll go if I pass and I'll go if I fail, but I won't go if I don't know whether I passed or failed."

Shafir (1994) describes a host of decision situations where this outcome obtains. Subjects prefer A to B when event X obtains, prefer A to B when X does not obtain, but prefer B to A when uncertain about the outcome X—a clear violation of the sure-thing principle. These violations are not limited to hypothetical problems or laboratory situations. Shafir provides some real-life examples, one involving the stock market just prior to the Bush/Dukakis election of 1988. Market analysts were nearly unanimous in their opinion that Wall Street preferred Bush to Dukakis. Yet subsequent to Bush's election, stock and bond prices declined and the dollar plunged to its lowest level in ten months. Of course, analysts agreed that the outcome would have been worse had Dukakis been elected. Yet if the market was going to go down subsequent to the election of Bush, and going to go down even further subsequent to the election of Dukakis, then why didn't it go down *before* the election in response to the absolute certainty that whoever was elected (Bush or Dukakis), the outcome would be bad for the market? The market seems to have violated the sure-thing principle.

The sure-thing principle is not the only rule of rational thinking that humans have been shown to violate. A substantial research literature—one comprising literally hundreds of empirical studies conducted over nearly four decades—has firmly established that people's responses often deviate from the performance considered normative on many reasoning tasks. For example, people assess probabilities incorrectly, they display confirmation bias, they test hypotheses inefficiently, they violate the axioms of utility theory, they do not properly calibrate degrees of belief, they overproject their own opinions onto others, they display illogical framing effects, they uneconomically honor sunk costs, they allow prior knowledge to become implicated in deductive reasoning, and they display numerous other information processing biases (for summaries of the large literature, see Arkes 1991; Baron 1994, 1998; Dawes 1998; Evans 1989; Evans & Over 1996; Kahneman, Slovic, & Tversky 1982; Nickerson 1998, Oskisson 1995, Piattelli-Palmarini 1994; Plous 1993; Shafir & Tversky 1995; Stanovich 1999, Tversky 1996).

The reader need not be familiar with all these principles of rational thinking. It is sufficient to appreciate that many of them are as fundamental as the sure-thing principle just discussed. It is also important to point out that these reasoning errors do cash out in real-life behaviors that are decidedly suboptimal and unpleasant for those displaying these processing biases. Because of the failure to follow the normative rules of rational thought— because of the processing biases listed above—physicians choose less effective medical treatments (McNeil et al. 1982; Redelmeier & Tversky 1990, 1992; Sutherland 1992); people fail to accurately assess risks in their environment (Lichtenstein et al. 1978; Margolis 1996; Yates 1992); information is misused in legal proceedings (Saks & Kidd 1980–1981); millions of dollars are spent on unneeded projects by government and private industry (Arkes & Ayton 1999; Dawes 1988, pp. 23–24); parents fail to vaccinate their children (Baron 1998); unnecessary surgeries are performed (Dawes 1988, pp. 73–75); animals are hunted to extinction (Baron 1998; Dawkins 1998); billions of dollars are wasted on quack medical remedies (Gilovich 1991); and costly financial misjudgments are made (Belsky 1995; Belsky & Gilovich 1999; Fridson 1993; Thaler 1992; Tversky 1996; Willis 1990).

Many of these examples concern what philosophers call pragmatic, or practical, rationality—how well individuals maximize the satisfaction of their desires, given their beliefs (Audi 1993; Harman 1995; Nathanson 1994). This is often contrasted with epistemic rationality, which is concerned with the consistency of a person's network of beliefs and how well it represents the external world (the so-called theoretical rationality of philosophy) (Audi 1993; Foley 1987; Harman 1995).

Smart People Doing Dumb Things: Resolving the Paradox

The findings from the reasoning and decision making literature and the many real-world examples of the consequences of irrational thinking (e.g., Belsky & Gilovich 1999; Gilovich 1991; Piattelli-Palmarini 1994; Shermer 1997; Sutherland 1992; Thaler 1992) create a seeming paradox. The physicians using ineffective procedures, the financial analysts making costly misjudgments, the retired professionals managing their money poorly—none of these are unintelligent people. The experimental literature is even more perplexing. Over 90 percent of the subjects in the studies in the literature are university students—some from the most selective institutions of higher learning in the world (Tversky and Shafir's subjects are from Stanford). Yet these are the very people who have provided the data indicating that a substantial proportion of people can sometimes violate the most basic strictures of rational thought, such as transitivity or the sure-thing principle. It appears that an awful lot of pretty smart people are doing some incredibly dumb things. How are we to understand this seeming contradiction?

The first step in understanding the seeming paradox is to realize that the question "How can so many smart people be doing so many dumb things?" is phrased in the language of folk psychology. The issue of how to interpret folk psychology is a topic of immense interest in cognitive science at present, and it is the subject of much controversy (Christensen & Turner 1993; Churchland & Churchland 1998; Davies & Stone 1995; Greenwood 1991; Stich 1996). Positions vary from those who think that most folk psychology needs to be eliminated from the terminology of scientific psychology to those who think that folk psychology should be the very foundation of a scientific psychology. My concern here is not with these classic issues but with how concepts in cognitive science can be used to make folk usage more precise in ways that serve to dissipate seeming paradoxes.[1] I propose to do just this with the "smart but dumb" phrase. In this chapter, I identify the folk term "smart" with the psychology concept of intelligence (defined as an amalgamation of cognitive capacities). The acts that spawn the folk term "dumb" I identify with violations of rationality as that term is conceptualized within cognitive science, philosophy, and decision science (Baron 1993a; Harman 1995; Jeffrey 1983; Kleindorfer, Kunreuther, & Schoemaker 1993; Nathanson 1994; Nozick 1993). This mapping does not immediately solve the problem, because there are several different ways of parsing the concepts intelligence and rationality—especially within psychology. Thus, I present one such partitioning that I think is useful in contextualizing the "smart but dumb" phenomenon and dissolving its seemingly paradoxical status. The partitioning that I prefer relies heavily on distinguishing levels of analysis in cognitive theory.

Levels of Analysis in Cognitive Science

Levels of analysis in cognitive theory have been discussed by numerous theorists (Anderson 1990, 1991; Dennett 1978, 1987; Horgan & Tienson 1993; Levelt 1995; Marr 1982; Newell 1982, 1990; Oaksford & Chater 1995; Pylyshyn 1984; Sterelny 1990). For example, Anderson (1990) defines four levels of theorizing in cognitive science: a biological level, which is inaccessible to cognitive theorizing; an implementation level, which is basically a comprehensible shorthand approximation to the biological; an algorithmic level, concerned with the computational processes necessary to carry out a

TABLE 7.1. Different Levels of Cognitive Theory as Characterized by Several Investigators and in This Chapter

Anderson	Marr	Newell	Dennett	This Chapter
Rational level	Computational level	Knowledge level	Intentional stance	Intentional level
Algorithmic level		Program symbol level		
	Representation and algorithm		Design stance	Algorithmic level
Implementation level		Register transfer level		
Biological level	Hardware implementation	Device	Physical stance	Biological level

task; and the rational level. The rational level provides a specification of the *goals* of the system's computations (*what* the system is attempting to compute and *why*) and can be used to suggest constraints on the operation of the algorithmic level. The rational level of analysis is concerned with the goals of the system, beliefs relevant to those goals, and the choice of action that is rational given the system's goals and beliefs (Bratman, Israel, & Pollack 1991; Dennett 1987; Newell 1982, 1990; Pollock 1995).

Many similar taxonomies exist in the literature. Sterelny (1990, p. 46) warns of the "bewildering variety of terms" used to describe these levels of analysis. Indeed, Anderson's (1990) draws heavily on the work of Marr (1982) and Newell (1982). Table 7.1 presents the alternative, but similar, schemes of Anderson (1990), Marr (1982), Newell (1982), Dennett (1987), and a compromise scheme that I used in a 1999 volume (Stanovich 1999) and that will be used in this chapter. The most fundamental level of analysis is termed the "biological level" in my taxonomy because I am largely concerned here with human information processing rather than computational devices in general. My scheme follows those of Marr (1982) and Dennett (1987) in collapsing Anderson's algorithmic and implementation levels into one, because for the purposes of the present discussion the distinction between these two levels is not important. This second level is termed "algorithmic"—a term that is relatively uncontroversial.

In contrast, the proper term for the remaining level is variable and controversial. Borrowing from Dennett (1987), I have termed this level of analysis the "intentional level" for the following reasons. First, Anderson (1990) has argued that Marr's (1982) terminology is confusing and inapt because "his level of computational theory is not really about computation but rather about the goals of the computation. His basic point is that one should state these goals and understand their implications before one worries about their computation, which is really the concern of the lower levels of his theory" (p. 6). Dennett (1987) reiterates this critique of Marr's terminology by noting that "the highest level, which he misleadingly calls computational, is in fact concerned not with computational processes but strictly (and more abstractly) with the question of what function the system in question is serving" (pp. 74–75). The term chosen by Newell (1982)—the "knowledge level"—is equally inapt in not signaling that this level is concerned with action selection based on expected goal attainment in light of current beliefs. Instead, I have adapted Dennett's terminology and referred to this level as the intentional level of analysis. Although Sterelny (1990, p. 45) argues that this level of analysis is not necessarily tied to an intentional psychology, like Dennett, I do want to conjoin the two—so in the present case, the term is apt.

Thinking Dispositions, Cognitive Capacities, and Levels of Analysis

In many areas of psychology, increasing attention is being paid to behavioral/cognitive concepts that reside at the borderline of cognitive psychology and personality (Ackerman & Heggestad 1997; Goff & Ackerman 1992; Haslam & Baron 1994; Keating 1990; Nickerson 1988; Perkins 1995; Perkins, Jay, & Tishman 1993; Rolfhus & Ackerman 1999; Siegel 1993; Stanovich & West 1997; Sternberg 1997b; Sternberg & Ruzgis 1994; Swartz & Perkins 1989). Moshman (1994), for instance, reminds us of the importance of "considerations of will and disposition [because they] lie at the interface of cognition with affect, motivation, social relations, and cultural context" (p. 143), and Sternberg (1988) likewise notes that "intellectual styles represent an important link between intelligence and personality, because they probably represent, in part, a way in which personality is manifested in intelligent thought and action" (p. 218). Terminology surrounding such notions is remarkably varied. The term "thinking dispositions" is used in this chapter (see Baron 1988; Ennis 1987; Perkins 1995; Stanovich & West 1997), although other theorists—in dealing with similar concepts—prefer terms such as intellectual style (Sternberg 1988, 1989), cognitive emotions (Scheffler 1991), habits of mind (Keating 1990), inferential propensities (Kitcher 1993, pp. 65–72), epistemic motivations (Kruglanski 1990), constructive meta-reasoning (Moshman 1994), styles of epistemic regulation (Sá, West, & Stanovich 1999; Stanovich 1999); cognitive styles (Messick 1984, 1994), and thinking styles (Sternberg 1997b). Despite this diversity of terminology, most authors use such terms similarly—to refer to relatively stable psychological mechanisms and strategies that tend to generate characteristic behavioral tendencies and tactics (see Buss 1991).

In this chapter, it is proposed that thinking dispositions should be distinguished from cognitive capacities because the two constructs are at different levels of analysis in cognitive theory and do separate explanatory work. This distinction motivates interest in a consistent empirical finding in the literature—that thinking dispositions can predict performance on reasoning and rational thinking tasks even after individual differences in measures of general cognitive ability have been partialled out.

The distinction between cognitive capacities and thinking dispositions has been drawn by many theorists (e.g., Baron 1985, 1988, 1993b; Ennis 1987; Moshman 1994; Norris 1992; Perkins et al. 1993; Schrag 1988). For example, in Baron's conceptualization (1985, 1988), capacities refer to the types of cognitive processes studied by information processing researchers seeking the underlying cognitive basis of performance on IQ tests. Perceptual speed, discrimination accuracy, working memory capacity, and the efficiency of the retrieval of information stored in long-term memory are examples of cognitive capacities that underlie traditional psychometric intelligence and that have been extensively investigated (Ackerman, Kyllonen, & Richards 1999; Carpenter, Just, & Shell 1990; Deary & Stough 1996; Engle et al. 1999; Fry & Hale 1996; Hunt 1978, 1987; Lohman 1989; Sternberg 1982; Vernon 1991, 1993). These cognitive capacities are what Baltes (1987) terms the "mechanics of intelligence." Psychometric g provides an overall index of the cognitive efficiency of a wide variety of such mechanisms in a given individual (Carroll 1993, 1997). According to Baron's (1985) conception, cognitive capacities cannot be improved in the short term by admonition or instruction. They are, nevertheless, affected by long-term practice.

Thinking dispositions, in contrast, are better viewed as cognitive styles that are more malleable: "Although you cannot improve working memory by instruction, you can tell someone to spend more time on problems before she gives up, and if she is so inclined, she can do what you say" (Baron 1985, p. 15). Rational thinking dispositions are those that relate to the adequacy of belief formation and decision making—things like "the disposition to weigh new evidence against a favored belief heavily (or lightly), the disposition to spend a great deal of time (or very little) on a problem before giving up, or the disposition to weigh heavily the opinions of others in forming one's own" (p. 15).

By and large, psychometric instruments such as IQ tests have tapped cognitive capacities almost exclusively and have ignored cognitive styles and thinking dispositions (Baron 1985, 1988; Stanovich 1994; Sternberg 1997b). Importantly, Baron (1988) argues that in ignoring dispositions, the IQ concept "has distorted our understanding of thinking. It has encouraged us to believe that the only general determinants of good thinking are capacities, and this attitude has led to the neglect of general dispositions" (p. 122; see also Sternberg 1997b). It will be argued here that the study of thinking dispositions balances this tendency by directing attention to the possibility of systematically suboptimal systems at the intentional level of analysis.

Recall that each level of analysis in cognitive theory frames a somewhat different issue. At the algorithmic level the key issue is one of computational efficiency, and at the biological level the paramount issue is whether the physical mechanism has the potential to instantiate certain complex algorithms. In contrast, it is at the intentional level that issues of rationality arise. Using this taxonomy, it is proposed here that omnibus measures of cognitive capacities such as intelligence tests are best understood as indexing individual differences in the efficiency of processing at the algorithmic level. In contrast, thinking dispositions as traditionally studied in psychology (e.g., Cacioppo et al. 1996; Kardash & Scholes 1996; Klaczynski, Gordon, & Fauth 1997; Kruglanski & Webster 1996; Schommer 1990, 1993, 1994; Stanovich & West 1997; Sternberg 1997b) index individual differences at the intentional level of analysis. They are telling us about the individual's goals and epistemic values (Sá et al. 1999)—and they are indexing broad tendencies of pragmatic and epistemic self-regulation. For example, in his model of mind as a control system, Sloman (1993) views desires as control states that can produce behavior either directly or through a complex control hierarchy by changing intermediate desire-states. He views dispositions (high-level attitudes, ideals, and personality traits) as long-term desire-states that "work through a control hierarchy, for instance, by changing other desire-like states rather than triggering behaviour" (p. 85).

Thus, thinking dispositions are reflective of intentional-level psychological structure. It has been the goal of our research program to determine whether such features of intentional-level psychology can serve as explanatory mechanisms in accounts of discrepancies between normative and descriptive models of behavior (Stanovich 1999). If thinking dispositions correlate with individual differences in the normative/descriptive gap, then this is prima facie evidence that the gap is caused by actual differences in intentional psychology. However, any such association might well arise because the variation in thinking dispositions is co-extensive with differences in computational capacity. Thus, it is important to examine whether intentional-level cognitive dispositions can explain unique variance—variance independent of cognitive capacity. This has been one of the major analytic tests we have used when examining individual differences across a variety of rational thinking tasks in the heuristics and biases literature (Stanovich 1999). In short, we have been searching for systematic differences in intentional-level psychology that are not explainable by variation in algorithmic capacity.

Thinking Dispositions as Predictors of Rational Thought

Discussions of critical thinking in the educational and psychological literature consistently point to the importance of the ability to evaluate arguments and evidence in a way that is not contaminated by one's prior beliefs. For example, Norris and Ennis (1989) list as one characteristic of critical thinkers the tendency to "reason from starting points with which they disagree without letting the disagreement interfere with their reasoning" (p. 12). Similarly, Nickerson (1987) and many other theorists (e.g., Lipman 1991; Paul 1984, 1987; Perkins 1995; Perkins et al. 1993; Swartz & Perkins 1989) stress that critical thinking entails the ability to recognize "the fallibility of one's own opinions, the probability of bias in those opinions, and the danger of differentially weighting evidence according to personal preferences" (Nickerson 1987, p. 30). The growing literature on informal or practical reasoning likewise emphasizes the importance of detaching one's own beliefs from the process of argument evaluation (Baron 1991, 1995; Brenner, Koehler, & Tversky 1996; Kardash & Scholes 1996; Klaczynski & Gordon 1996; Klaczynski et al. 1997; Kuhn 1991, 1993; Perkins 1985; Stanovich & West 1997; Voss, Perkins, & Segal 1991).

In light of the emphasis in the critical thinking literature on the importance of evaluating arguments independently of prior belief, it is noteworthy that there are increasing indications in the research literature that individual differences in this skill can be predicted by thinking dispositions even after differences in general cognitive ability have been partialled out. For example, Schommer (1990) found that a measure of the disposition to believe in certain knowledge predicted the tendency to draw one-sided conclusions from ambiguous evidence even after verbal ability was controlled. Kardash and Scholes (1996) found that the tendency to properly draw inconclusive inferences from mixed evidence was related to belief in certain knowledge and to a measure of need for cognition (Cacioppo et al., 1996). Furthermore, these relationships were not mediated by verbal ability, because a vocabulary measure was essentially unrelated to evidence evaluation. Likewise, Klaczynski (1997; see also Klaczynski & Gordon 1996; Klaczynski et al. 1997) found that the degree to which adolescents criticized belief-inconsistent evidence more than belief-consistent evidence was unrelated to cognitive ability (see also Perkins, Farady, & Bushey 1991).

Results from our own studies have converged with those of Schommer (1990) and Kardash and Scholes (1996) in indicating that thinking dispositions can predict argument evaluation skill once cognitive ability is partialled out. We have developed an argument evaluation task in which we derive an index of the degree to which argument evaluation is associated with argument quality independent of prior belief (see Stanovich & West 1997; Sá et al. 1999). Our methodology involves assessing, on a separate instrument, the participant's prior beliefs about a series of controversial propositions. On an argument evaluation measure, administered at a later time, the participants evaluate the quality of arguments related to the same propositions. The arguments have an operationally determined objective quality that varies from item to item. Our analytic strategy is to regress each subject's evaluations of the argument simultaneously on the objective measure of argument quality and on the strength of the belief he or she had about the propositions prior to reading the argument. The standardized beta weight for argument quality then becomes an index of that subject's reliance on the quality of the arguments independent of the subject's beliefs concerning the issues in question. The magnitude of the former statistic becomes an index of argument-driven, or data-driven processing (to use Norman's (1976) term).

Our methodology is different from the traditional logic used in critical thinking tests, and it is a more sensitive one for measuring individual differences (see Stanovich, 1999, for a discussion). For example, standardized critical thinking tests often simply try to balance opinions across items by utilizing a variety of issues and relying on chance to ensure that prior belief and strength of the argument are relatively balanced from respondent to respondent (Watson & Glaser 1980). In contrast, we actually *measured* the prior opinion and took it into account in the analysis (for related techniques, see Klaczynski & Gordon 1996; Kuhn 1991, 1993; Kuhn, Amsel, & O'Loughlin 1988; Slusher & Anderson 1996). The technique allowed us to examine thought processes in areas of "hot" cognition where biases are most likely to operate (Babad & Katz 1991; Klaczynski & Narasimham 1998; Kunda 1990, 1999; Pyszczynski & Greenberg 1987).

We have consistently found (see Stanovich & West 1997; Sá et al. 1999) that *even after controlling for cognitive ability,* individual differences on our index of argument-driven processing can be predicted by measures of dogmatism and absolutism (Rokeach 1960), categorical thinking (Epstein & Meier 1989), openness (Costa & McCrae 1992), flexible thinking (Stanovich & West 1997), belief identification (Sá et al. 1999), counterfactual thinking, superstitious thinking (Stanovich 1989; Tobacyk & Milford 1983), and actively open-minded thinking as conceptualized by Baron (1985, 1988, 1993b; see also, Facione 1992; Norris & Ennis 1989; Perkins et al. 1993). These findings converge with those of Schommer (1990) and Kardash and Scholes (1996) in supporting a conceptualization of human cognition that emphasizes the potential separability of cognitive capacities and thinking styles/ dispositions as predictors of reasoning skill (e.g., Baron 1985, 1988; Ennis, 1987; Kitchener & Fischer 1990; Klaczynski et al. 1997; Norris 1992; Schrag 1988; Siegel 1993; Sternberg 1997b).

Such a separation in psychological constructs makes sense if indeed they do map onto different levels of analysis in cognitive theory. I proposed earlier in this chapter that variation in cognitive ability refers to individual differences in the efficiency of processing at the algorithmic level. In contrast, thinking dispositions index individual differences at the intentional level. They are telling us about the individual's goals and epistemic values (King & Kitchener 1994; Kitcher 1993; Kruglanski & Webster 1996; Pintrich, Marx, & Boyle 1993; Schommer, 1990, 1993, 1994; Stanovich 1999). For example, consider an individual who scores high on our measures of actively open-minded thinking (see Stanovich & West 1997) and low on measures of dogmatism and absolutism—a person who agrees with statements such as "People should always take into consideration evidence that goes against their beliefs" and who disagrees with statements such as "No one can talk me out of something I know is right." Such a response pattern indicates that this person values belief change in order to get closer to the truth. This individual is signaling that she values having an accurate *belief forming system* more than she values holding onto her current beliefs (see Cederblom, 1989, for an insightful discussion of this distinction and our scale based on this notion in Sá et al. 1999).

In contrast, consider a person scoring low on actively open-minded thinking measures and high on measures of absolutism and categorical thinking—a person who disagrees with statements such as "A person should always consider new possibilities" and who agrees with statements such as "There are a number of people I have come to hate because of the things they stand for." Such a response pattern indicates that retaining current beliefs is an important goal for this person. This individual is signaling that he values highly the beliefs he currently has and that he puts a very small premium on mechanisms that might improve belief accuracy (but that involve belief change).

In short, thinking dispositions of the type studied by Schommer (1990, 1993, 1994), Kardash and Scholes (1996), and Stanovich and West (1997) provide information about epistemic goals at the rational level of analysis. Within such a conceptualization, we can perhaps better understand why such thinking dispositions predict additional variance in argument evaluation even after cognitive ability is partialled out. This result may indicate that to understand variation in reasoning in such a task we need to examine more than just differences at the algorithmic level (computational capacity)—*we must know something about the epistemic goals of the reasoners.*

Thus, performance on tasks requiring reasoning about previously held beliefs, while certainly somewhat dependent upon the cognitive capacity of the subject, also depends on the balance of epistemic goals held by the reasoners. The instructions for many tasks that require reasoning in the face of belief bias (Baron 1995; Evans, Newstead, Allen, & Pollard 1994; Oakhill, Johnson-Laird, & Garnham 1989; Stanovich & West 1997) dictate that prior belief be totally discounted in evaluating the argument. But individuals may differ in their willingness and/or ability to adapt to such instructions. Some individuals may put a low priority on allocating computational capacity to evaluate the argument. Instead, for them, capacity is engaged to assess whether the conclusion is compatible with prior beliefs (Evans, Barston, & Pollard 1983; Evans et al. 1994). Other individuals—of equal cognitive ability—may marshal their cognitive resources to decouple (see Navon 1989a, 1989b) argument evaluation from their prior beliefs as the instructions demand. These individuals may easily engage in such a processing strategy because it does not conflict with their epistemic goals. Many problems in practical reasoning may have a similar logic (Baron 1991, 1995; Foley 1991; Klaczynski & Gordon 1996; Kuhn 1991; Perkins et al. 1991; Schoenfeld 1983). Such problems—although they obviously stress algorithmic capacity to varying degrees—might also differ greatly in how they engage people's goal structure.

Thus, to fully understand variation in evidence evaluation performance, we might need to consider variation at the rational level as well as at the algorithmic level of cognitive analysis. Indeed, this may be true for other measures of rational and critical thought as well. In fact, we have linked various measures of thinking dispositions to statistical reasoning tasks of various types (Stanovich 1999; Stanovich & West 1998, 2000). For example, Nisbett and Ross (1980) have demonstrated how human judgment is overly influenced by vivid but unrepresentative personal and testimonial evidence and is underinfluenced by more representative and diagnostic statistical information. Studying the variation in this response tendency is important because, as Griffin and Tversky (1992) argue, "the tendency to prefer an individual or 'inside' view rather than a statistical or 'outside' view represents one of the major departures of intuitive judgment from normative theory" (pp. 431–432). The quintessential problem (see Fong, Krantz, & Nisbett 1986) involves choosing between contradictory car purchase recommendations—one from a large-sample survey of car buyers and the other the heartfelt and emotional testimony of a single friend. Fong and colleagues (1986) and Jepson, Krantz, and Nisbett (1983) have studied a variety of such problems, and we have examined a number of them in our own research. We have consistently found that even though these problems are presented to participants as having no right or wrong answers, dispositions toward actively open-minded thinking (Baron 1993b) are consistently associated with reliance on the statistical evidence rather than the testimonial evidence. Furthermore, this association remains even after cognitive ability has been controlled.

We have examined a variety of other critical and rational thinking tasks and have consistently found the same pattern. For example, we have examined the phenomenon of outcome bias in decision evaluation (Baron & Hershey 1988)—the tendency to rate decision quality according to the outcome of the decision even when the outcome provides no cues to the information available to the decision maker. We again found that the ability to avoid outcome bias was associated with dispositions toward actively open-minded thinking and that this tendency was not due solely to differences in cognitive ability. Similar results were found for a variety of other hypothesis testing and reasoning tasks (Stanovich 1999; Stanovich & West 1998, 2000).

Throughout several of our studies, normative responding on a variety of problems from the heuristics and biases literature (see Arkes & Hammond 1986; Kahneman & Tversky 2000; Kahneman et al. 1982) was moderately correlated with cognitive ability. Nevertheless, these algorithmic-level limitations were far from absolute. The magnitude of the associations with cognitive ability left much room for the possibility that the remaining reliable variance might indicate there are systematic irrationalities in intentional-level psychology. It was rarely the case that once capacity limitations had been controlled, the remaining variations from normative responding were unpredictable (which would have indicated that the residual variance consisted largely of performance errors). In several studies, we have shown that there was significant covariance among the scores from a variety of tasks in the heuristics and biases literature after they had been residualized on measures of cognitive ability (Stanovich 1999). The residual variance (after partialling cognitive ability) was also systematically associated with questionnaire responses that were conceptualized as intentional-level styles relating to epistemic regulation (Sá et al. 1999; Stanovich 1999; Stanovich & West

1997, 1998, 2000). Both of these findings are indications that the residual variance is systematic. They falsify models that attempt to explain the normative/ descriptive gap entirely in terms of computational limitations and random performance errors. Instead, the findings support the notion that the normative/descriptive discrepancies that remain after computational limitations have been accounted for reflect a systematically suboptimal intentional-level psychology.

The Rationality/Intelligence Demarcation: Dissolving the Smart but Dumb Paradox

The empirical work summarized above illustrates why I think the distinction between cognitive capacities and thinking dispositions is useful to psychological theory. I further propose that it might clarify folk usage like the "smart but dumb" phrasing if the concept of intelligence is restricted to the domain of individual differences in cognitive capacities—in short, that the expression be restricted to discussions of computational capacity at the algorithmic level of analysis. In contrast, the term "rationality" is used here to refer to styles of epistemic and response regulation at the intentional level of analysis.

Using this terminology, we see that the results summarized above can be taken to indicate that while the algorithmic level constrains the intentional level—as it is standard to assume in cognitive science (Cherniak 1986; Goldman 1978; Harman 1995; Oaksford & Chater 1993, 1995)—from an individual differences perspective, the correlation between individual differences at the two levels is less than unity. Thus, dissociations between intentional-level individual differences and algorithmic-level individual differences are indeed possible. Rationality can dissociate from intelligence on this view.

A little mapping of folk psychological terms now resolves the paradox with which we opened this chapter. In the vernacular, we often say "What a dumb thing to do" when irrational thinking has led to a maladaptive behavioral act—an act best analyzed by positing suboptimal action regulation at the intentional level of analysis. For example, Baron (1985) notes that "When we disapprovingly call a person 'stupid' because of some action, for example, a political leader, we do not often mean that the action was done too slowly, or that it would not have been done if the doer had a larger working memory capacity. . . . When we call someone stupid, we are really saying he is irrational, not that he is retarded" (p. 235).

The problem here is that for many, the antonym for dumb and stupid is often "smart" and this, to most people, often connotes intelligence—here viewed as an algorithmic-level concept having to do with cognitive capacity. If the folk psychological view shades the connotation of "dumb" a little more toward rationality than toward intelligence, and the connotation of "smart" a little less toward rationality and a little more toward intelligence, then there is no paradox at all. There is nothing strange in smart people acting dumb, because people can have considerable algorithmic capacity yet still display irrational behavior and thought as a result of systematic sub-optimalities in their intentional-level psychologies—in the systems that regulate epistemic functioning and action determination (see Stanovich 1999). This is one way to view what the heuristics and biases literature has been demonstrating now for over thirty years (e.g., Arkes 1991; Dawes 1998; Kahneman, Slovic, & Tversky 1982; Kahneman & Tversky 2000; Nickerson 1998; Piattelli-Palmarini 1994; Shafir & Tversky 1995). In short, if the folk usage is parsed in this manner, then there emerges a thirty-year research history of demonstrations of "smart people acting dumb."

Dysrationalia: Demarcating Intelligence and Rationality

In previous publications (Stanovich 1993, 1994) I have tried to draw attention to the intelligence/rationality distinction by proposing a new discrepancy-based disability category termed "dysrationalia"—the inability to think and behave rationally despite adequate intelligence. The coining of this term (which was called an "epistemological bender" by one commentator; see Metcalf 1998) served not only as a critique of discrepancy definitions in learning disabilities but also as a tool for exploring whether conceptual work could be done by differentiating intelligence and rationality in the manner described above.

I recognize that such a differentiation cuts against the grain of current trends in terminological practice. Specifically, it is the case that many prominent theorists depart from the distinction suggested above and prefer to conflate the terms "rationality" and "intelligence" in a manner more in line with folk psychology.[2] For example, Baron's (1985) use of the distinction between cognitive capacities and rational thinking dispositions is somewhat different from that exemplified in the concept of dysrationalia. He proposes that these dispositions be *folded into* our view of intelligence—that intelligence be made to encompass rationality. Perkins (1995; Perkins et al. 1993) likewise subsumes rationality under the construct of intelligence.

Similarly, Sternberg (1997a) explicitly defines intelligence in a manner that subsumes *both* epistemic and pragmatic rationality: "A more intelligent, adaptive person has achieved a higher degree of external correspondence and internal coherence in his or her knowledge base and belief structures. People think unintelligently to the extent that they make errors in achieving external correspondence or internal coherence. For example, in believing the gambler's fallacy, a person fails in achieving external correspondence; in touching a hot stove despite knowledge of the danger of doing so, a person fails in achieving internal coherence" (p. 1031). Thus, in appropriating external correspondence for the concept of intelligence, Sternberg (1997a) encompasses epistemic rationality—the "hot stove" example is a clear case of pragmatic rationality. This intelligence conception thoroughly incorporates notions of rationality. Likewise, characterizations of intelligent behavior as that which helps us achieve our goals or that which helps us to adapt to the environment (Sternberg & Detterman 1986) conceptualize intelligence as something overlapping with rationality, even if actual operationalizations of the concept do not reflect this.

All these theorists have made progress with their conflated conceptions of intelligence and rationality, and thus my program differentiating the two should not be seen as replacing these efforts. There is more than one way to carve this particularly complex part of nature at its joints, and each of the parsings has various strengths and weaknesses. I have alluded to some of these tradeoffs previously (Stanovich 1993, 1994). For example, the conflated definition perhaps serves as a better platform for a critique of the properties of current IQ tests (a critique I am in some sympathy with; see Stanovich 1991, 1994). Allowing intelligence to subsume rationality highlights the fact that we *cannot* identify current IQ tests with the concept of intelligence defined in this sense. In contrast, from the standpoint of a nonconflated definition, the tests—taken as omnibus indicators of overall functioning at the algorithmic level of analysis only—are less problematic first approximations.

Accord with vernacular usage (Neisser 1979; Sternberg 1985; Sternberg et al. 1981) might be deemed another advantage of the conflated definition, although, as I have argued previously (Stanovich 1990), convergence with folk psychology is very much a two-edged sword (Churchland 1979; Churchland & Churchland 1998). For example, the disability of dysrationalia disappears under this view, which many may view as a virtue. But there is a cost to this disappearance: we can no longer explain the "strangeness" of the notion of smart people acting dumb. Instead, we must accept the implication of the conflated view—smart people acting dumb really aren't as smart as we thought they were! Rational behavior is part of intelligence under the conflated view. What my view identifies as irrationality in the face of intelligence (dysrationalia) the conflated view calls impeached intelligence.

Despite some drawbacks, I have explored an alternative parsing of the psychological concepts in this chapter in order to give its advantages a fuller airing. First, as I have argued, the parsing I have argued for dissolves the somewhat paradoxical connotations of the "smart but acting dumb" phrase. Even more important, there are other significant issues raised and at least partially answered by my distinctions. In the remainder of the chapter, I will highlight a few of these.

Individual Differences at the Intentional Level of Analysis

If we conflate intelligence and rationality in discussions of individual differences, we lose the ability to address an issue of immense interest in philosophy and cognitive science: whether there can be actual (as opposed to apparent) variation in intentional-level psychologies. As discussed in Stanovich (1999), there are three powerful traditions in philosophy that argue against this possibility. Arguments from charity (Dennett 1987; Quine 1960; Stein 1996; Stich, 1990), from reflective equilibrium (Cohen 1981; Stein 1996; Stich 1990), and from evolution (Dennett 1987; Stich 1990) have famously claimed to have demonstrated uniformly optimal functioning of intentional-level psychologies in human beings.

I think all these arguments are mistaken (Stanovich 1999), but the more important point is that in order to produce empirical data relevant to the issue, we need to clearly demarcate concepts at the intentional level. Finding nonartifactual variation in a conflated notion of intelligence obscures the critical issue of whether the individual differences are best understood as arising from variation in algorithmic-level or intentional-level functioning. In contrast, by taking the demarcation as fundamental, I believe that the work summarized above (see Stanovich 1999) has demonstrated that some smart people do a lot of dumb things and some don't—and that this is an indication of variation in intentional-level psychologies, a variation in degrees of rationality that some philosophers have denied (see Cohen 1981; Stanovich 1999; Stein 1996; Stich 1990).

Fostering Actively Open-Minded Thinking: The Normative Issue

I also believe that drawing the intelligence/rationality distinction helps to provide a needed educational rationale for attempts to foster critical thinking. Specifically, if one's goal is to *aid* people in their thinking, then it is essential that one have some way of *evaluating* thinking. For example, in the current educational literature, teachers are constantly exhorted to "teach children how to think" or to "foster critical thinking" and "encourage creative problem solving." However, the problem here is that "thinking" is not a domain of knowledge. As Baron (1993b) notes, "We teach Latin or calculus because students do not already know how to speak Latin or find integrals. But, by any reasonable description of thinking, students already know how to think, and the problem is that they do not do it as effectively as they might" (p. 199). Thus, the admonition to educators to teach thinking skills and foster critical thinking contains implicit evaluative assumptions. Children *already* think; educators are charged with getting them to think *better* (Adams 1989, 1993). This of course implies a normative model of what we mean by "better thinking" (Baron, Badgio, & Gaskins 1986; Haslam & Baron 1994).

A somewhat analogous issue arises when thinking dispositions are discussed in the educational literature of critical thinking. Why do we want people to think in an actively open-minded fashion? Why do we want to foster "multiplist" and evaluative thinking (Kuhn 1992) rather than absolutist thinking? Why do we want people to be reflective? It can be argued that the superordinate goal we are actually trying to foster is that of rationality (Stanovich 1994). That is, much of what educators are ultimately concerned about is rational thought in both the epistemic sense and the practical sense. We value certain thinking dispositions because we believe they will at least aid in the former and are essential for the latter. But at least in principle we could imagine a person with excellent epistemic rationality (her degree of confidence in propositions being well calibrated to the available evidence relevant to the proposition) and optimal practical rationality (she optimally satisfies her desires given her beliefs) who is *not* actively open-minded. We might still want to mold such an individual's dispositions in the direction of open-mindedness for the sake of society as a whole, but from a purely individual perspective, we would now be hard-pressed to find reasons for *wanting* to change such a person's thinking dispositions if—whatever they were—they had led to rational thought and action in the past.

In short, a large part of the rationale for educational interventions to change thinking dispositions derives from a tacit assumption that actively open-minded thinking dispositions make the individual a more rational person (Baron 1985, 1988, 1993b; Stanovich 1994). But that puts a burden of proof upon the shoulders of advocates of such educational interventions. They must show that thinking dispositions are associated with the responses and thought patterns that are considered normative (and that the association is causal). This is precisely the empirical evidence that we (Stanovich 1999; Stanovich & West 1997, 1998, 2000) and other investigators (Kardash & Scholes 1996; Klaczynski et al. 1997; Kuhn 1991, 1993, 1996; Schaller et al.

1995; Schommer 1990, 1994; Smith & Levin 1996) have begun to compile. Although the trends are sometimes modest, there has been a consistent tendency for people who are high in actively open-minded thinking to give the normative response on hypothesis testing and reasoning tasks, to avoid belief bias in their reasoning, and to properly calibrate their beliefs to the state of the evidence. Therefore, the field is beginning to develop a normatively justified foundation for an emphasis on thinking dispositions.

The Paradoxical Relation Between Rationality and Emotion

Identifying rationality with the intentional level of analysis in cognitive science and intelligence with the algorithmic level can potentially help to dissolve another seeming paradox: the disconnect between the folk theory of emotions and conceptions of the emotions in cognitive science. In folk psychology the emotions are ostensibly the cause of irrationality. Quintessentially, they are thought to interfere with rational thought. Yet despite the fact that folk psychology assigns them a disruptive role, most conceptions of emotions in cognitive science stress the adaptive regulatory powers of the emotions. For example, in their discussion of the rationality of emotions, Johnson-Laird and Oatley (1992; see Oatley 1992) conceptualize emotions as interrupt signals supporting goal achievement. They see emotions as intentional-level constructs that are particularly important in the characterization of systems whose behavior is governed by neither fixed action patterns nor impeccable rationality. Other cognitive scientists concur in this view (see Damasio 1994; de Sousa 1987). The basic idea is that emotions serve to stop the combinatorial explosion of possibilities that would occur if an intelligent system tried to calculate the utility of all possible future outcomes. Emotions are thought to constrain the possibilities to a manageable number based on somatic markers (see Damasio 1994) stored from similar situations in the past.

How are we to square this view with the folk psychological notion of the emotions as the enemies of reason? One potential resolution may reside in two-process models of cognitive activity that have been proposed by numerous investigators in the past two decades. These theories propose two structured cognitive systems with separable goal structures and separate algorithmic mechanisms to implement those structures. The details and terminology of these models differ, but they all share a family resemblance, and the specific differences are not material to the present discussion. The dual-process terms of several major theorists are presented in Table 7.2. In order to emphasize the prototypical view adopted here, the two systems

TABLE 7.2. Terms for the Two Systems Used by a Variety of Theorists, and the Properties of Dual-Process Theories of Reason

	SYSTEM 1	SYSTEM 2
Dual-process theories		
Sloman (1996)	Associative system	Rule-based system
Evans (1984, 1989)	Heuristic processing	Analytic processing
Evans & Over (1996)	Tacit thought processes	Explicit thought processes
Reber (1993)	Implicit cognition	Explicit learning
Levinson (1995)	Interactional intelligence	Analytic intelligence
Epstein (1994)	Experiential system	Rational system
Pollock (1991)	Quick and inflexible modules	Intellection
Klein (1998)	Recognition-primed decisions	Rational choice strategy
Johnson-Laird (1983)	Implicit inferences	Explicit inferences
Chaiken, Liberman, & Eagly (1989)	Heuristic processing	Systematic processing
Gibbard (1990)	Animal control system	Normative control system
Shiffrin & Schneider (1977)	Automatic processing	Controlled processing
Posner & Snyder (1975)	Automatic activation	Conscious processing system
Evans & Wason (1976)	Type 1 processes	Type 2 processes
Properties	Associative	Rule-based
	Holistic	Analytic
	Automatic	Controlled
	Relatively undemanding of cognitive capacity	Demanding of cognitive capacity
	Relatively fast	Relatively slow
	Acquisition by biology, exposure, and personal experience	Acquisition by cultural and formal tuition
	Highly contextualized	Decontextualized
Goal structure	Largely genetically determined	Utility maximizing for the organism and constantly updated because of changes in environment
Type of intelligence indexed	Interactional (conversational implicature)	Analytic (psychometric IQ)

have simply been generically labeled System 1 and System 2. The key differences in the properties of the two systems are listed next. System 1 is characterized as automatic, heuristic-based, and relatively undemanding of computational capacity. Thus, it conjoins properties of automaticity and heuristic processing as these constructs have been variously discussed in the literature. System 2 conjoins the various characteristics that have been viewed as typifying controlled processing. At the algorithmic level, System 2 encompasses the processes of analytic intelligence that have traditionally been studied in psychometric work and that have been examined by information processing theorists trying to uncover the computational components underlying psychometric intelligence. At the intentional level, the goal structure of System 1 has been determined largely by evolutionary adaptation, whereas the goal structure of System 2 is more flexible and reflects ongoing goal evaluation at the personal level as an individual is shaped by environmental experience (see Stanovich 1999).

The work of Pollock (1991) is particularly relevant to the present discussion of the role of the emotions. In his view, heavily influenced by work in artificial intelligence, System 1 is composed of quick and inflexible (Q&I) modules that perform specific computations. System 2 processes are grouped under the term "intellection" in his model and refer to all explicit reasoning in the service of theoretical or practical rationality: "The advantage of Q&I modules is speed. The advantage of intellection, on the other hand, is extreme flexibility. It seems that it can in principle deal with any kind of situation, but it is slow" (p. 192).

As an example, Pollock mentions the Q&I trajectory module that predicts the movement path of objects in motion. The Q&I module for this computation is quite accurate, but it relies on certain assumptions about the structure of the world. When these assumptions are violated, the module must be overridden by System 2 processing. So when a baseball approaches a telephone pole "We had best wait until it ricochets before predicting its trajectory. Our built-in trajectory module cannot handle this situation accurately, so we use intellection to temporarily override it until the situation becomes one that can be handled accurately by the trajectory module" (p. 191). Pollock stresses, however, that Q&I modules do not just operate in the domains of movement and perception but instead that "Everyday inductive and probabilistic inference is carried out by Q&I modules" (p. 191). Indeed, we (1999; Stanovich & West 2000) stress the importance of the override function of System 2 in explaining individual differences in rational thought.

It is important to note that Pollock (1995) conceptualizes emotions within his cognitive architecture in a manner that helps to dissolve the emotion/rationality paradox described above. In Pollock's model, emotions are conceived as Q&I modules for practical reasoning. As examples, he notes that "Being afraid of tigers initiates quick avoidance responses without our having to think about it—a very useful reaction for anyone who is likely to encounter tigers unexpectedly. Embarrassment, indignation, and so forth, may similarly be practical Q&I modules whose purpose is to supplement explicit practical reasoning in social situations. This provides a computational role for these emotions and throws light on why humans are subject to them" (p. 11).

Pollock's (1991, 1995) view is consistent with that of Johnson-Laird and Oatley (1992) and offers an explanation of the seeming discontinuity between the folk psychological view of the relation between emotions and rationality and the view of modern cognitive science. The key insight is that if we view emotions as Q&I modules for practical reasoning there are two ways in which the rational regulation of behavior could go wrong.[3] These two ways might be termed "module failure" and "override failure," respectively. First, Q&I emotion modules might be missing or might malfunction. In this case, the automatic and rapid regulation of goals is absent and System 2 is faced with a combinatorial explosion of possibilities because the constraining function of the emotions is missing. A module failure of this type represents a case where there is not too much emotion but, instead, too little.

The second way that behavioral regulation can go awry has the opposite properties. It is a situation analogous to Pollock's (1995) trajectory example. Here, the Q&I module has fired but it happens to be one of those instances where the module's output is inappropriate and needs to be overridden by the controlled processing of System 2. Behavioral regulation is suboptimal when the System 2 override function does not work properly. In this situation, the emotions of the Q&I practical reasoning module are too pervasive and unmodifiable. The problem in cases of override failure is indeed a problem of too much emotion, rather than too little.

It is clear that the folk psychological notion of the emotion/rationality relationship refers to the latter situation—failure to override System 1 Q&I modules for practical reasoning. This leads to the folk psychological cliché that emotion interferes with rational thought. But what folk psychology leaves out is irrationality of the first type—and here the emotions play the opposite role. It is their absence that is the problem. Behavioral regulation is not aided by crude but effective emotional signals that help to prioritize goals for subsequent action.

Folk psychology is thus incomplete in the sense that it recognizes override-based irrationality but not irrationality owing to emotion module failure. Several architectures in cognitive science would, in contrast, recognize both possibilities (Damasio 1994; Johnson-Laird & Oatley 1992; Oatley 1992; Pennington & Ozonoff 1996; Pollock 1991, 1995; Stanovich 1999). More important, there is empirical evidence for rationality failures of the two different types. Dorsolateral prefrontal damage has been associated with executive functioning difficulties (and/or working memory difficulties) that can be interpreted as the failure of System 2 to override automatized processes being executed by System 1 (Duncan et al. 1996; Kimberg, D'Esposito, & Farah 1998; Kolb & Wilshaw 1990; McCarthy & Warrington 1990; Shallice 1988). In contrast, ventromedial damage to the prefrontal cortex has been associated with problems in behavioral regulation that are accompanied by affective disruption (Bechara et al. 1994; Bechara et al. 1997; Damasio 1994). Difficulties of the former but not the latter kind are associated with lowered intelligence (Damasio 1994; Duncan et al. 1996)—consistent with the association of System 2 with psychometric intelligence (see Table 7.2) and the relative independence of System 1 and algorithmic computational capacity of the type measured by IQ tests.

In summary, our developing understanding of the relation between emotion and rationality might provide another instance where cognitive science could well help to shape folk psychology in the direction of more accurate conceptions of human mental life (Bruner 1990).

Epistemic Irrationality in the Face of Substantial Computational Power

It is not just practical rationality that can become dissociated from algorithmic efficiency. Epistemic rationality can also display marked dissociations. In fact, there is no dearth of examples of smart people believing ridiculous things—an indication that aspects of epistemic rationality (the proportional calibration of belief to evidence) can go awry. Studies of leading Holocaust deniers (see Lipstadt 1994; Shermer 1997), for example, have revealed that their ranks contain the holder of a Master's degree from Indiana University in European history, the author of several well-known biographies of World War II figures, a professor of literature at the University of Lyon, an author of textbooks used in Ivy League universities, a professor of English at the University of Scranton, a professor at Northwestern University, and the list goes on (see Lipstadt 1994).

A cognitive science that demarcates the intentional level also promises to throw some light on the puzzling phenomenon of epistemic irrationality coexisting with substantial cognitive power—the educated Holocaust deniers studied by Lipstadt (1994), creationists who are physical scientists, and many similar examples (Shermer 1997; Stanovich 1993). Philosopher Hilary Kornblith (1993) provides one form of the argument that can unlock this seeming puzzle. In discussing the phenomenon of belief perseverance: "Mistaken beliefs will, as a result of belief perseverance, taint our perception of new data. By the same token, however, belief perseverance will serve to color our perception of new data when our preexisting beliefs are accurate.... If, overall, our belief-generating mechanisms give us a fairly accurate picture of the world, then the phenomenon of belief perseverance may do more to inform our understanding than it does to distort it" (p. 105).

This argument—that in a natural ecology where most of our prior beliefs are true, projecting our beliefs onto new data will lead to faster accumulation of knowledge—I have termed the "knowledge projection argument" (Stanovich 1999), and it reappears in a remarkably diverse set of contexts throughout the reasoning and decision making literature. For example, Koehler (1993) demonstrated that scientists' prior beliefs about a hypothesis influence their judgments of evidence quality. In a Bayesian analysis of whether this evaluation tendency could ever be normatively justified, Koehler found that under certain conditions it could. One of those conditions was that the prior hypotheses influencing evidence evaluation were more likely than not to be true. When evidence is evaluated with reference to a pool of hypotheses that are largely true, that evidence will lead to belief convergence faster if the prior beliefs do influence evidence evaluation— another version of the knowledge projection argument.

Evans, Over, and Manktelow (1993) rely on a variant of the knowledge projection argument when considering the normative status of belief bias in syllogistic reasoning. They consider the status of selective scrutiny explanations of the belief bias phenomenon. Such theories posit that subjects accept conclusions that are believable without engaging in logical reasoning at all. Only when faced with unbelievable conclusions do subjects engage in logical reasoning about the premises. Evans and colleagues (1993) consider whether such a processing strategy could be rational in the sense of serving to achieve the person's goals, and they conclude that it could. They argue that any adult is likely to hold a large number of true beliefs that are interconnected in complex ways. Because single-belief revision has interactive effects on the rest of the belief network, it may be computationally costly. According to them, under such conditions it is quite right that conclusions that contradict one's beliefs "should be subjected to the closest possible scrutiny and refuted if at all possible" (p. 174). Again, the argument works when the selective scrutiny mechanism is applied using a subset of beliefs that are largely true in the domain to which the scrutiny strategy is being applied.

Finally, Alloy and Tabachnik (1984) echo the knowledge projection argument in their review of the covariation detection literature on humans and other animals: "When individuals' expectations accurately reflect the contingencies encountered in their natural environments . . . it is not irrational for them to assimilate incoming information about covariation between events to these expectations. . . . Because covariation information provided in an experiment may represent only one piece of conflicting evidence against the background of the large body of data about event covariations summarized by an expectation, it would be normatively appropriate for organisms to weight their expectations more heavily than situational information in the covariation judgment process" (p. 140). Of course, Alloy and Tabachnik (1984) emphasize that we must project from a largely *accurate* set of beliefs in order to obtain the benefit of knowledge projection. In a sea of inaccurate beliefs, the situation is quite different. And herein lies the key to understanding the creationist or Holocaust denier.

The caveat here is critical: When the subset of beliefs that the individual is projecting contains substantial false information, selective scrutiny will *delay* the assimilation of the correct information. This caveat creates the possibility of observing a so-called Matthew effect—a cumulative advantage phenomenon—in the acquisition of knowledge (Stanovich 1986). Walberg (Walberg et al. 1984; Walberg & Tsai 1983), following Merton (1968), dubbed cumulative advantage effects in education "Matthew effects," after the Gospel according to Matthew: "For unto every one that hath shall be given, and he shall have abundance: but from him that hath not shall be taken away even that which he hath" (XXV:29). In the educational literature, the term springs from findings that individuals who have advantageous early educational experiences are able to utilize new educational experiences more efficiently and thus increase their advantage. How might the knowledge projection process lead to Matthew effects in knowledge acquisition? Imagine two scientists, A and B, working in domain X. The bulk of hypotheses in domain X held by scientist A are true, and the bulk of hypotheses in domain X held by scientist B are false. Imagine that they both then begin to project those prior beliefs on the same new evidence in the manner demonstrated experimentally by Koehler (1993)—with stronger tendencies to undermine the evidence when it contradicts prior belief. It is clear that scientist A—who already exceeds B in number of true beliefs—will increase that advantage as new data come in.

The knowledge projection tendency, efficacious in the aggregate, may have the effect of isolating certain individuals on "islands of false beliefs" from which—because of the knowledge projection tendency—they are unable to escape. In short, there may be a type of knowledge isolation effect when projection is used in particularly ill-suited circumstances. Thus, knowledge projection, which in the aggregate might lead to more rapid induction of new true beliefs, may be a trap in cases where people, in effect, keep reaching into a bag of beliefs which are largely false, using these beliefs to structure their evaluation of evidence, and hence more quickly adding incorrect beliefs to the bag for further projection.

Knowledge projection from an island of false beliefs might explain the phenomenon of otherwise intelligent people who get caught in a domain-specific web of falsity and because of projection tendencies cannot escape (e.g., the otherwise competent physical scientists who believe in creationism). Indeed, such individuals often use their considerable computational power to rationalize their beliefs and to ward off the arguments of skeptics (Evans 1996; Evans & Wason 1976; Margolis 1987; Nisbett & Wilson 1977; Wason 1969). The cognitive machinery recruited to aid in knowledge projection might be extremely potent in individuals high in cognitive capacity—but when the projection occurs from an island of false belief, it merely results in a belief network even more divergent from that of individuals not engaged in such projection or with less computational power.

Further research is needed to examine whether such Matthew effects and knowledge isolation effects can be documented. Nevertheless, there is a statistical rationale for the *presence* of such a bias, because across individuals—and across beliefs held by an individual—most of what is believed is true. Thus, on an overall statistical basis, knowledge projection may well increase the rate of acquisition of true beliefs. But this does not prevent particular individuals with particularly ill-formed initial beliefs from projecting them and developing beliefs that correspond even less with reality. Neither does it prevent an individual (with an otherwise generally accurate belief network) from getting caught on an island of false beliefs with respect to a particular domain, projecting those beliefs, and with time developing even more bizarre theories about this domain. These effects might explain how some individuals could have their beliefs detached from reality in ways so extreme that an attribution of irrationality would seem justified. Such a case would be an example of a generally efficacious mechanism resulting in seriously suboptimal belief structures. Knowledge projection is thus a mechanism that could be generally normative in a statistical sense but still be the cause of a minority of actions and beliefs that are seriously irrational.

NOTES

Preparation of this chapter was supported by a grant from the Social Sciences and Humanities Research Council of Canada to Keith E. Stanovich.

1. Bruner (1986, 1990) has argued that researchers should display a greater awareness of their influence on folk psychology because the intuitive psychologies of the layperson provide the motivation for social policies. Rationality assumptions of various types form an important part of folk

concepts of the nature of human cognition and, as Bruner (1990) notes, "It is through folk psychology that people anticipate and judge one another, draw conclusions about the worthwhileness of their lives, and so on. Its power over human mental functioning and human life is that it provides the very means by which culture shapes human beings to its requirements" (p. 15).

2. The terms must be somewhat conflated, or else the smart but acting dumb phrasing would not sound strange at all.

3. Obviously there may be more than two. I am focusing on one particular contrast here.

REFERENCES

Ackerman, P. L., & E. D. Heggestad (1997). Intelligence, personality, and interests: Evidence for overlapping traits. *Psychological Bulletin, 121,* 219–245.

Ackerman, P. L., P. Kyllonen, & R. Roberts (Eds.) (1999). *The future of learning and individual differences research: Processes, traits, and content.* Washington, D.C.: American Psychological Association.

Adams, M. J. (1989). Thinking skills curricula: Their promise and progress. *Educational Psychologist, 24,* 25–77.

——. (1993). Towards making it happen. *Applied Psychology: An International Review, 42,* 214–218.

Alloy, L. B., & N. Tabachnik (1984). Assessment of covariation by humans and animals: The joint influence of prior expectations and current situational information. *Psychological Review, 91,* 112–149.

Anderson, J. R. (1990). *The adaptive character of thought.* Hillsdale, N.J.: Erlbaum.

——. (1991). Is human cognition adaptive? *Behavioral and Brain Sciences, 14,* 471–517.

Arkes, H. R. (1991). Costs and benefits of judgment errors: Implications for debiasing. *Psychological Bulletin, 110,* 486–498.

Arkes, H. R., & P. Ayton (1999). The sunk cost and Concorde effects: Are humans less rational than lower animals? *Psychological Bulletin, 125,* 591–600.

Arkes, H., & K. Hammond (Eds.) (1986). *Judgment and decision making.* Cambridge, England: Cambridge University Press.

Audi, R. (1993). *Action, intention, and reason.* Ithaca, N.Y.: Cornell University Press.

Babad, E., & Y. Katz (1991). Wishful thinking—Against all odds. *Journal of Applied Social Psychology, 21,* 1921–1938.

Baltes, P. B. (1987). Theoretical propositions of life-span developmental psychology: On the dynamics between growth and decline. *Developmental Psychology, 23,* 611–626.

Baron, J. (1985). *Rationality and intelligence.* Cambridge: Cambridge University Press.

——. (1988). *Thinking and deciding.* Cambridge, England: Cambridge University Press.

——. (1991). Beliefs about thinking. In J. Voss, D. Perkins, & J. Segal (Eds.), *Informal reasoning and education* (pp. 169–186). Hillsdale, N.J.: Erlbaum.

——. (1993a). *Morality and rational choice.* Dordrecht: Kluwer.

——. (1993b). Why teach thinking?—An essay. *Applied Psychology: An International Review, 42,* 191–214.

——. (1994). Nonconsequentialist decisions. *Behavioral and Brain Sciences, 17,* 1–42.

——. (1995). Myside bias in thinking about abortion. *Thinking and Reasoning, 1,* 221–235.

——. (1998). *Judgment misguided: Intuition and error in public decision making.* New York: Oxford University Press.

Baron, J., P. C. Badgio, & I. W. Gaskins (1986). Cognitive style and its improvement: A normative approach. In R. J. Sternberg (Ed.), *Advances in the psychology of human intelligence* (Vol. 3) (pp. 173–220). Hillsdale, N.J.: Erlbaum.

Baron, J., & J. C. Hershey (1988). Outcome bias in decision evaluation. *Journal of Personality and Social Psychology, 54,* 569–579.

Bechara, A., A. R. Damasio, H. Damasio, & S. Anderson (1994). Insensitivity to future consequences following damage to human prefrontal cortex. *Cognition, 50,* 7–15.

Bechara, A., H. Damasio, D. Tranel, & A. R. Damasio (1997, Feb. 26). Deciding advantageously before knowing the advantageous strategy. *Science, 275,* 1293–1295.

Belsky, G. (1995, July). Why smart people make major money mistakes. *Money Magazine,* pp. 76–85.

Belsky, G., & T. Gilovich (1999). *Why smart people make big money mistakes—And how to correct them: Lessons from the new science of behavioral economics.* New York: Simon & Schuster.

Bratman, M. E., D. J. Israel, & M. E. Pollack (1991). Plans and resource-bounded practical reasoning. In J. Cummins & J. Pollock (Eds.), *Philosophy and AI: Essays at the interface* (pp. 7–22). Cambridge, Mass.: MIT Press.

Brenner, L. A., D. J. Koehler, & A. Tversky (1996). On the evaluation of one-sided evidence. *Journal of Behavioral Decision Making, 9,* 59–70.

Bruner, J. (1986). *Actual minds, possible worlds.* Cambridge, Mass.: Harvard University Press.

——. (1990). *Acts of meaning.* Cambridge, Mass.: Harvard University Press.

Buss, D. M. (1991). Evolutionary personality psychology. *Annual Review of Psychology, 42,* 459–491.

Cacioppo, J. T., R. E. Petty, J. Feinstein, & W. Jarvis (1996). Dispositional differences in cognitive motivation: The life and times of individuals varying in need for cognition. *Psychological Bulletin, 119,* 197–253.

Carpenter, P. A., M. A. Just, & P. Shell (1990). What one intelligence test measures: A theoretical account of the processing in the Raven Progressive Matrices Test. *Psychological Review, 97,* 404–431.

Carroll, J. B. (1993). *Human cognitive abilities: A survey of factor-analytic studies.* Cambridge: Cambridge University Press.

——. (1997). Psychometrics, intelligence, and public perception. *Intelligence, 24,* 25–52.

Cederblom, J. (1989). Willingness to reason and the identification of the self. In E. Maimon, D. Nodine, & F. O'Conner (Eds.), *Thinking, reasoning, and writing* (pp. 147–159). New York: Longman.

Chaiken, S., A. Liberman, & A. H. Eagly (1989). Heuristic and systematic information within and beyond the persuasion context. In J. S. Uleman & J. A. Bargh (Eds.), *Unintended thought* (pp. 212–252). New York: Guilford Press.

Cherniak, C. (1986). *Minimal rationality.* Cambridge, Mass.: MIT Press.

Christensen, S. M., & D. R. Turner (Eds.) (1993). *Folk psychology and the philosophy of mind.* Hillsdale, N.J.: Erlbaum.

Churchland, P. M. (1979). *Scientific realism and the plasticity of mind.* Cambridge: Cambridge University Press.

Churchland, P. M., & P. S. Churchland (1998). *On the contrary: Critical essays, 1987–1997.* Cambridge, Mass.: MIT Press.

Cohen, L. J. (1981). Can human irrationality be experimentally demonstrated? *Behavioral and Brain Sciences, 4,* 317–370.

Costa, P. T., & R. R. McCrae (1992). *Revised NEO personality inventory.* Odessa, Fla.: Psychological Assessment Resources.

Damasio, A. R. (1994). *Descartes' error.* New York: Putnam.

Davies, M., & T. Stone (Eds.) (1995). *Folk psychology.* Oxford: Blackwell.

Dawes, R. M. (1988). *Rational choice in an uncertain world.* San Diego, Calif.: Harcourt, Brace Jovanovich.

——. (1998). Behavioral decision making and judgment. In D. T. Gilbert, S. T. Fiske, & G. Lindzey (Eds.), *The handbook of social psychology* (Vol. 1) (pp. 497–548). Boston: McGraw-Hill.

Dawkins, R. (1998). *Unweaving the rainbow.* Boston: Houghton Mifflin.

Deary, I. J., & C. Stough (1996). Intelligence and inspection time. *American Psychologist, 51,* 599–608.

Dennett, D. C. (1978). *Brainstorms: Philosophical essays on mind and psychology*. Cambridge, Mass.: MIT Press.

———. (1987). *The intentional stance*. Cambridge, Mass.: MIT Press.

de Sousa, R. (1987). *The rationality of emotion*. Cambridge, Mass.: MIT Press.

Duncan, J., H. Emslie, P. Williams, R. Johnson, & C. Freer (1996). Intelligence and the frontal lobe: The organization of goal-directed behavior. *Cognitive Psychology, 30,* 257–303.

Engle, R. W., S. W. Tuholski, J. E. Laughlin, & A. R. A. Conway (1999). Working memory, short-term memory, and general fluid intelligence: A latent-variable approach. *Journal of Experimental Psychology: General, 128,* 309–331.

Ennis, R. H. (1987). A taxonomy of critical thinking dispositions and abilities. In J. Baron & R. Sternberg (Eds.), *Teaching thinking skills: Theory and practice* (pp. 9–26). New York: Freeman.

Epstein, S. (1994). Integration of the cognitive and the psychodynamic unconscious. *American Psychologist, 49,* 709–724.

Epstein, S., & P. Meier (1989). Constructive thinking: A broad coping variable with specific components. *Journal of Personality and Social Psychology, 57,* 332–350.

Evans, J. St. B. T. (1984). Heuristic and analytic processes in reasoning. *British Journal of Psychology, 75,* 451–468.

———. (1989). *Bias in human reasoning: Causes and consequences*. London: Erlbaum.

———. (1996). Deciding before you think: Relevance and reasoning in the selection task. *British Journal of Psychology, 87,* 223–240.

Evans, J. St. B. T., J. Barston, & P. Pollard (1983). On the conflict between logic and belief in syllogistic reasoning. *Memory & Cognition, 11,* 295–306.

Evans, J. St. B. T., S. Newstead, J. Allen, & P. Pollard (1994). Debiasing by instruction: The case of belief bias.

European Journal of Cognitive Psychology, 6, 263–285.

Evans, J. St. B. T., & D. E. Over (1996). *Rationality and reasoning*. Hove, England: Psychology Press.

Evans, J. St. B. T., D. E. Over, & K. Manktelow (1993). Reasoning, decision making and rationality. *Cognition, 49,* 165–187.

Evans, J. St. B. T., & P. C. Wason (1976). Rationalization in a reasoning task. *British Journal of Psychology, 67,* 479–486.

Facione, P. (1992). *California Critical Thinking Dispositions Inventory*. La Cruz, Calif.: California Academic Press.

Foley, R. (1987). *The theory of epistemic rationality*. Cambridge, Mass.: Harvard University Press.

———. (1991). Rationality, belief, and commitment. *Synthese, 89,* 365–392.

Fong, G. T., D. H. Krantz, & R. E. Nisbett (1986). The effects of statistical training on thinking about everyday problems. *Cognitive Psychology, 18,* 253–292.

Fridson, M. S. (1993). *Investment illusions*. New York: Wiley.

Fry, A. F., & S. Hale (1996). Processing speed, working memory, and fluid intelligence. *Psychological Science, 7,* 237–241.

Gibbard, A. (1990). *Wise choices, apt feelings: A theory of normative judgment*. Cambridge, Mass.: Harvard University Press.

Gilovich, T. (1991). *How we know what isn't so*. New York: Free Press.

Goff, M., & P. L. Ackerman (1992). Personality-intelligence relations: Assessment of typical intellectual engagement. *Journal of Educational Psychology, 84,* 537–552.

Goldman, A. I. (1978). Epistemics: The regulative theory of cognition. *Journal of Philosophy, 55,* 509–523.

Greenwood, J. D. (Ed.) (1991). *The future of folk psychology: Intentionality and cognitive science*. Cambridge: Cambridge University Press.

Griffin, D., & A. Tversky (1992). The

weighing of evidence and the determinants of confidence. *Cognitive Psychology, 24,* 411–435.

Harman, G. (1995). Rationality. In E. E. Smith & D. N. Osherson (Eds.), *Thinking* (Vol. 3) (pp. 175–211). Cambridge, Mass.: MIT Press.

Haslam, N., & J. Baron (1994). Intelligence, personality, and prudence. In R. J. Sternberg & P. Ruzgis (Eds.), *Personality and intelligence* (pp. 32–58). Cambridge: Cambridge University Press.

Horgan, T., & J. Tienson (1993). Levels of description in nonclassical cognitive science. In C. Hookway & D. Peterson (Eds.), *Philosophy and cognitive science* (pp. 159–188). Cambridge: Cambridge University Press.

Hunt, E. (1978). Mechanics of verbal ability. *Psychological Review, 85,* 109–130.

——. (1987). The next word on verbal ability. In P. A. Vernon (Ed.), *Speed of information-processing and intelligence* (pp. 347–392). Norwood, N.J.: Ablex.

Jeffrey, R. C. (1983). *The logic of decision* (second edition). Chicago: University of Chicago Press.

Jepson, C., D. Krantz, & R. Nisbett (1983). Inductive reasoning: Competence or skill? *Behavioral and Brain Sciences, 6,* 494–501.

Johnson-Laird, P. N. (1983). *Mental models.* Cambridge, Mass.: Harvard University Press.

Johnson-Laird, P., & K. Oatley (1992). Basic emotions, rationality, and folk theory. *Cognition and Emotion, 6,* 201–223.

Kahneman, D., P. Slovic, & A. Tversky (Eds.) (1982). *Judgment under uncertainty: Heuristics and biases.* Cambridge: Cambridge University Press.

Kahneman, D., & A. Tversky (Eds.) (2000). *Choices, values, and frames.* Cambridge: Cambridge University Press.

Kardash, C. M., & R. J. Scholes (1996). Effects of pre-existing beliefs, epistemological beliefs, and need for cognition on interpretation of controversial issues. *Journal of Educational Psychology, 88,* 260–271.

Keating, D. P. (1990). Charting pathways to the development of expertise. *Educational Psychologist, 25,* 243–267.

Kimberg, D. Y., M. D'Esposito, & M. J. Farah (1998). Cognitive functions in the prefrontal cortex—working memory and executive control. *Current Directions in Psychological Science, 6,* 185–192.

King, P. M., & K. S. Kitchener (1994). *Developing reflective judgment.* San Francisco: Jossey-Bass.

Kitchener, K., & K. W. Fischer (1990). A skill approach to the development of reflective thinking. In D. Kuhn (Eds.), *Developmental perspectives on teaching and learning thinking skills* (pp. 48–62). Basil: Karger.

Kitcher, P. (1993). *The advancement of science.* New York: Oxford University Press.

Klaczynski, P. A. (1997). Bias in adolescents' everyday reasoning and its relationship with intellectual ability, personal theories, and self serving motivation. *Developmental Psychology, 33,* 273–283.

Klaczynski, P. A., & D. H. Gordon (1996). Self-serving influences on adolescents' evaluations of belief-relevant evidence. *Journal of Experimental Child Psychology, 62,* 317–339.

Klaczynski, P. A., D. H. Gordon, & J. Fauth (1997). Goal-oriented critical reasoning and individual differences in critical reasoning biases. *Journal of Educational Psychology, 89,* 470–485.

Klaczynski, P. A., & G. Narasimham (1998). Development of scientific reasoning biases: Cognitive versus ego-protective explanations. *Developmental Psychology, 34,* 175–187.

Klein, G. (1998). *Sources of power: How people make decisions.* Cambridge, Mass.: MIT Press.

Kleindorfer, P. R., H. C. Kunreuther, & P. J. H. Schoemaker (1993). *Decision*

sciences: An integrative perspective.
Cambridge: Cambridge University Press.

Koehler, J. J. (1993). The influence of prior beliefs on scientific judgments of evidence quality. *Organizational Behavior and Human Decision Processes, 56,* 28–55.

Kolb, B., & I. Whishaw (1990). *Fundamentals of human neuropsychology* (third edition). New York: Freeman.

Kornblith, H. (1993). *Inductive inference and its natural ground.* Cambridge, Mass.: MIT Press.

Kruglanski, A. W. (1990). Lay epistemics theory in social-cognitive psychology. *Psychological Inquiry, 1,* 181–197.

Kruglanski, A. W., & D. M. Webster (1996). Motivated closing the mind: "Seizing" and "freezing." *Psychological Review, 103,* 263–283.

Kuhn, D. (1991). *The skills of argument.* Cambridge: Cambridge University Press.

——. (1992). Thinking as argument. *Harvard Educational Review, 62,* 155–178.

——. (1993). Connecting scientific and informal reasoning. *Merrill-Palmer Quarterly, 38,* 74–103.

——. (1996). Is good thinking scientific thinking? In D. R. Olson & N. Torrance (Eds.), *Modes of thought: Explorations in culture and cognition* (pp. 261–281). New York: Cambridge University Press.

Kuhn, D., E. Amsel, & M. O'Loughlin (1988). *The development of scientific thinking skills.* San Diego: Academic Press.

Kunda, Z. (1990). The case for motivated reasoning. *Psychological Bulletin, 108,* 480–498.

——. (1999). *Social cognition: Making sense of people.* Cambridge, Mass.: MIT Press.

Levelt, W. (1995). Chapters of psychology. In R. L. Solso & D. W. Massaro (Eds.), *The science of the mind: 2001 and beyond* (pp. 184–202). New York: Oxford University Press.

Levinson, S. C. (1995). Interactional biases in human thinking. In E. Goody (Ed.), *Social intelligence and interaction* (pp. 221–260). Cambridge: Cambridge University Press.

Lichtenstein, S., P. Slovic, B. Fischhoff, M. Layman, & B. Combs (1978). Judged frequency of lethal events. *Journal of Experimental Psychology: Human Learning and Memory, 4,* 551–578.

Lipman, M. (1991). *Thinking in education.* Cambridge: Cambridge University Press.

Lipstadt, D. (1994). *Denying the Holocaust.* New York: Plume.

Lohman, D. F. (1989). Human intelligence: An introduction to advances in theory and research. *Review of Educational Research, 59,* 333–373.

Margolis, H. (1987). *Patterns, thinking, and cognition.* Chicago: University of Chicago Press.

——. (1996). *Dealing with risk.* Chicago: University of Chicago Press.

Marr, D. (1982). *Vision.* San Francisco: Freeman.

McCarthy, R. A., & E. K. Warrington (1990). *Cognitive neuropsychology: A clinical introduction.* San Diego: Academic Press.

McNeil, B., S. Pauker, H. Sox, & A. Tversky (1982). On the elicitation of preferences for alternative therapies. *New England Journal of Medicine, 306,* 1259–1262.

Merton, R. K. (1968). The Matthew effect in science. *Science, 159,* 59–63.

Messick, S. (1984). The nature of cognitive styles: Problems and promise in educational practice. *Educational Psychologist, 19,* 59–74.

——. (1994). The matter of style: Manifestations of personality in cognition, learning, and teaching. *Educational Psychologist, 29,* 121–136.

Metcalf, S. D. (1998, March). Attention deficits. *Lingua Franca, 8*(2), 60–64.

Moshman, D. (1994). Reasoning, metareasoning, and the promotion of rationality. In A. Demetriou & A. Efklides (Eds.), *Intelligence, mind, and reasoning: Structure and development* (pp. 135–150). Amsterdam: Elsevier.

Nathanson, S. (1994). *The ideal of rationality.* Chicago: Open Court.

Navon, D. (1989a). The importance of being

visible: On the role of attention in a mind viewed as an anarchic intelligence system: I. Basic tenets. *European Journal of Cognitive Psychology, 1,* 191–213.

———. (1989b). The importance of being visible: On the role of attention in a mind viewed as an anarchic intelligence system: II. Application to the field of attention. *European Journal of Cognitive Psychology, 1,* 215–238.

Neisser, U. (1979). The concept of intelligence. In R. J. Sternberg & D. K. Detterman (Eds.), *Human intelligence* (pp. 179–189). Norwood, N.J.: Ablex.

Newell, A. (1982). The knowledge level. *Artificial Intelligence, 18,* 87–127.

———. (1990). *Unified theories of cognition.* Cambridge, Mass.: Harvard University Press.

Nickerson, R. (1987). Why teach thinking? In J. Baron, & R. Sternberg (Eds.), *Teaching thinking skills: Theory and practice* (pp. 27–40). New York: Freeman.

———. (1988). On improving thinking through instruction. In E. Z. Rothkopf (Ed.), *Review of Research in Education* (Vol. 15) (pp. 3–57). Washington, D.C.: American Educational Research Association.

———. (1998). Confirmation bias: A ubiquitous phenomenon in many guises. *Review of General Psychology, 2,* 175–220.

Nisbett, R., & L. Ross (1980). *Human inference: Strategies and shortcomings of social judgment.* Englewood Cliffs, N.J.: Prentice-Hall.

Nisbett, R., & Wilson, T. (1977). Telling more than we know: Verbal reports on mental processes. *Psychological Review, 84,* 231–259.

Norman, D. A. (1976). *Memory and attention: An introduction to human information processing* (second edition). New York: Wiley.

Norris, S. P. (1992). Testing for the disposition to think critically. *Informal Logic, 14,* 157–164.

Norris, S. P., & R. H. Ennis (1989). *Evaluating critical thinking.* Pacific Grove, Calif.: Midwest Publications.

Nozick, R. (1993). *The nature of rationality.* Princeton, N.J.: Princeton University Press.

Oakhill, J., P. N. Johnson-Laird, & A. Garnham (1989). Believability and syllogistic reasoning. *Cognition, 31,* 117–140.

Oaksford, M., & N. Chater (1993). Reasoning theories and bounded rationality. In K. Manktelow & D. Over (Eds.), *Rationality: Psychological and philosophical perspectives* (pp. 31–60). London: Routledge.

———. (1995). Theories of reasoning and the computational explanation of everyday inference. *Thinking and Reasoning, 1,* 121–152.

Oatley, K. (1992). *Best laid schemes: The psychology of emotions.* Cambridge: Cambridge University Press.

Osherson, D. N. (1995). Probability judgment. In E. E. Smith & D. N. Osherson (Eds.), *Thinking* (Vol. 3) (pp. 35–75). Cambridge, Mass.: MIT Press.

Paul, R. W. (1984). Critical thinking: Fundamental to education for a free society. *Educational Leadership, 42*(1), 4–14.

Paul, R. W. (1987). Critical thinking and the critical person. In D. N. Perkins, J. Lockhead, & J. Bishop (Eds.), *Thinking: The second international conference* (pp. 373–403). Hillsdale, N.J.: Erlbaum.

Pennington, B. F., & Ozonoff, S. (1996). Executive functions and developmental psychopathology. *Journal of Child Psychology and Psychiatry, 37,* 51–87.

Perkins, D. N. (1985). Postprimary education has little impact on informal reasoning. *Journal of Educational Psychology, 77,* 562–571.

———. (1995). *Outsmarting IQ: The emerging science of learnable intelligence.* New York: Free Press.

Perkins, D. N., M. Farady, & B. Bushey (1991). Everyday reasoning and the roots of intelligence. In J. Voss, D. Perkins, & J. Segal (Eds.), *Informal reasoning and*

education (pp. 83–105). Hillsdale, N.J.:
Erlbaum.

Perkins, D. N., E. Jay, & S. Tishman (1993).
Beyond abilities: A dispositional theory
of thinking. *Merrill-Palmer Quarterly, 39,*
1–21.

Piattelli-Palmarini, M. (1994). *Inevitable
illusions: How mistakes of reason rule our
minds.* New York: Wiley.

Pintrich, P. R., R. Marx, & R. Boyle (1993).
Beyond cold conceptual change: The role
of motivational beliefs and classroom
contextual factors in the process of
conceptual change. *Review of Educational
Research, 63,* 167–199.

Plous, S. (1993). *The psychology of judgment and
decision making.* New York: McGraw-Hill.

Pollock, J. L. (1991). OSCAR: A general theory
of rationality. In J. Cummins & J. L.
Pollock (Eds.), *Philosophy and AI: Essays at
the interface* (pp. 189–213). Cambridge,
Mass.: MIT Press.

———. (1995). *Cognitive carpentry: A blueprint for
how to build a person.* Cambridge, Mass.:
MIT Press.

Posner, M. I., & C. R. R. Snyder (1975).
Attention and cognitive control. In R. L.
Solso (Eds.), *Information processing and
cognition: The Loyola Symposium* (pp. 55–
85). New York: Wiley.

Pylyshyn, Z. (1984). *Computation and cognition.*
Cambridge, Mass.: MIT Press.

Pyszczynski, T., & J. Greenberg (1987).
Toward an integration of cognitive and
motivational perspectives on social
inference: A biased hypothesis-testing
model. In L. Berkowitz (Ed.), *Advances in
Experimental Social Psychology* (pp. 297–
340). San Diego: Academic Press.

Quine, W. (1960). *Word and object.* Cambridge,
Mass.: MIT Press.

Reber, A. S. (1993). *Implicit learning and tacit
knowledge.* New York: Oxford University
Press.

Redelmeier, D. A., & A. Tversky (1990).
Discrepancy between medical decisions
for individual patients and for groups.

New England Journal of Medicine, 322, 1162–
1164.

———. (1992). On the framing of multiple
prospects. *Psychological Science, 3,* 191–193.

Rokeach, M. (1960). *The open and closed mind.*
New York: Basic Books.

Rolfhus, E. L., & P. L. Ackerman (1999).
Assessing individual differences in
knowledge: Knowledge, intelligence,
and related skills. *Journal of Educational
Psychology, 91,* 511–526.

Sá, W., R. F. West, & K. E. Stanovich (1999).
The domain specificity and generality of
belief bias: Searching for a generalizable
critical thinking skill. *Journal of Educational
Psychology, 91,* 497–510.

Saks, M., & R. Kidd (1980–1981). Human
information processing and adjudication:
Trial by heuristics. *Law and Society Review,
15,* 123–160.

Savage, L. J. (1954). *The foundations of statistics.*
New York: Wiley.

Schaller, M., C. Boyd, J. Yohannes, &
M. O'Brien (1995). The prejudiced
personality revisited: Personal need for
structure and formation of erroneous
stereotypes. *Journal of Personality and Social
Psychology, 68,* 544–555.

Scheffler, I. (1991). *In praise of the cognitive
emotions.* New York: Routledge.

Schoenfeld, A. H. (1983). Beyond the
purely cognitive: Belief systems, social
cognitions, and metacognitions as driving
forces in intellectual performance.
Cognitive Science, 7, 329–363.

Schommer, M. (1990). Effects of beliefs
about the nature of knowledge on
comprehension. *Journal of Educational
Psychology, 82,* 498–504.

———. (1993). Epistemological development
and academic performance among
secondary students. *Journal of Educational
Psychology, 85,* 406–411.

———. (1994). Synthesizing epistemological
belief research: Tentative understandings
and provocative confusions. *Educational
Psychology Review, 6,* 293–319.

Schrag, F. (1988). *Thinking in school and society*. New York: Routledge.

Shafir, E. (1994). Uncertainty and the difficulty of thinking through disjunctions. *Cognition, 50*, 403–430.

Shafir, E., & A. Tversky (1995). Decision making. In E. E. Smith & D. N. Osherson (Eds.), *Thinking* (Vol. 3) (pp. 77–100). Cambridge, Mass.: MIT Press.

Shallice, T. (1988). *From neuropsychology to mental structure*. Cambridge: Cambridge University Press.

Shermer, M. (1997). *Why people believe weird things*. New York: Freeman.

Shiffrin, R. M., & W. Schneider (1977). Controlled and automatic human information processing: II. Perceptual learning, automatic attending, and a general theory. *Psychological Review, 84*, 127–190.

Siegel, H. (1993). Not by skill alone: The centrality of character to critical thinking. *Informal Logic, 15*, 163–177.

Sloman, A. (1993). The mind as a control system. In C. Hookway & D. Peterson (Eds.), *Philosophy and cognitive science* (pp. 69–110). Cambridge: Cambridge University Press.

Sloman, S. A. (1996). The empirical case for two systems of reasoning. *Psychological Bulletin, 119*, 3–22.

Slusher, M. P., & C. A. Anderson (1996). Using causal persuasive arguments to change beliefs and teach new information: The mediating role of explanation availability and evaluation bias in the acceptance of knowledge. *Journal of Educational Psychology, 88*, 110–122.

Smith, S. M., & I. P. Levin (1996). Need for cognition and choice framing effects. *Journal of Behavioral Decision Making, 9*, 283–290.

Stanovich, K. E. (1986). Matthew effects in reading: Some consequences of individual differences in the acquisition of literacy. *Reading Research Quarterly, 21*, 360–407.

——. (1989). Implicit philosophies of mind: The dualism scale and its relationships with religiosity and belief in extrasensory perception. *Journal of Psychology, 123*, 5–23.

——. (1990). Concepts in developmental theories of reading skill: Cognitive resources, automaticity, and modularity. *Developmental Review, 10*, 72–100.

——. (1991). Discrepancy definitions of reading disability: Has intelligence led us astray? *Reading Research Quarterly, 26*, 7–29.

——. (1993). Dysrationalia: A new specific learning disability. *Journal of Learning Disabilities, 26*, 501–515.

——. (1994). Reconceptualizing intelligence: Dysrationalia as an intuition pump. *Educational Researcher, 23*(4), 11–22.

——. (1999). *Who is rational? Studies of individual differences in reasoning*. Mahwah, N.J.: Erlbaum.

Stanovich, K. E., & R. F. West (1997). Reasoning independently of prior belief and individual differences in actively open-minded thinking. *Journal of Educational Psychology, 89*, 342–357.

——. (1998). Individual differences in rational thought. *Journal of Experimental Psychology: General, 127*, 161–188.

——. (2000). Individual differences in reasoning: Implications for the rationality debate? *Behavioral and Brain Sciences, 23*, 645–726.

Stein, E. (1996). *Without good reason: The rationality debate in philosophy and cognitive science*. Oxford: Oxford University Press.

Sterelny, K. (1990). *The representational theory of mind: An introduction*. Oxford: Basil Blackwell.

Sternberg, R. J. (Ed.) (1982). *Handbook of human intelligence*. Cambridge: Cambridge University Press.

Sternberg, R. J. (1985). Implicit theories of intelligence, creativity, and wisdom. *Journal of Personality and Social Psychology, 49*, 607–627.

——. (1988). Mental self-government: A theory of intellectual styles and their development. *Human Development, 31,* 197–224.

——. (1989). Domain-generality versus domain-specificity: The life and impending death of a false dichotomy. *Merrill-Palmer Quarterly, 35,* 115–130.

——. (1997a). The concept of intelligence and its role in lifelong learning and success. *American Psychologist, 52,* 1030–1037.

——. (1997b). *Thinking styles.* Cambridge: Cambridge University Press.

Sternberg, R. J., B. Conway, J. Ketron, & M. Bernstein (1981). People's conceptions of intelligence. *Journal of Personality and Social Psychology, 41,* 37–55.

Sternberg, R. J., & D. K. Detterman (1986). *What is intelligence?* Norwood, N.J.: Ablex.

Sternberg, R. J., & P. Ruzgis (Eds.). (1994). *Personality and intelligence.* Cambridge: Cambridge University Press.

Stich, S. P. (1990). *The fragmentation of reason.* Cambridge, Mass.: MIT Press.

Stich, S. P. (1996). *Deconstruction of the mind.* New York: Oxford University Press.

Sutherland, S. (1992). *Irrationality: The enemy within.* London: Constable.

Swartz, R. J., & D. N. Perkins (1989). *Teaching thinking: Issues & approaches.* Pacific Grove, Calif.: Midwest Publications.

Thaler, R. H. (1992). *The winner's curse: Paradoxes and anomalies of economic life.* New York: Free Press.

Tobacyk, J., & G. Milford (1983). Belief in paranormal phenomena. *Journal of Personality and Social Psychology, 44,* 1029–1037.

Tversky, A. (1996). Contrasting rational and psychological principles of choice. In R. Zeckhauser, R. Keeney, & J. Sebenius (Eds.), *Wise choices* (pp. 5–21). Boston, Mass.: Harvard Business School Press.

Tversky, A., & E. Shafir (1992). The disjunction effect in choice under uncertainty. *Psychological Science, 3,* 305–309.

Vernon, P. A. (1991). The use of biological measures to estimate behavioral intelligence. *Educational Psychologist, 25,* 293–304.

Vernon, P. A. (1993). *Biological approaches to the study of human intelligence.* Norwood, N.J.: Ablex.

Voss, J., D. Perkins, & J. Segal (Eds.) (1991). *Informal reasoning and education.* Hillsdale, N.J.: Erlbaum.

Walberg, H. J., B. F. Strykowski, E. Rovai, & S. S. Hung (1984). Exceptional performance. *Review of Educational Research, 54,* 87–112.

Walberg, H. J., & S. Tsai (1983). Matthew effects in education. *American Educational Research Journal, 20,* 359–373.

Wason, P. C. (1969). Regression in reasoning? *British Journal of Psychology, 60,* 471–480.

Watson, G., & E. M. Glaser (1980). *Watson-Glaser Critical Thinking Appraisal.* New York: Psychological Corporation.

Willis, C. (1990, June). The ten mistakes to avoid with your money. *Money Magazine,* pp. 84–94.

Yates, J. F. (Ed.) (1992). *Risk-taking behavior.* Chichester, England: Wiley.

ELENA L. GRIGORENKO & DONNA LOCKERY

8 Smart Is as Stupid Does

EXPLORING BASES OF ERRONEOUS REASONING OF SMART PEOPLE REGARDING LEARNING AND OTHER DISABILITIES

In 1925, Samuel Orton, director of an Iowa State Psychiatric Hospital, upon the request of the Iowa Conference of Social Work, sent a number of mental health clinic workers to rural Greene County. According to Lyday (1926), the caseworkers evaluated 173 referrals (originating primarily from the county schools). Of these referrals, 84 of the children were described by their teachers as "dull, backward, or retarded," and 30 were described as "nervous, peculiar, or unruly." This group of children was rather heterogeneous, with IQs ranging from 70 to 122; but the common feature was that all of them had learning difficulties in school. Among these children with a variety of different diagnoses, the clinic distinguished 15 children with specific reading problems.

Lyday's account is one of the first reports on specific diagnostic professional evaluations of a group of children referred by a school system as having problems in school. In the nineteenth and early twentieth centuries, on more than one occasion, school systems describing students who fell behind their peers and who could not reach age-appropriate educational standards nondiscriminatingly made a reference to the "stupidity" of these students (*U.S. News & World Report*, Apr. 14, 1997). According to estimates, these children constituted approximately 2 percent of the population of schoolchildren (Kerr 1897).

In the first half of the twentieth century, great advances in medical, educational, and psychological professions resulted in differentiation of students who were deemed to fall below a standard category of "educability" into a number of specific categories (e.g., children with mental retardation, children with learning disabilities) (Solity 1992). The Institution of Special Education originated in order to meet the needs of these students: to remediate their difficulties, and to help them become "smarter." Today the intention of institutions of special education is to attempt to find the best possible fit between an individual's profile of abilities and the educational program in which he or she participates in order to maximize the learning outcome of that individual.

However, something has gone off track somewhere. Somehow good intentions, in a number of directions, have turned into serious problems. First, the system of special education has become a financial threat to the system of mainstream education in the United States. Describing this rising conflict, Meredith and Underwood (1995) have concluded that the cost of educating students with disabilities is threatening society's ability to educate those students without disabilities, therefore placing the entire public education edifice at risk. Second, public laws intended to guarantee the rights of people with disabilities, partially as a result of the imprecision of the definition of "disabilities," have overwhelmed court dockets with justified and not-so-well justified complaints (Kelman & Lester 1997). Third, the system of educational privileges established for students with special needs has created tension between academic and professional standards and special accommodation given to those who qualify for these privileges (Sternberg & Grigorenko 1999).

These outcomes, from our point of view, are indicators of society's thinking "stupidly" about problems of those who have temporal, content, and/or sequential difficulties with learning. Etymologically, the word *stupid* originates from the Latin *stupidus,* which means to be numb or stunned (*Webster's Dictionary* 1996, p. 1889). Having dealt inadequately with disabilities, society is currently stupefied by the unfolding system of problems it has largely created itself. In this chapter we describe some of the symptoms indicative of society's inadequate thinking about disabilities, and we point out some reasoning fallacies that might, partially, account for the current societal attitude toward disabilities.

Enormous human and economic resources are invested in the system of special education. According to the National Center for Policy Analysis website (www.ncpa.org/pi/edu), the Department of Education estimates that federal, state, and local governments spent as much as $35 billion on special education programs in the 1995–1996 school year. Currently services are provided to 5.2 million children and adults with learning disabilities from birth to twenty-two years of age (*Associated Press State & Local Wire,* Dec. 12, 1999).

These numbers are particularly impressive when the changes in these numbers are analyzed over time. The Office of Special Education of the U.S. Department of Education has released longitudinal data on the number of children served by the system of special education. The department lists thirteen disabilities: specific learning disabilities, speech or language impairments, mental retardation, emotional disturbances, multiple disabilities, hearing impairments, orthopedic impairments, other health impairments, visual impairments, autism, deafness/blindness, traumatic brain injury, and developmental delay. For the age group six to twenty-one years of age, 4,173,512 children received special services in 1988–1989; 4,499,824 in 1991–1992; 4,907,511 in 1994–1995; and 5,401,282 in 1997–1998. This shows a steady increase of about 204,720 children with disabilities per year. For the category of specific learning disabilities, 1,995,186 children received services in 1988–1989; 2,247,004 in 1991–1992; 2,510,224 in 1994–1995; and 2,756,046 in 1997–1998. These numbers suggest that, on average, 126,810 new cases of learning disabilities are identified and accommodated in the system of special education every year. Overall, about 12 percent of the youngsters in the United States between six and twenty-one years of age are being served by the special education system (Guidelines for Identifying Children with Learning Disabilities, Connecticut State Department of Education, 1999). The discrepancy between estimates obtained in the late nineteenth century (2 percent) and frequencies observed now (25 percent) is stunning.

Among the 1.6 million first-time, full-time freshmen enrolled at 3,100 institutions of higher education in the United States in 1998 (the most recent figure available), some 154,520 (9.4 percent of the total) had claimed some kind of disability that qualified them for special education accommodations. In 1978, by contrast, fewer than 3 percent of freshmen reported having a disability (*Cincinnati Enquirer,* Feb. 10, 2000). According to the National Education Council report (*Denver Rocky Mountain News,* Feb. 15, 2000), the number of college freshmen describing themselves as having learning disabilities increased by 35 percent between 1988 and 1998. In 1999, 24,106 students with various disabilities asked for special accommodations when they took the SAT—a dramatic number when compared with 14,994 in 1994. Today, approximately 1 out of every 30 college students identifies him- or herself as having a learning disability.

According to the American Disability Association estimates, between 16 million and 27 million Americans suffer from some form of learning disability. A number of issues are relevant when clarifying the nature of these astonishing numbers.

The first issue is that of overidentification. According to Alice Parker, California's director of special education, as many as 250,000 students statewide have been designated as having learning disabilities because of reading difficulties but should not be receiving special education (*Los Angeles Times,* Dec. 12, 1999). Recent reports (e.g., Goldman et al. 1998) have made references to overdiagnosis of attention deficit/hyperactivity disorder (a category that is usually included in the "specific learning disabilities" category or the "multiple disabilities" category). Overall, special education enrollments have grown by 19 percent between 1992–1993 and 1997–1998 in relation to public school enrollment increases of just over 6 percent (*Evaluation of Special Education Funding,* State of Wisconsin, 1999).

Second, the system of special education is tightly linked to that of mainstream education because both identification of special needs and provision of special services are obtained through the regular education system. Thus, it is possible that the special education system is being used to shield the failures of the regular system. According to G. Reid Lyon, chief of the Child Development and Behavior Branch of the National Institutes of Health, who oversees federal government–supported research on learning disabilities, the situation in the American education system is alarming: more than 40 percent of fourth-grade students performed below basic levels of academic performance (i.e., below grade standards for fourth graders) as established by the National Assessment of Educational Progress (NAEP) in 1994 and again in 1998. Still worse, more than 10 percent of fourth-grade children could not participate in the NAEP because of severe reading difficulties (*Baltimore Sun,* Apr. 2, 2000). The more state and local officials continue to raise the bar for student achievement and to heighten the sanction for school failure, the more tempting it becomes for general educators to refer students for individualized treatment through special education (http://nces.ed.gov). Summarizing the situation, Lyon said that learning disabilities have become "a sociological sponge to wipe up the spills of general education" (http://nces.ed.gov).

Third, one of the traditional beliefs of Americans reflecting upon the deep cultural foundations of society is that social status reflects educational achievement (Carrier 1986). Success is often equated with ability. Thus, educational success is thought of as both reflecting students' intrinsic abilities and providing students with the knowledge and skills with which to succeed in adult life. Consequently, educational success and failure are intimately connected to societal success and failure. Thus, educational achievement is both an indicator of the current socioeconomic status and a predictor of future status. Achievement test scores are of high stakes to local communities. In other words, advantages offered by the special education system are of interest not only to those who want better education for their children because of the children's disabilities, but also to those who want better education for their children, irrespective of the children's abilities and disabilities.

Owing to both financial and value considerations related to the institution of special education in the United States, many special education–related issues (e.g., identification, enrollment, eligibility, benefits, rights) are among the most contentious issues faced by communities today. The system of special education is not constrained *solely* to the domain of education anymore; it is a complex sociological and psychological phenomenon tightly linked to a number of major aspects of American life. And, as with any complex phenomenon, it has multiple layers of representations—in public laws, in courtrooms, in classrooms, and in people's minds.

In the remainder of this chapter we explore some peculiarities of people's reasoning about abilities and disabilities and the system of special education.

Smart and Stupid Behaviors of Smart and Stupid People

People's implicit definitions of abilities and disabilities do not come out of the blue. They are formed on the bases of their everyday interactions with the real world and real people. The system described above has resulted not from some kind of abstract scientific theorizing or research, but from people trying to cope educationally, politically, and societally with a group of children who were not performing well in school. In trying to explain the puzzles of everyday life, people make inferences, but not all these inferences are correct or justified. People are especially susceptible to this type of faulty reasoning when they make conjectures about abilities and disabilities. When classifying types of erroneous inferences, researchers studying reasoning refer to *fallacies* of various kinds. The concept of fallacy is closely linked to the concepts of both intuition (a judgment made without preliminary reasoned cogitation) and counterintuition (a judgment made despite intuition). Fallacies are often difficult to detect—they are simply errors in reasoning or thinking that produce a conclusion that is seemingly true but actually false. It is this falseness in an argument that, curiously enough, seems sound. Fallacies can be made at any step of the reasoning process—while encoding information (i.e., formulating premises), engaging in reasoning (i.e., establishing connections between premises), or deriving conclusions (i.e., making inferences).

This portion of the chapter is intended to demonstrate how stereotypes of people with learning disabilities (or disabilities in general), as is the case with any stereotype, are based on fallacies—in other words, mistakes in reasoning—held by people who otherwise are intelligent. There are many reasons why people make mistakes in reasoning. A major cause is lack of information. American society as a whole did not become aware of the problems of individuals with mental challenges and learning problems until the middle of the nineteenth century (when, in 1843, Dorothea Dix delivered a speech to the Massachusetts state legislature calling for humane treatment of the mentally ill). Since then, society has learned about, described, and classified a whole spectrum of disabilities. It also has learned that people with disabilities deserve better treatment than they have received in the past. They did not ask to be disabled—their weaknesses are as integral to and characteristic of them as their strengths. People with disabilities cannot look for fairness in the way they are "constructed"; they can only search for fairness in the way other people react to them, interact with them, and treat them.

The expression of group norms in mass media (art, literature, drama, and film) reflects, and often reinforces, stereotypes. Unfortunately, stereotypes prevalent in a society often serve to justify existing social inequalities, portraying various disadvantaged groups as "deserving" their social roles and positions. Paul Darke, an author with a disability, referred to the media's perspective toward disability as one of "betrayal, hypocrisy, and ignorance" (*The Scotsman,* Aug. 28, 1998).

To stress the importance of delivering accurate information about people with disabilities to a general audience, One in Eight, a disability pressure group whose name originates from the frequency estimates of recognized disabilities in the general population, organized the disability Oscars—awards for the best and worst portrayals of disabled people in the media. Richard Riese, coordinator of One in Eight, has stated that film and TV producers should use realistic and varied portrayals of people with disabilities rather than the stereotypical images that have been dominating the mass media. These stereotypic images portray disabilities as (1) rare; (2) abnormalizing (i.e., excluding a person from "normal" society); (3) taking away fundamental human qualities, motivations, and desires (e.g., participation in certain occupational, athletic, scholastic, or community activities); (4) prohibiting those who have them from forming and developing close relationships (love, friendship, commitment, dedication); (5) a burden to society in general, as well as to local communities and to their own families. By the very nature of their impairment, people with disabilities are accompanied by stereotyped or even iconic (Darke 1998) status. Even to an unsophisticated observer, it is noticeable that disability is usually presented as a central rather than incidental characteristic with no more significance than nose shape or hair length (Pointon, Davies, & Pointon 1998). It is also noticeable that the frequency of portrayals of people with disabilities in media productions does not reflect the statistical incidence of various disabilities within society at large (Marks 1999). There is some debate regarding whether those employed by the mass media do or do not know the facts pertaining to the objects of their creation (whether they are newspaper articles or PG-13 rated movies) (Zillmann & Vorderer 2000); lack of accuracy contributes to the formation and crystallization of stereotypes about the disabled. The disability Oscars, or "Raspberry Ripple" awards (the Cockney[1] rhyme with "cripple"[2]), first bestowed in 1996, are endorsed by more than a hundred celebrities, including actors, film directors, and movie industry administrators.

Many famous names (e.g., Liz Hurley, Hugh Grant, the Walt Disney Corporation) have been selected to receive a Raspberry Ripple Award for the worst betrayals of people with disabilities. These awards are intended as a "beware" sign for those who shape the media to think about how they portray this sector of the population. The message here is that these images might be responsible for the formation of false images and negative stereotypes, which may in turn lead to increased intolerance. This, of course, is not to say that the media target people with disabilities exclusively. Mass media is one of the most powerful and effective agents capable of enhancing the stereotypic images of everything and everyone. These include stereotypes of sexuality, ethnicity, physical appearance, and so on. Consequently, religious groups, feminist organizations, advocacy groups, and ethnic groups also battle these stereotypical and often unfair and inaccurate presentations.

Besides movies, the other major source of images of people with disabilities is the print medium. Journalism transmits as well as shapes the narratives of a culture (Barkin 1984; Bird & Dardenne 1988). Researchers have investigated cultural images of disability and the way the disabled are treated in different societies and cultures and subcultures within those societies (e.g., Cumberbatch & Negrine 1992; Darke 1994; Evans 1992; Gartner & Joe 1987; Hevey 1992; Klobas 1988; Longmore 1987; Morris 1991). Opinions range from the position that disabilities are out there, and therefore we need to acknowledge and understand them, to the position that there are no disabilities but only human variation and cultural labels. For example, Longmore (1987) has argued for the necessity of increasing the number of positive representations of people with disabilities who occupy typical as well as powerful positions. Darke (1998), on the contrary, has argued that "negative" portrayals of people with disabilities and the way "normal" society reacts to them may in fact be an accurate reflection of how these people are subjected to societal dismissal, isolation, infantilization, and lack of appreciation.

Images of disabilities in the mass media have been multifaceted and multipurpose. They have appeared in horror, romance, science fiction, mystery, and comedy films. These images have been used as a metaphor for violence and innocence, saintliness and sinfulness. Mass media portrayals of people with disabilities have been a mirror, reflecting society's attempts to deal with the issue of humane attitudes toward people who are less fortunate. Societal issues of equal access to various aspects of life, rehabilitation, acceptance, and support for people with disabilities have been examined in the mass media since its establishment. These issues continue to occupy a place in the spectrum of media attention. For people who have limited exposure to those with disabilities, mass media, especially film—whether the information embedded in these sources is accurate or not—becomes a major source of knowledge about disabilities. Depictions in the media can serve as the basis for acceptance and understanding or lack of acceptance and misunderstanding. Lack of exposure to people with disabilities and non-critical acceptance of media portrayals of these people have led to erroneous reasoning by people about those with disabilities. Even though the mechanisms underlying the formation of stereotypes of people with learning disabilities are diverse, there are some specific reasoning fallacies that appear to underlie the formation of these stereotypes. So, what are the fallacies underlying some major stereotypes of people with disabilities?

THE BASE-RATE FALLACY

This fallacy is easy to detect. For example, in making inferences about people with learning disabilities, the typical person tends to ignore the fact that the proportion of people with these disabilities in the general population is relatively large. However, this proportion is grossly underrepresented on the large screen, on TV shows, in fictional literature, and in journalistic presentations (as is the proportion of portrayals of people who lead well-adjusted lives or who are only average in physical attractiveness). Thus, the mass media leads the public to believe that the proportion of people with learning disabilities is negligible, and, therefore, that their issues can be ignored.

When statements are made about "inaccuracy" in the media presentation of a given issue, the typical counterargument is that the mass media is concerned primarily with the issues of entertainment value and sale revenues, not with accurate representations (e.g., in television fiction, there is usually a time and sequence-of-event warp between the first meeting and sexual intercourse and between sexual intercourse and love—everything happens very quickly on TV). But it is society that gives the media the power to influence mass consciousness, and it is society that can take these powers away or reshape them. One attempt at changing "the way things are" is that of the British Film Institute's project from and about people with disabilities. It is already being seen as a role model for other European film organizations. The hope is that the project will create an impetus for change in the attitudes of the film industry and the public on the issue of disability (*The Scotsman,* Aug. 28, 1998).

PART-WHOLE FALLACY (THE FALLACY OF DIVISION)

The fallacy of division is committed when people reason that what is true of the whole is necessarily true of each individual part of the whole. In other words, if X is diagnosed with a learning disability, then X will have all the components of the diagnostic definition present in his or her behavior. For example, if person X has a learning disability and exhibits particular behaviors, then, based on this fallacy, person Y, solely on the basis of his or her label as a person having the same learning disability, *should* also manifest all (or at least some) behaviors of person X.

The influence of stereotype rather than reality was, among other factors, what produced problems for Jon Westling of Boston University a few years ago. Westling, past provost and current president of the university, invented a stereotypical student with learning disabilities who had all the worst qualities of such students. According to Westling, the student had told him after class that she had a learning disability "in the area of auditory processing" and would need copies of lecture notes, a seat in front, extra time on exams, and a separate room to take them in. And, he said, he was told that the student, Samantha, might fall asleep in class, so he would need to fill her in on material she missed while she dozed (*New York Times,* Apr. 8, 1997). Westling, to stress the nature of these demands, nicknamed the student "Somnolent Samantha." It may well be that somewhere there exists a student with learning disabilities with all Samantha's traits and worse, but, real or imagined, the trouble with Samantha-as-representative is that she was an invention and a stereotype. Westling tried using Samantha to present the worst-case scenario as normative. In this way, he could challenge the reality of her excesses. However, the excesses in Samantha's image crossed far into the realm of the ridiculous. Westling spoke of Samantha on multiple occasions, affirmed that the case was real in an interview with the *New York Times* in 1996, and cited the case, as if it were real, in a letter to the mother of a child with a disability. Although the case of Somnolent Samantha was not the *only* reason, it was almost certainly one of the reasons that students with various learning disabilities at Boston University filed a highly visible lawsuit against the university and its policy regarding people with learning disabilities; the plaintiffs won (for more details on the case see http://www.elibrary.com; Kelman & Lester 1997; Sternberg & Grigorenko 1999).

Like many other educational institutions, Boston University is struggling to determine the best and most fair-minded accommodations for students with learning disabilities. If accommodations are too generous, the student might become overly reliant on assistance and, therefore, might be unprepared for performance in real-world situations, jeopardizing the reputation of the school from which he or she graduated. If accommodations are not provided fairly, the university will not meet the requirements of the public laws and will not be providing its best in educational opportunities to its students. This dilemma is not an easy one to resolve, and Boston University has attempted to contribute to the debate. This contribution, however, would have seemed more credible if Westling had not fabricated Somnolent Samantha.

THE FALLACY OF ROLE SUBSTITUTION
(THE FALLACY OF DIFFERENTIAL REASONING)

This fallacy refers to a type of reasoning, the structure and content of which changes depending on the position from which the arguing is done. The fallacy invokes the acceptability of two different lines of reasoning (e.g., one for friends and one for enemies). As an illustration of this fallacy, consider the following.

The City of Manchester Democratic Party Committee endorsed Peter Leonard, a fifty-three-year-old man with a specific reading disability who had an IQ of 80 and reading skills at a third-grade level (*Good Morning America,* Mar. 19, 1998). Mr. Leonard had won a seat on the Manchester school board. The city's Republican leader, Marc Pappas, said that Leonard was a nice man who had the best intentions, but he questioned whether Leonard would be able to represent his constituents adequately. What is noteworthy, however, is that Pappas admitted that if Leonard had been a Republican with this same learning disability, the Republicans would have supported him (*Union Leader,* Nov. 12, 1999).

Here, while reasoning as a Republican opposing a Democratic Party candidate, Mr. Pappas questioned the quality of the candidate—the concern being not whether Mr. Leonard did or did not have a learning disability, but whether he could represent his constituents adequately. Mr. Pappas's reasoning changed, however, when he was asked what he and his party colleagues would do were Mr. Leonard a Republican. Put in this conditional position, Mr. Pappas did not bring up the question of Mr. Leonard's personal qualities but concentrated instead on his group membership. This kind of reasoning, which stresses the importance of being correctly affiliated politically rather than of making justified and consistent inferences following common sense, is quite effective in creating the stereotype according to which people with learning disabilities will be given special considerations.

The fallacy of hasty generalization is committed when only exceptional (or rare) cases are considered and a generalization is drawn from those cases to create a rule that fits only those exceptions.

In the context of this chapter, two examples of the use of this fallacy in the formation and propagation of stereotypes of people with learning disabilities are especially relevant. The first stereotype emerges from the fallacy that problems with learning are accompanied by delinquent and violent behavior. Whereas there is a significant amount of evidence pointing to comorbidity between learning problems and delinquent and aggressive behaviors (e.g., Duane 1991; Rasmussen, Storsaeter, & Levander 1999), there is no evidence that *every* individual with learning disabilities demonstrates antisocial behavior. The second stereotype has to do with the fallacy that people with learning disabilities are inferior and therefore deserve to be treated badly.

As an illustration of the first stereotype, consider the *aggressive moron* stereotype.

Gregg Nitzberg, forty-three, a student with learning disabilities at William Paterson University, found himself summarily suspended after his father allegedly told a staff member in the governor's office that his son could cause "a lot of students to be hurt" (*New Jersey Law Journal*, Oct. 4, 1999). The university's written policy allows for "interim suspensions" without a hearing if a student presents a "clear and present danger." Based on this policy, the school's dean of student development, without any warnings or investigations, suspended Nitzberg by means of a formal letter. In addition, a few days after the suspension, Nitzberg received a letter notifying him that the school had cut off his financial aid and dropped him from classes for the remainder of the term. Although Nitzberg challenged the university on other issues, he was not violent and had no police record. He filed suit in Newark federal court, asking to be reinstated immediately, and sued for other damages.

The impact of this kind of stereotype on people's reasoning was depicted in *Let Him Have It,* a film about a gentle youth with learning problems who falls in with a crowd of boys he admires and is badgered by one of them into going along on a break-in. He is caught, and a jury subsequently deems him responsible for the murder of a policeman. Ultimately, he is sentenced to death.

As an illustration of the second stereotype, consider the numerous examples of the *inferior person* (*"infeperson"*) stereotype. This stereotype is exhibited in criminal behavior motivated by hatred toward people with disabilities. On January 30, 1999, a group of young people committed a hate crime against a person with a learning disability (*Asbury Park Press*, May 17, 2000). One of the defendants lured the victim from his job at a McDonald's to a party at an apartment shared by two of the defendant's friends. The victim was a special-education student, appeared to be slow, wore a hearing aid, had a heart problem, and was short. For the next few hours the victim was tortured, humiliated, and beaten by several people. The victim was told that his parents' house would be burned down if he went to the police. After the "party," he was taken to a deserted area, where he was assaulted once again and dumped. According to the prosecution, no fewer than two of the abusers knew about their victim's learning disabilities, and this knowledge at least partially motivated their behavior.

However heinous this crime is, the most horrifying aspect of it is that it is not unique. Indeed, even a superficial, quick search of the news in 1999 and 2000 reveals a number of hate crimes against people with learning disabilities, allegedly in response to those disabilities. For example, an entrepreneur and longtime church/youth-group volunteer was sentenced to a six-month jail term for repeatedly molesting an eleven-year-old girl with learning disabilities (*Buffalo News*, Apr. 6, 2000). Allegedly, the girl's learning disabilities were the reason and excuse for molestation. A retired priest was arrested for sodomizing a boy with learning disabilities (*Daily News*, May 17, 2000). The boy's disability was a factor contributing to the priest's conduct. A teacher's aide was arrested for allegedly slamming a student with learning disabilities against a wall in a Queens public school and, as a result, breaking his forearm and wrist (*Daily News*, Dec. 10, 1999). A driver was sentenced to six months in jail and five years' probation after admitting to charges that he sodomized a young passenger with learning disabilities (*Time Union*, Aug. 21, 1999). In New Hampshire, three frequently homeless friends terrorized a man with learning disabilities, robbing him of all his possessions, strangling him, and dumping him in a river (*Associate Press State & Local Wire*, Aug. 5, 1999). Two women were imprisoned for kidnapping and torturing their roommate with learning disabilities (*Record*, July 27, 1999). A former Wall Street consultant was convicted on multiple counts of rape and sodomy for repeatedly having sex with a fourteen-year-old girl with learning disabilities (*Times Union*, May 28, 1999). A gym teacher pleaded guilty to having sex on school premises with a teenage student with learning disabilities who later bore his child (*Washington Post*, July 27, 1999). Although it is not clear that these crimes were committed as a cause of the victims' learning disabilities, these crimes were more easily committed because these individuals were more easily manipulated than are people without disabilities.

Even though people with disabilities are protected like all other citizens— and, indeed, more so (by state hate-crime laws protecting victims who have

disabilities)—given the frequency of learning disabilities in the general population, the crime rate against this subpopulation is much higher than might
be expected by chance. The National Center for Victims of Crime (NCVC)
website reports that the rates of violent crime against people with developmental or other severe disabilities are four to ten or more times higher than
the rate of violent crime among the general population (http://www.ncvc
.org/newsltr/disabled.htm).

THE FALLACY OF IRRELEVANT CONCLUSION
(IRRELEVANT REASONS): THE CURE FALLACY

The fallacy of irrelevant conclusion occurs when a conclusion is irrelevant to the line of reasoning that led to it.

It is interesting to note that the number of Academy Award–winning
films portraying individuals with disabilities has dramatically increased since
the Oscars were first handed out in 1928. To appreciate this change, consider
that up to 1939, only one award (2.6 percent of the total) was given to a film
portraying a person with a mental disability (Fredric March in *Dr. Jekyll and
Mr. Hyde*). From 1990 to 1997, ten films (56 percent of the total) featured a
person with some kind of disability. The disabilities portrayed were, most
frequently, psychiatric disturbances, followed by physical disabilities, sen-
sory disabilities, and intellectual disabilities. Commenting on the increase in
the number of people with disabilities seen both on the big screen and on
TV, Steve Safran (see http://www.ohiou.edu) observed that this increase
reflects the trend of those with disabilities becoming more visible members
of society; but, unfortunately, the contents of these portraits often provide
viewers with a skewed perspective that may have little to do with reality.

Winners of Oscars by actors without disabilities playing people with
disabilities include Dustin Hoffman in *Rain Man,* Al Pacino in *Scent of a
Woman,* Tom Hanks in *Forrest Gump,* Daniel Day-Lewis in *My Left Foot,* Cliff
Robertson in *Charly,* John Mills in *Ryan's Daughter,* Holly Hunter in *The Piano,*
and Patty Duke in *The Miracle Worker*. Anne Bancroft also won an Oscar for
The Miracle Worker for her portrayal of Annie Sullivan, Helen Keller's teacher.
One exception to this list is the performance of Marlee Matlin (who is
deaf) in *Children of a Lesser God,* for which Matlin won a Best Actress Oscar
in 1988.

During a radio broadcast, Alex Cox, a movie director, asked a number of
other directors for an explanation of the phenomenon of "the portrayal of
people with disabilities by people without disabilities." According to the
respondents, there are two major reasons for this: (1) acting is about pretending, so it is natural to use people without disabilities to play people
with disabilities, and (2) there is a shortage of actors with disabilities. The

reasoning underlying the first argument is skewed because if this reasoning were correct, there would also be people with disabilities playing people without disabilities. However, it is difficult to find even a single example of such a portrayal. The second argument is also questionable: Actors' Equity has a list of 500 actors with disabilities, and there are a number of people affiliated with disabilities-related acting companies, such as Graear and Strathcona in Great Britain. A notable exception was during the 1981–1984 run of the television sitcom *The Facts of Life,* in which Geri Jewell made several guest appearances as "Cousin Geri," a remarkably upbeat young woman with cerebral palsy. Some audiences found this portrayal uncomfortable, but they nevertheless applauded Jewell's determination and willingness to bring disabilities into the open. (In one episode she remarked to the girls, "Questions don't hurt, ignorance does.") Remarkably, her disability was not the central theme of her appearance on the show. Unfortunately, she never was integrated into the cast, and she left the show during the 1984 season. During a television interview many years later, she lamented that no roles had been offered to her after her groundbreaking appearances on *The Facts of Life,* and at times she was so destitute that she could not afford to pay her rent. She has not appeared as an actress elsewhere, but is currently a freelance motivational speaker. Another example is Chris Burke—a person with Down's syndrome, who played one of the central characters in the more recent television series *Life Goes On.* Burke's performance was acknowledged by way of a number of awards.

Marks (1999) has argued that the real reason for not employing people with disabilities is that knowing "it is only pretend" reassures viewers and gives them an opportunity to project on an actor without disabilities their fears of dependency and loss. Knowing that Leonardo Di Caprio (in *What's Eating Gilbert Grape*) is not really autistic and Mercedes Ruehl (in *Lost in Yonkers*) does not really have learning disabilities helps the viewer maintain a safe distance and detach the "movie tears" from the experience of real disabilities in real lives. Director Stanley Kubrick (as cited by the Australian National Council on Intellectual Disability, 1995) once commented that knowing that a character with a disability is played by a person without a disability makes all the difference: people feel much more comfortable viewing these performances because they know that after the movie is over, the actors will return to their "normal" lives. It is knowing that there will be no change, that their disability will never go away, that many people with disabilities refer to as the hardest adjustment they have to make.

Thus, by hiring typical actors and actresses to perform roles of people with disabilities, Hollywood, willingly or unwillingly, contributes to the erroneous reasoning that people can be cured (as soon as the movie is over) or that they really do not suffer from their disabilities but only pretend to be suffering. Hollywood will consistently put forth a sentiment of hope—that although this person has a disability, he or she will someday be able to function perfectly within society. The harsh reality of having a disability and the battle of the person with a disability for independence and acceptance are glossed over. Children, however, are portrayed on film as more accepting of people with disabilities. Frequently, a child will befriend an individual with a learning disability and accept him or her without exception (e.g., *Dominick and Eugene* and *Sling Blade*).

THE FALLACY OF REPRESENTATIVENESS

This fallacy is committed when people decide that two or more things or events are related simply because they resemble each other.

Movie portrayals of people with learning disabilities often depict such people as being more intuitive, "childlike," spontaneous, and innocent—but also as more uncivilized, unpredictable, and dangerous—than are people without disabilities. Consider the main characters in *Of Mice and Men, What's Eating Gilbert Grape, Rain Man, Forrest Gump,* and *Sling Blade:* people with disabilities are depicted in these movies as both concerned and humane yet lacking in common sense and understanding, and therefore as threatening to themselves and others. In other words, even when portrayed with great sympathy, people with learning disabilities are viewed as having the potential to cause great damage, and therefore as incapable of integration into "normal" society (e.g., because they are untrustworthy and also capable of erratic behavior). When they are lucky (*Forrest Gump*), they find their unique and atypical (and thus abnormal) niche; when unlucky (*Rain Man, Sling Blade*), they try (or other people try for them) to succeed in the real world, but fail and must return to the institution where they lived at the beginning of the story. Marks (1999) summarizes the message of such movies: despite dreams of inclusion, there is only one place for people with disabilities—outside of the "normal" society.

In *Charly,* a 1968 film based on the book "Flowers for Algernon," by Daniel Keyes, Cliff Robertson plays a middle-aged man who has an IQ of 70. We see Charly in a playground romping with school-aged children, struggling in night school without improvement in his reading or writing abilities, and standing outside the gates of a university or college, observing and imitating the individuals within. Although Charly has a learning impairment, he is wise enough to know that there is higher intellect—something he aspires to. After undergoing experimental cerebral surgery, Charly develops a genius IQ—absorbing all elementary-school material in five weeks and secondary-school material in three weeks, and advancing beyond the level of his instructors. However, Charly soon discovers that the results of the surgery are temporary. He comments that this experiment has allowed him to see the world—he sees things as they are. However, with his new intellect he also observes that there are brave new hates, brave new bombs, and brave new wars. He also comments on society's suicide. When asked "Who is Charly Gordon?" he replies, "A fella who will very shortly be what he used to be." In the closing scene, we see Charly Gordon once again happily playing with children on the playground. The message appears to be that Charly is better off as he was, outside rather than inside "normal" society.

Movies about real people tend to distort real images: they tend to take real-life facts and fill in the holes with fictional reasoning that explains the missing (or unknown) links. Ben Godar (2000) insightfully points out that Hollywood's versions of real lives often resemble slanted storytelling rather than artistic interpretations of real people's stories. Godar, then, formulates a task for moviegoers: employ critical-thinking skills in viewing Hollywood productions and take movies for what they are—fiction—and recognize that the events of everyday life (both important and compelling) are what constitute the truth.

Films that deal directly with disability, depict the "boring routine" of the everyday life of a person with disabilities, and do not have the typical Hollywood happy ending have not been box office successes. Critics were embarrassed and angered by the film *A Child Is Waiting* (1963). A music teacher who wants to find some meaning in her life applies for a position at a state institution for children with mental retardation. She becomes emotionally involved with one of the students and makes an error in judgment regarding his management, against the director's wishes. The child's father arrives to transfer the child to a private school. While at the school, the father attends a Thanksgiving show in which all the children perform. When he hears his son haltingly recite a poem and respond to the audience's applause, he better understands his son's need to achieve something for himself. All but one of the children (the lead actor) in the film were patients with mental retardation in the Pacific State Hospital in Pomona, California. Although the movie and actors were praised by some critics, it was not a box office success—presumably due to the strong theme of the film. Some critics faulted the film for its sentimental and melodramatic portrayals.

The Men (1950) also resulted in little box office income. A young lieutenant is shot in the spine at the end of World War II. He returns a paraplegic to a Veterans Hospital, where he is bitter and suicidal, rejecting the woman he was to have married. He gradually begins to adjust and struggles for mental and physical rehabilitation. On his wedding night, he and his new wife quarrel and he returns to the hospital, losing the ground that he gained. The loss of biological function (especially sexual) is discussed only indirectly, but concern and fears are communicated nonverbally. During his extended hospital stay, he is asked to leave by his peers because of his drinking and fighting. He wants to stay at the hospital, but through counseling and his wife's support, he leaves the hospital with his wife. Their future together is left open-ended and hopeful, but uncertain. *The Men* was filmed at a Veterans Hospital for paraplegics outside of Los Angeles and a number of patients were cast as extras.

Although not considered a big box office success, one exception may be *Dominick and Eugene,* a 1988 film depicting the story of two brothers: Dominick, who is intellectually impaired from a childhood traumatic brain injury, and Eugene, who is struggling to complete medical school. Dominick works as a garbage collector in Pittsburgh, supporting them both and partially financing Eugene's education. Eugene is accepted at Stanford Medical School for his residency training and struggles with his responsibility to Dominick. He believes that Dominick will not adapt well to the relocation, but he also has doubts about Dominick's ability to be self-sufficient. We see Dominick struggling to remember his responsibilities and being taken advantage of and coerced by others, which deepens Eugene's doubts and guilt about leaving his brother behind. Eugene tells Dominick that he can still think, see, hear, and keep himself strong, and that he should believe in those strengths. The brothers experience a personal crisis and revelation, and at the close of the film, we see Eugene leaving for California and Dominick remaining behind, more confident in his abilities and not having Eugene to rely on anymore.

THE CONJUNCTION FALLACY:
ASEXUALITY OF PEOPLE WITH DISABILITIES

The fallacy of conjunction appears when the co-occurrence of two events is viewed to be more likely than the probability of a component event. In the context of this chapter, the fallacy results in the stereotype that the probability of both having a disability and being asexual (i.e., not engaging in sexual relationships) is higher than that expected based on the probability of either having a disability or of being asexual.

According to Nemeth (2000), the societal message about sexuality and disability indicates that the American public does not perceive people with learning disabilities as sexual beings. A remarkable observation here is that, almost irrespective of *what* disability the portrayed person has, people with disabilities (with rare exceptions such as *Children of a Lesser God*) are portrayed as asexual. Zola (1982) states that this image is an outcome of a narrow definition of what sex, sexual relationships, and sexual activities consist of. According to this narrow definition, sex is associated with values of health, youth, beauty, and physical and mental perfection; this definition renders the conjunction of sexuality and disability taboo. People with disabilities are typically not expected to have desires or to be desired. This lack of desire is viewed as characteristic of people with disabilities, irrespective of age (e.g., as young as Leonardo DiCaprio, who was in his teens in *What's Eating Gilbert Grape,* and as old as Peter Sellers, who was fifty to sixty years of age in *Being There*).

The most noticeable manifestation of this stereotype is found in Hollywood images. In general, films rarely show romantic and sexual images of people with learning disabilities. Typically, either no such images are shown (e.g., *Rain Man*) or sexual relationships are "generously given as a gift" (*Forrest Gump*) to the previously untouched (*Children of a Lesser God*). Tom Hanks's Gump is emotionally and sexually monogamous while waiting for his childhood sweetheart to consider him seriously. The film does not bother explaining to the audience what actually happens with his sexual life when they do marry and his spouse has AIDS. Chance, the character played by Peter Sellers in *Being There*, mimics a scene he has viewed on TV— embracing and attempting to kiss a woman—while being totally unaware of the sexual meaning of his behavior.

The stereotype of asexuality is promoted not only through images of people with disabilities, but also through images of their relatives. In the film *The Other Sister,* for example, Carla, a rich San Francisco girl of seventeen, returns home after several years in a special-education institution because of learning problems. She has the ambition to train as a veterinarian's assistant and encounters her mother, who, without considering that Carla might have changed, insists that her daughter is not ready for junior college, dating, dancing, sex, living in her own apartment, or anything else characteristic of a mature individual.

Tim was a revolutionary (though unrealistic) story of a friendship that progressed to love and marriage between an older woman and a handsome character with a mental disability, performed by Mel Gibson. According to many accounts of people with disabilities, the sexuality of these people is not necessarily diminished or childlike in its manifestations (for a review, see Nemeth 2000).

Thus, typical people's perceptions of the disabled are replete with erroneous inferences, based in part or even largely on stereotypes. These stereotypes, which are often unquestioned by otherwise intelligent people, can, by means of sheer repetition, eventually assume "the ring of truth." By applying such stereotypes uncritically, smart people do not appear to be quite so smart. In the 1980 comedy *Being There,* based on the novel by Jerzy Kosinski, Peter Sellers plays Chance, a sheltered man who is described as "feebleminded" and who cannot read or write. Chance's only knowledge about life is through his garden and what he sees on television. Through a series of mishaps, Chance is taken in by a wealthy and politically influential couple in Washington, D.C. Due to several misunderstandings, Chance the Gardener becomes Chauncey Gardener, a man whose opinion regarding the American economy is widely sought after. Although he speaks simply of his love of gardening, his words are misinterpreted as gardening analogies for the state of the American economy (e.g., fertilize it, water it, watch it grow). Chance becomes the center of media attention as it is rumored that he has become a financial advisor to the president of the United States. (He is also rumored to possess medical and legal degrees and to speak three languages). Throughout the film, Chauncey is described as intuitive, intense, possessing a great sense of humor, centered, and showing remarkable trustworthiness—as "a truly peaceful man with a down-to-earth philosophy." It is said that "more like him are needed on Capitol Hill." All the while, Chance is just being Chance.

There are many causes for such stereotyping, one of which, as pointed out by Marks (1999), is that those aspects of disability that generate the most anxiety are in precisely those areas of human experience with which many "typical" people struggle. Most people have wondered whether their weaknesses will someday be discovered and lead to the withholding of love and appreciation, and to loneliness and exclusion. Marks has outlined a number of anxieties about identity and difference that are commonly dealt with by projection onto people with learning disabilities. Klobas (1988), however, has offered a more sociologically based hypothesis, suggesting that stereotyping of people with learning disabilities can be traced to mainstream society's reluctance to acknowledge and recognize people with disabilities as "typical" members of society. This hypothesis asserts that typical members of a society have some advantages in being typical and therefore do not want to share these advantages with other "atypical" members. Inversely, atypical members want to get a share of the pluses associated with membership in the society. Klobas's hypothesis, then, is verifiable by assuming that the "borderline" between typical and atypical, and between smart and stupid, can be easily shifted by offering differential advantages to the atypical group. With the introduction of the Americans with Disabilities Act (ADA),[3] the Individuals with Disabilities Education Act (IDEA),[4] and the Carl Perkins Vocational and Applied Technology Act (P.L. 101–392),[5] this line has moved.

We will now consider the degree of flexibility of this borderline.

"Learning disability" is a noticeably flexible category. In addition to the federal definition, each of the fifty states has its own. The range of these definitions is such that more than 80 percent of all schoolchildren in the United States could qualify as students with learning disabilities under one specification or another (*Washington Monthly*, June 1, 1999).

If the line between the categories of "stupidity" and "non-stupidity" (or "smartness" and "non-smartness") is blurry and people can move (both willingly and unwillingly) between the two categories, then

1. there are examples of smart people who 'migrate' into the category of not-so-smart people and
2. there are examples of not-so-smart people who are recognized as smart.

Let us investigate whether there is support for these arguments.

Mercedes Ruehl, playing Bella, a woman with a learning disability, in *Lost in Yonkers* (1993), stressed the tragic disproportion of Bella's abilities to her appearance, so obvious in situations which she was incapable of handling or unprepared to negotiate. The story is of two young boys who are sent to live with their tyrannical grandmother in Yonkers after the death of their mother. The boys become attached to their Aunt Bella (Mercedes Ruehl), who is rumored to be mentally ill (although how is not specified). She is flighty, optimistic, and enthusiastic, yet plagued by tormenting doubts. Aunt Bella lives in a fantasy world of the movies, and the boys are drawn in. They meet her boyfriend, a movie usher, who also seems to be mentally unbalanced, but introspectively so. The film is a series of small discoveries and victories over life, over disabilities, and especially over the grandmother's tyranny. At the end of the movie, Aunt Bella finds a way to live life on her own terms.

FROM SMART TO STUPID: UNWILLING MIGRATIONS

When smart people think or feel they have done something stupid (that is, they have unwillingly migrated, at least temporarily, from one category to another), they deal with their feelings of stupidity in different ways. Some try to hide areas of ignorance and difficulties in learning. Some try to devalue certain kinds of knowledge they cannot master. Some demonstrate defensive pessimism by trying to defend themselves in advance, announcing after the failure that they had anticipated it. Some try to play the fool, limiting themselves publicly to a very narrow domain of knowledge. Whatever people choose to do, the purpose of their behavior is to conceal their inability to learn and to avoid experiencing the sense of humiliation that often accompanies this lack of ability. In short, most often people do not like to show their limitations or their fear of having them.

One of the best known examples of a significant public figure who successfully hid his disability is that of President Franklin D. Roosevelt. Gallagher (1985) demonstrated how Roosevelt used a carefully orchestrated strategy to hide the extent of his paralysis. The president could "walk" only with the help of leg braces. He was often supported on one side and used a walking stick on the other. So, he developed a set of strategies (e.g., arriving first at a meeting so he could be seated before the others arrived, using a wheelchair primarily in private, never being lifted in public, having his secret service agents prevent photographers from documenting the extent of his paralysis) to camouflage his disability and to propagate the myth that his illness was merely an "episode" from which he had recovered. His biographers compared his triumph over polio with America's recovery from the Great Depression (Marks 1999).

People perceive disabilities (or inabilities) as weaknesses not only in themselves but also in their children. The Emily Hall Tremaine Foundation polled 1,700 adults nationwide (for the entire report online, see www.LD Online.org/pressroom) and reported that 48 percent of them agreed that having their children labeled as learning disabled was more painful than struggling privately with an undiagnosed problem. There are many reasons why some parents preferred their children to remain undiagnosed.

First, it has been documented that teachers' expectations of children are reduced if they are labeled "learning disabled" (Richey & Ysseldyke 1983). Parents who are aware of this reduction in expectations may have mixed feelings about whether their child would be better off without formal identification. Second, parents are very concerned about whether their children, if stigmatized by a label, will be able to establish and maintain adequate social relationships with their peers (Marshak, Seligman, & Prezant 1999). Third, many parents are worried about their children's self-esteem. For example, one of the results of the Tremaine Foundation survey was that from the very early stages of their child's life, about 25 percent of the survey parents considered that their child might have a serious problem with learning and schoolwork. Among these parents, 44 percent waited for their child to manifest signs of difficulty for a year or more before acknowledging that their child might have a problem. Many parents are aware of some worrisome statistics implying a possible failure of the labeling system. For example, only 52 percent of students identified with learning disabilities will actually graduate with a high school diploma: diagnosed students drop out of high school at more than twice the rate of their peers without disabilities (*Congressional Quarterly Researcher*, December 1993). Sixty-two percent of students identified with learning disabilities have been reported to be unemployed one year after graduation (*National Longitudinal Transition Study*, 1991, as cited at http://forgottenkids.virtualave.net). Fourth, many parents do not trust the school system with taking adequate care of the needs of their children.

The results also showed that parents who tackled the problem privately were more likely to blame themselves for their children's learning disability, believing that it was a hereditary problem or that they were not adequate parents. These results were recorded in the *Fort Worth Star-Telegram* (May 17, 2000).

However, not all people perceive disabilities as disadvantageous for themselves and their children. Some even view disabilities as advantages.

FROM SMART TO STUPID: WILLING MIGRATION

Before Congress passed the nation's special education law, the Individuals with Disabilities Education Act (IDEA), an estimated one million children in need of special services were not getting adequate education, and a vastly disproportionate number of minority students were labeled as *educably mentally retarded*. At first, accommodating children with special needs did not seem to be a problem. The total cost of special education programs in the United States in 1977 was about $1 billion. However, little by little, Congress has added new categories to the originally adopted list of thirteen disabilities. Currently, special education costs the nation over $35 billion, with some estimates running close to $60 billion.

It is hard not to sympathize with the person (or the family) in each specific case. The trouble for legislators and educators comes when the law pits the single interest of every person with learning disabilities against the broader interest of the school. The issue of definition recurs because, if the law was intended to promote the interests of a special group of individuals, this "pie" should go to them, while everyone else gets an equally attractive piece of a different pie.

Unfortunately, neither the 1990 Americans with Disabilities Act (ADA) nor the 1997 Individuals with Disabilities Education Act (IDEA) provides a clear definition of disability. Therefore, the courts are flooded with both reasonable and unreasonable complaints. Moreover, both the ADA and the IDEA have generated some difficult administrative problems. For example, after the National Collegiate Athletic Association revised its regulations to forbid recruiting of high school athletes unprepared for college work, the Justice Department threatened to sue, claiming discrimination against students with learning disabilities who have not taken college preparatory courses (http://www.ncpa.org).

Some critics of the ADA say they are concerned that the act turns disabilities into valuable legal assets and therefore encourages tens of thousands of lawsuits against private companies, municipalities, and school systems, creating an incentive to maximize the number of Americans who claim to have disabilities (*Washington Times,* May 20, 1996). For example, Marilyn Bartlett, a fifty-year-old law school graduate who failed the New York Bar Examination four times, asserted that she suffered from a reading disability (after managing to get through high school, college, graduate school, and law school without special accommodations for her condition) and filed a lawsuit against the State of New York (*Denver Post,* Dec. 3, 1998). She is also said to have earned a Ph.D. in educational administration from New York University (*New York Law Journal,* Sept. 15, 1998). Bartlett sued under the ADA and won. However, when she took the exam under the relaxed rules, she failed again. The United States Supreme Court has recently decided to set aside the ruling for review by the federal appeals court in Manhattan (*The New York Times,* June 25, 1999), stating that Dr. Bartlett had developed accommodations to improve her reading skills so that they were comparable to those of an average person and therefore should not be covered by the Americans with Disabilities Act.

How far are people willing to go in order to get to where they want to be? Sinanson (1992), trying to address this question, came up with the term *stupefy.* In the sense she uses it, *stupefy* means to make society look stupid for the sake of reaching your own goal by making yourself look stupid.

How easily can some people stupefy themselves if they see an advantage in doing so? Recently there appears to have been a remarkable increase in the number of students diagnosed with learning disabilities on the campuses of America's elite private and most affluent public secondary schools. Specifically, the number of adolescents diagnosed with learning disabilities in areas with the wealthiest ZIP codes has jumped by almost 50 percent. Paul Campos, a professor of law at the University of Colorado, has commented that in Palo Alto, California, where the average price of a house is roughly $1 million, the percentage of high school students identified with learning disabilities is approximately seven times greater than in the roughest districts of nearby Oakland (*Denver Rocky Mountain News,* Feb. 15, 2000). Michele Norris, an ABC correspondent, was curious about why the affluent community of Greenwich, Connecticut, has one of the nation's highest percentages of students identified with learning disabilities—30 percent (twice the national average) of the high school students in this town are legally entitled to special education services (*Times Union,* June 1, 1999).

National Education Council data reveal that freshmen whose parents make under $75,000 per year are 15 percent less likely to report themselves as having a learning disability than is the freshman population as a whole, whereas those whose parents make $75,000 and above are 36 percent more likely than the general student population to describe themselves as having a learning disability (*Denver Rocky Mountain News,* Feb. 15, 2000). One possible reason for this is that the average, or C, student who is labeled with a learning disability will be granted certain advantages in school and has a better opportunity of becoming an A student, and thus will more likely be eligible for admission into a prestigious university. As we pointed out at the beginning of the chapter, education is an indicator of success (and social class). By pushing a child into special education, parents try to maintain for the child the parents' own high socioeconomic level.

To examine this issue of stupefication and its costs to society, let us look in detail at the case of a Phillips Academy (former) student, Nicholas Axelrod Panagopoulos. Phillips Academy, an elite prep school, expelled Nicholas, age eighteen, in the middle of his senior year, after he violated the terms of his academic probation by missing several assignments and turning in others late. His mother, Nancy Axelrod, had paid Phillips $90,000 over the four years of her son's education. Nicholas is the grandson of Evelyn Axelrod and the late Harry Axelrod, a prominent Andover hotel owner and Republican activist. Nicholas's mother attended Abbot Academy, Phillips's sister school, and his uncle had gone to Phillips as well. According to Axelrod, Nicholas's grandfather had also donated money to Phillips Academy.

The boy had received low grades in his classes since his first year at the academy, maintaining only a C average. He and his mother were told numerous times that Nicholas could not handle the work load and should consider withdrawing. However, he returned to the school despite this advice. Nicholas had been diagnosed as having a disability (Attention Deficit/ Hyperactivity Disorder).

In March 1999, Nicholas and his mother sued the school, hoping to force administrators to readmit Nicholas and to give him a chance to graduate from the academy. The plaintiff claimed that the school had violated the Americans with Disabilities Act because teachers and administrators did not recognize that the appearance of a lack of effort was a classic symptom of Nicholas's disability.

In court (www.earletribune.com), the plaintiff's lawyer, Marc Redlich, argued that (1) Phillips knew about Nicholas's learning disorder and did not tell his teachers; (2) Phillips did not accommodate him by extending assignment deadlines or allowing him to hire a private tutor; (3) Nicholas had maintained a C average, better than some students who would graduate; and

(4) the academy had expelled Nicholas in the middle of his senior year, after it had received $90,000 in fees. Phillips Academy's lawyer, Douglas Seaver, argued that (1) Nicholas and his mother had been warned many times that the boy could not handle the work; (2) accommodations *had* been made for his disability, such as waiving the foreign language requirement, encouraging the student to get a peer tutor, and giving him a quiet place to study; (3) neither the student nor his mother had requested additional accommodations; (4) Nicholas did not meet the school's academic standards; and (5) twenty-four other Phillips students had ADHD and were meeting the school's academic standards.

Based on the presented evidence, U.S. District Court Judge Edward Harrington ruled in favor of Phillips Academy, saying that the school had provided, as required by law, the necessary accommodations for Nicholas and that the student had showed a willful lack of effort to capitalize on these accommodations and to succeed in school. In his order, Harrison wrote that if it ruled otherwise, the court would send a devastating message to academia that might result in teachers being reluctant to set high standards and to give honest grades for fear of being dragged into court. It also might result in students learning that effort and achievement are less important than a handy excuse. The essence of Harrington's order is that schools must (as the academy did) give reasonable accommodations to students with learning disabilities, but that such students are obliged to ask for help when they need it and to demonstrate a willful effort to succeed.

Perhaps this should be added to the definition of "learning disability": the "willful effort to succeed." One has to try. Otherwise, the system of special education and special accommodations is not there to help students in need of equal rights to an education; it is there to rob "typical" children of their right to a decent education.

FROM DISABILITIES TO ABILITIES

There are numerous success stories of people with learning difficulties. We, as admirers of our own civilization and its major contributors, are fascinated by the handwriting and spelling errors in Leonardo da Vinci's manuscripts and journals (was Leonardo dyslexic?), by Albert Einstein's trouble with basic arithmetic (was Einstein dyscalculic?), and by the strange sounds and gestures of Wolfgang Amadeus Mozart (did Mozart have Tourette's Syndrome?). It is somewhat reassuring to know that even when one has a disability, success is possible. At some level, perhaps everyone has some type of disability!

The movie version of the character Forrest Gump introduced into the field of disabilities the late twentieth-century emphasis on productivity and success. Gump succeeds in obtaining a military education, starting his own business, making a substantial profit, and establishing a reliable social network. An interesting aspect of Gump is his lack of apparent effort to succeed. Success simply comes to him. Gump does what he does, honestly and openly, and his humble nature brings him good luck.

Stories abound concerning diverse kinds of people working together to help each other. In the film *Mighty,* the two main characters are Maxwell, who has learning disabilities and repeats seventh grade for the third time, and Kevin, who is dying of a degenerative disease (Morquio's syndrome). They find that when they work together, they are capable of accomplishing much more than either of them can do alone. Kevin and Maxwell form a bond because nobody else is interested in them. Kevin teaches Maxwell, who discovers that he can learn much more than he thought.

This idea of making one perfect person out of two, each of whom has a particular challenge, was also developed in *Of Mice and Men,* a novel by John Steinbeck. Lennie, with his great strength and mental simplicity, and George, with his intelligence and cunning, work together smoothly as a functional unit. George does the thinking and Lennie does the work, and the duo functions well.

In addition to historical and fictional stories, there are many examples of success in everyday life that we tend to overlook simply because we do not pay as much attention to the success of real people who have disabilities. But for a young woman, Kristen Rawles, suffering from both spina bifida and a learning disability, who lands her first job at a car dealership and buys her first self-earned car at the age of twenty-two (*Virginian Pilot,* Mar. 19, 2000), her achievement is a great victory. So are the accomplishments of Jonathan Mooney, a Brown University senior with dyslexia, who spells on a third-grade level and whose reading skills match those of the lower 10 percent of the population, but who majors in English, manages to maintain a 4.0 grade-point average, has a book contract with a major publishing house, and plans to go national with his tutoring program for children with learning disabilities (*Detroit News,* Mar. 16, 2000).

The borderline between the two categories of *smart* and *not-so-smart* is a blurred one. Many people define this line for themselves. Jonathan Mooney, in promoting a broader understanding of abilities and disabilities, has provided suggestions to college candidates with disabilities on how to conduct their discussions with admissions counselors. He has shared what he would say: "I have strengths and weaknesses. This (spelling) is one of my profound weaknesses" (*Detroit News,* Mar. 16, 2000). The best way to avoid stupidity is not to be afraid of looking stupid. "Shall I tell you what it is to know? To say when you know, and to say you do not when you do not, that is knowledge" (*Confucian Analects,* as cited in Do-sai 1880).

NOTES

1. Cockney refers to lower-income working class in Great Britain.

2. In this context, cripple refers to everyone who is crippled (i.e., disabled or impaired) in any way.

3. The Americans with Disabilities Act of 1990 (P.L. 101–336) is landmark federal legislation that ensures equal access to individuals with disabilities in employment, public accommodations, transportation, telecommunications, and government services.

4. The Individuals with Disabilities Education Act of 1990 (P.L. 101–476) is an amended and reauthorized version of the Education for All Handicapped Children Act of 1975 (P.L. 94–142). The IDEA guarantees needed services and education to children from birth to age three (Part H) and from ages three to twenty-one (Part B). According to the law, the following categories are used to define exceptions: mental retardation, hearing impairments and deafness, serious emotional disturbance, orthopedic impairments, autism, traumatic brain injury, other health impairments, specific learning disabilities, deaf blindness, or multiple disabilities.

5. The Carl Perkins Vocational and Applied Technology Act (P.L. 101–392) provides for the assessment and assistance of students in special populations to complete vocational educational programs, including modifications of curriculum, equipment, and classrooms; the provision of instructional aids and supports; and counseling and career development activities by specialized personnel.

REFERENCES

Barkin, S. M. (1987). Local television news. *Critical Studies in Mass Communication; 4* (1), 79–82.

Braithwait, D. O., & T. L. Thompson (Eds.) (2000). *Handbook of communications and people with disabilities: Research and application.* Mahwah, N.J.: Erlbaum.

Carrier, J. G. (1986). *Learning disability: Social calls and the construction of inequality in American education.* New York: Greenwood Press.

Cumberbatch, G., & R. Negrine (1992). *Images of disability on television.* London: Routledge.

Darke, P. A. (1994). *The Elephant Man* (David Lynch, EMI Films, 1990): An analysis from a disabled perspective. *Disability and Society, 9,* 327–342.

——. (1998). Don't turn me into the invisible man. *The Scotsman,* The Scotsman Publications, Ltd., August 28.

Do-sai, K. (1880). *Confucian analects.* Osaka, Japan.

Duane, D. D. (1991). Dyslexia: Neurobiological and behavioral correlates. *Psychiatric Annals, 21,* 703–708.

Elliott, T. R., & Byrd, E. K. (1982). Media and disability. *Rehabilitation Literature (Attitudes), 43* (11–12), 348–355.

Evans, J. (1992). Infantilism, projection and naturalism in the construction of mental disablement. In D. Hevey (Ed.), *The creature time forgot: Photography and disability imagery.* London: Routledge.

Gallagher, H. (1996). The politics of polio. *Social Education, 60* (5), 264–266.

Gartner, A., & T. Joe (Eds.) (1987). *Images of the disabled, disabling images.* New York: Praeger.

Godar, B. (2000). Hollywood glitz tarnishes reality. *Iowa State Daily,* March 31.

Goldman, L. S., M. Genel, R. J. Bezman, & P. J. Slanetz (1998). Diagnosis and treatment of attention-deficit/hyperactivity disorder in children and adolescents. Council on Scientific Affairs,

American Medical Association. *JAMA, 279,* 1100–1107.

Hevey, D. (Ed.) (1992). *The creature time forgot: Photography and disability imagery*. London: Routledge.

Kelman, M., & C. Lester (1997). *Jumping the queue: An inquiry into the legal treatment of students with learning disabilities*. Cambridge, Mass.: Harvard University Press.

Kerr, J. (1897). School hygiene, in its mental, moral, and physical aspects. *Journal of the Royal Statistical Society, 3,* 613–680.

Klobas, L. E. (1988). *Disability drama in television and film*. Jefferson City, Mo.: McFarland and Company.

Longmore, P. (1987). Screening stereotypes: Images of disabled people. *Social Policy, 16,* 31–37.

———. (1987). Screening stereotypes: Images of disabled people in television and motion pictures. In A. Gartner & T. Joe (Eds.), *Images of the disabled, disabling images* (pp. 65–78). New York: Praeger.

Lyday, J. F. (1926). The Green Country Mental Clinic. *Mental Hygiene, 10,* 759–786.

Marks, D. (1999). *Disability: Controversial debates and psychosocial perspective*. New York: Routledge.

Marshak, L. E., M. Seligman, & F. Prezant (1999). *Disability and the family cycle*. New York: Perseus.

Meredith, B., & J. Underwood (1995). Irreconcilable differences? Defining the rising conflict between regular and special education. *Journal of Law & Education, 24,* 195–226.

Morris, J. (1991). *Pride against prejudice: Transforming attitudes towards disability*. London: The Women's Press.

Nemeth, S. A. (2000). Society, sexuality, and disabled/ablebodied romantic relationships. In D. O. Braithwait & T. L. Thompson (Eds.), *Handbook of communication and people with disabilities* (pp. 37–48). Mahwah, N.J.: Erlbaum.

Pointon, A., C. Davies, & A. Pointon (Eds.) (1998). *Framed: Interrogating disability in the media*. Bloomington: Indiana University Press.

Rasmussen, K., O. Storsaeter, & S. Levander (1999). Personality disorders, psychopathy, and crime in a Norwegian prison population. *International Journal of Law & Psychiatry, 22,* 91–97.

Richey, L. S., & J. E. Ysseldyke (1983). Teachers' expectations of the younger siblings of learning disabled students. *Journal of Learning Disabilities, 16,* 610–615.

Sinanson, V. (1992). *Mental handicap and the human condition*. London: Free Association Books.

Solity, J. (1992). *Special education*. London: Cassell Educational.

Sternberg, R. J., & E. L. Grigorenko (1999). *Our labeled children. (What every parent and teacher needs to know about learning disabilities)*. Reading, Mass.: Perseus.

Webster's new universal unabridged dictionary (1996). New York: Barnes & Noble Books.

Wolfson, K., & M. F. Norde (2000). Film images of people with disabilities. In D. O. Braithwait & T. L. Thompson (Eds.), *Handbook of communication and people with disabilities* (pp. 289–306). Mahwah, N.J.: Erlbaum.

Zillmann, D., & Vorderer, P. (eds.). (2000). *Media entertainment: The psychology of its appeal*. Mahwah, N.J.: Erlbaum.

Zola, I. K. (1982). Denial of emotional needs to people with handicaps. *Archives of Physical Medicine and Rehabilitation, 63,* 63–67.

ELIZABETH J. AUSTIN & IAN J. DEARY

9 Personality Dispositions

In this chapter we consider the contribution of personality to "state stupidity." It is necessary to first adopt a meaningful definition of the term "stupid." Scores on personality and ability tests are only weakly related to each other (Ackerman & Heggestadt 1997), so personality does not strongly affect intelligence. This means that, for example, the proportions of highly extraverted and introverted people in groups of all levels of intelligence are very similar. Personality does, however, strongly affect behavior. This provides a mechanism for smart individuals to be stupid, owing to the effects of noncognitive aspects of their dispositions. In order to explore this idea in more detail, a dynamic/behavioral definition of intelligence/stupidity rather than a purely psychometric one is adopted in this chapter. This working definition is embedded in the effects of personality on quality of life, and in this context we have chosen to use the term "maladaptive." We focus on those aspects of an individual's personality which can cause behavior that is in some sense socially or personally maladaptive. Hence it can lead to distress and an impaired quality of life. While almost anyone may behave stupidly or foolishly under conditions of extreme fear or stress, even in normal daily life personality can on occasion override high levels of cognitive ability and lead to negative outcomes. This idea of individual differences in adaptivity is linked to concepts such as emotional intelligence (Mayer & Salovey 1993) and wisdom (Staudinger, Lopez, & Baltes 1997).

We first briefly review ways in which personality affects various aspects of quality of life and then turn to the topic of personality disorders. It is in this area that personality dispositions can become catastrophically maladaptive, with the potential for disrupting the lives of sufferers and their associates, regardless of their level of intelligence. Finally, a reconnection with the idea of "state stupidity" is established by inquiring whether intelligence is in any sense protective against maladaptive personality traits or behavior and, if so, to what extent.

Personality Traits

Personality traits can be defined as persistent dispositional differences between individuals. They refer to those parts of our mental styles unrelated to intellectual abilities. Modern personality research often adopts a dimensional view. This is based on the observation that among those people who have undergone personality testing, most score in the medium-level range, with a few people at the extremes. This view replaces the older idea of personality "types," based on the idea that, for example, everyone can be classified as either an extravert or an introvert. Astrology is a nonscientific type theory of personality because it separates people into twelve pigeonholes. There is little evidence to support type theories of personality. As an analogy, consider height in human adults. Most people have heights close to the average for the population, with very few being much taller or shorter than average. If we think of "rulers" to measure personality differences, how many do we need? Many researchers now think that a relatively small number of measures, usually called traits or dimensions, are just about sufficient to describe important personality differences among individuals. There is still some disagreement about the actual number. However, many psychologists are convinced by the scientific evidence for a five-factor model of personality (FFM, also called the "Big Five"). Table 9.1 lists these factors and their constituent facets. Two impressive bodies of evidence support the FFM. Versions of these five dimensions have been obtained from a wide range of personality questionnaires. In addition, the five factors emerge from "lexical" studies that seek clusters of personality terms existing in all human languages (Goldberg 1990). Indeed, many studies have found that the FFM trait structure of human personality applies across languages and cultures. These studies are important because they confirm the existence of personality traits as a component of human nature rather than as culturally determined.

Examination of Table 9.1 prompts an obvious question: How might each of these traits be maladaptive? We first review some effects of Neuroticism and Extraversion on quality of life. Quality of life outcomes associated with the other three traits are then recounted. Life outcomes associated with the effects of a mismatch between an individual's disposition and his or her

TABLE 9.1. Traits and Facets of the Five-Factor Model of Personality

Neuroticism (N)	Anxiety, angry hostility, depression, self-consciousness, impulsiveness, vulnerability
Extraversion (E)	Warmth, gregariousness, assertiveness, activity, excitement-seeking, positive emotions
Openness (O)	Fantasy, aesthetics, feelings, actions, ideas, values
Agreeableness (A)	Trust, straightforwardness, altruism, compliance, modesty, tender-mindedness
Conscientiousness (C)	Competence, order, dutifulness, achievement striving, self-discipline, deliberation

Source: P. T. Costa and R. R. McCrae, *Revised NEO Personality Inventory and NEO Five Factor Personality Manual,* Odessa, Fla.: Psychological Assessment Resources, 1992.

environment are also discussed, mainly in the context of findings on occupational performance.

NEUROTICISM

There is massive scientific evidence showing that people with high Neuroticism scores suffer more personal distress and have impaired quality of life. (This is hinted at by one widely used definition of Neuroticism as a "tendency to experience and express negative emotions.") Compared to the general population, individuals with high scores on Neuroticism are at increased risk for, among other things, stress-proneness, self-reported ill-health, medically unexplained conditions, eating disorders, divorce, and voluntarily leaving employment. These risks can be divided into three broad categories: stress, health, and relationships. Each of these is now discussed briefly.

1. *Stress and stress-proneness.* Individuals scoring high on Neuroticism (high-N) report higher levels of psychological distress, anxiety, and depression than do low-N scorers (see, for example, Deary et al. 1996). High-N individuals report higher levels of job stress and have stronger adverse emotional reactions to everyday stressors such as overwork and arguments than do their low-N counterparts (Bolger & Schilling 1991; Gustavsson et al. 1997). This dynamic of increased negative reactions to the stresses of everyday life provides a mechanism for the increased unhappiness reported by high-N scorers (Argyle & Lu 1990; Furnham & Brewin 1990). People with higher N scores also tend to make more pessimistic evaluations of potentially stressful situations, and they tend to adopt less effective coping styles. (Coping

styles and their associations with personality are discussed in more detail below.)

2. *Health.* High-N individuals report higher levels of psychological distress. There are related phenomena: in studies of physical health, they report both more physical illnesses and more medically unexplained physical symptoms (Deary, Scott, & Wilson 1997; Watson & Pennebaker 1989). Self-reported health satisfaction is also lower in high-N individuals (Gustavsson et al. 1997). These reports notwithstanding, there are no associations between high Neuroticism and an increased risk of serious diseases. High-N scorers report more physical problems but do not contract more actual diseases (Watson & Pennebaker 1989). Inasmuch as self-reported symptoms, including those that are medically unexplained, cause real distress, the Neuroticism-illness effect is undoubtedly a genuine one in terms of a poorer quality of life.

3. *Relationships.* High levels of Neuroticism are associated with problems in relationships with others; for example, high-N scorers are more likely to be shy (Crozier 1982). More specific patterns emerge concerning personal and work relationships. High Neuroticism is associated with an increased risk of both marital problems and divorce (Bolger & Schilling 1991; Gustavsson et al. 1997; O'Leary & Smith 1991). And there is an increased likelihood of leaving a job (Barrick & Mount 1996). The observations on relationship breakdown shed light on the finding that high levels of Neuroticism are associated with a greater exposure to negative life events (Bolger & Schilling 1991). High Neuroticism is a risk factor for apparently independent (i.e., supposedly not under the person's control) events such as divorce and unemployment (Magnus et al. 1993). As indicated above, such events do not fall randomly from the sky; the causal link appears to be the problematic social interactions of high-N individuals.

EXTRAVERSION

High scores on the personality trait of Extraversion are associated with the possession of good social skills. Perhaps unsurprisingly, therefore, extraverts tend to be happier than introverts (Argyle & Lu 1990). Indeed, personality accounts for a substantial proportion of individual differences in happiness, with Extraversion (positively) and Neuroticism (negatively) making the largest contributions (Brebner et al. 1995; Furnham & Cheng 1997). Hence it can be argued that introversion (particularly in combination with high N) is maladaptive, or at least predisposes individuals to self-confessed unhappiness. However, a nontrivial portion of the differences between individuals' happiness levels is unaccounted for by personality, showing that personality is by no means the sole determinant of quality of life. These findings support the commonsense assumption that social and other factors in a person's life are also important determinants of happiness.

OPENNESS, AGREEABLENESS, AND CONSCIENTIOUSNESS

Concerning the other three traits of the FFM, evidence for global effects on the quality of day-to-day life are generally less pronounced than for Neuroticism and Extraversion. There are some interesting findings associated with health and mortality. Recent research on risk factors associated with coronary heart disease and related conditions has increasingly focused on hostility. The personality trait of hostility is associated with higher levels of cardiovascular reactivity (the reaction of the heart and blood vessels to an external event, for example, harassment by another person) (Felsten & Leitten 1993). And people with higher trait hostility levels have an increased risk of peripheral artery disease. This condition is caused by a clogging up process in the leg arteries similar to that which precipitates heart attacks (Deary et al. 1994). In the FFM, hostility appears both as a facet of Neuroticism and as an aspect of low Agreeableness. More detailed studies suggest that it is the (low-A) tendency to express hostility rather than the (high-N) tendency to hostile feelings that is associated with cardiovascular reactivity and health problems (Felsten & Leiten 1993; Whiteman et al. in press).

A second important finding is an association between Conscientiousness (measured in childhood) and mortality; higher C is associated with longer life. This association (and a negative association between the childhood trait of Cheerfulness and longevity) was found in an analysis of data from the Terman Life-Cycle Study of Children, begun in 1921/1922 (Friedman et al. 1993). An association between Conscientiousness and positive health behaviors and/or risk avoidance seems likely, which may explain the result. The finding for Cheerfulness is harder to interpret; an association between cheerfulness, optimism, and risk-taking is a possible explanation. For example, an optimistic person might underestimate the risks involved in activities such as smoking and mountain climbing. It should be noted that the Terman sample comprised gifted children. It is currently not known if these findings extend to the general population.

PERSONALITY AND OCCUPATIONAL PERFORMANCE

Intelligence is the most consistent predictor of career success independent of the specifics of the job (Gottfredson 1997). While its predictive power is somewhat weaker than that of intelligence, the personality trait of

Conscientiousness has a similar, occupation-independent effect (Barrick & Mount 1991; Tett, Jackson, & Rothstein 1991). Higher C scorers tend to have greater career successes. There is also some evidence for a negative association between Neuroticism and job proficiency (Tett, Jackson, & Rothstein 1991). Thus a person with low Conscientiousness and/or high Neuroticism scores is mildly disadvantaged in making a successful career. For Neuroticism, however, the most consistently discovered effect is a negative association with job satisfaction (Furnham & Zacherl 1986). This is almost certainly related to the stress vulnerability and problems with interpersonal relationships that are general features of high N scorers. The findings on job proficiency may be related to a large body of results on performance on laboratory tasks. These show that subjects high on trait N tend to perform less well on complex, demanding tasks than do their low-N counterparts. A number of explanations of these findings have been proposed. One possibility is that the high-N person's tendency to worry about performance uses up working memory powers that would otherwise be devoted to the task at hand, thus impairing performance (M. W. Eysenck 1992).

Extraversion is related to the ability to perform specific types of laboratory task (Matthews & Deary 1998). These abilities are likely to be relevant to aspects of job performance. For example, extraverts are superior to introverts on tasks that require several things to be attended to at the same time. On the other hand, introverts excel on vigilance tasks—for example, watching for the very occasional flash of light on a TV screen. Extraverts are also advantaged in careers, such as selling, that require good social skills. Agreeableness and Openness are not often associated with occupational outcomes, although reference to Table 9.1 suggests that low- and high-A individuals have very different social styles, while low- and high-O individuals have very different intellectual and problem-solving styles.

In terms of occupational success, then, C and N appear to have global effects. Another important consideration is the extent to which the combination of personality traits that individuals *possess* matches those they *need* to succeed in their chosen careers. In particular it is likely that the cognitive and social aspects of extraversion influence career choice and success. There is clear evidence of occupational self-selection. Thus, the personality profiles of many occupational groups show differences from those of the general population (see, for example, Bartram 1995; Matthews & Oddy 1993). In terms of adaptive behavior, it seems probable that an extravert who chooses a career in librarianship or an introvert who ventures into sales will encounter more difficulties than those who pay more attention to their own personality traits when choosing a career.

PERSONALITY AND OCCUPATIONAL BEHAVIOR—AN EXAMPLE

To illustrate the effects of personality in an occupational context, we take an example obtained from a recent survey of Scottish farmers. This survey (Willock et al. 1999) measured a wide range of personality, ability, attitudinal, and behavioral variables. For farmers, one behavioral variable of interest is environmentally oriented behavior—for example, the active pursuit of conservation strategies. A framework for explaining differences in this type of behavior was constructed using a statistical modeling package (Bentler 1995). An initial look at the data suggested that the following factors contributed to actions more geared toward preserving the environment: higher fluid intelligence (problem-solving ability), higher crystallized intelligence (general knowledge), higher Openness, an innovative management style, a tendency to seek information and help from others, more negative attitudes toward the use of agrichemicals, and more environmentally oriented goals. The model obtained (Edwards-Jones, Deary, & Willock 1998) is shown in Figure 9.1. Environmentally oriented behavior is affected by both intelligence level and the personality trait of Openness; a farmer with high levels of either or both traits is more likely to be interested in land conservation. A more innovative management style, an information gathering strategy, and certain goals and attitudes also affect farming behavior. As indicated in the diagram, some of these relationships are indirect. The key conclusion from this model and others obtained from the survey data (Austin et al. 1998; Edwards-Jones, Deary, & Willock 1998) is that personality trait levels have direct and observable effects on behavior. Other findings are that high scores on Extraversion and Openness are associated with innovative management, and high scores on Extraversion and Conscientiousness with a production-oriented management style. These results suggest situational aspects of adaptive behavior. Farmers in Scotland are certainly under pressure to adopt environmentally friendly practices but also need to pursue efficient production methods as a business survival strategy. These goals can conflict, so a farmer's decision to take conservation measures, perhaps driven by high levels of Openness, might, depending on circumstances, eventually prove to be either "smart" or "stupid."

OTHER ASPECTS OF TRAIT THEORY—
"ADAPTIVE" INDIVIDUAL DISPOSITIONAL DIFFERENCES

Trait theory has been extended by studying individual dispositional differences that relate explicitly to adaptivity. These resemble personality traits in that they capture stable individual differences, but the theoretical approach in this area is a cognitive one that focuses on the way a person appraises and

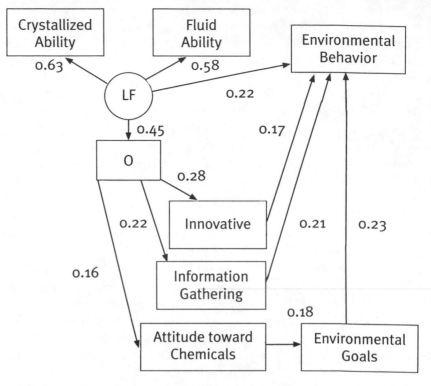

FIGURE 9.1. Model of environmentally oriented behavior. O = openness; LF = an underlying factor derived from fluid ability (problem solving), crystallized ability (knowledge), and O; Innovative = innovative management style. Further information about the measures used in the survey can be found in Edwards-Jones, Deary, & Willock (1998) and Willock et al. (1999). The number on each path can be squared to give a measure of the strength of the association between the corresponding pair of variables. *Source:* Redrawn from G. Edwards-Jones, I. J. Deary, and J. Willock, Incorporating psychological variables in models of farmer behaviour: Does it make for better predictions? *Etudes de Reserches sur les Sysemes Agraires et le Development, 31* (1998), 153–173.

deals with problems, challenges, and stressors. Recent reviews of some of these individual dispositional differences are given by Matthews and Deary (1998) and Schaubroeck and Ganster (1991). Here, two of these—coping styles and wisdom—are discussed.

Coping styles. The idea of coping styles is associated with individual differences in the choice of strategy for dealing with a stressful situation. A detailed account of this topic is given in the *Handbook of Coping Theory,* edited by Zeidner and Endler (1996). Three broad dimensions of coping have been identified: task-focused, emotion-focused, and avoidance coping. Task-focused coping involves actively attempting to deal with an external problem. Emotion-focused coping involves concentration on feelings arising from the stressful situation. Avoidance coping involves escaping from or ignoring the problem. Task-focused coping is frequently described as being the most adaptive style. This view is reinforced by studies showing that Neuroticism is associated with a tendency to make negative appraisals of stressful situations and to react by choosing an emotion-focused or avoidance rather than a task-focused strategy (Deary et al. 1996). However, it is simplistic to assume that there is a single "ideal" coping style that fits all situations. While there are many situations in which a problem-solving approach is helpful, some problems cannot be resolved by rational means, so emotion-focused or avoidance coping may be appropriate (Zeidner & Saklofske 1996). Coping style questionnaires explore individuals' typical reactions to stress but cannot be used to characterize the degree of flexibility with which they deal with different types of stressors. Nonetheless, examination of how coping styles are associated with intelligence and personality does provide useful data. As an illustration, Table 9.2 shows findings from the survey of Scottish farmers discussed earlier (Willock et al. 1999). The large association between Neuroticism and the tendency to use emotion-focused coping is particularly striking. The main overall finding is that Neuroticism is associated with an increased tendency to use emotion-focused and avoidance coping rather than task-focused coping, while both Extraversion and Conscientiousness are associated with the use of task-focused coping and Extraversion and Openness with avoidance coping. A full analysis of these associations is complicated by the fact that scores on N, E, and C have some overlaps and this contributes to the personality/coping style associations. Corrected figures are also shown in Table 9.2. Assuming that task-focus is at least on average the "best" coping choice, these findings mirror the general results on the adaptivity of E, N, and C discussed above. In this particular sample, the more able individuals were found to be less likely to use avoidance coping, but intelligence level was found to be unrelated to use of the other two coping styles.

Wisdom.   Research on wisdom focuses on judgment and problem-solving, types of behavior that are located at the interface between personality, intelligence, and social functioning (Staudinger, Lopez, & Baltes 1997). Measures of wisdom are usually based on reactions to imaginary scenarios involving complex practical and moral decisions. Wisdom is clearly an adaptive trait related to, but by no means the same as, intelligence. The adaptivity of wisdom has been demonstrated in a study showing that elderly people with high wisdom scores also tend to report higher levels of life satisfaction (Ardelt 1997). A study of how wisdom is associated with intelligence and

TABLE 9.2. Associations Between Coping Styles, General Ability (*g*), and Personality for a Group of Scottish Farmers

	Task	Emotion	Avoidance
N	−0.18** (0.01)	0.68*** (0.63***)	0.19* (0.25***)
E	0.22*** (0.13**)	−0.24*** (0.02)	0.14** (0.23**)
O	0.09	0.06	0.23***
A	−0.05	−0.09	0.02
C	0.36*** (0.31***)	−0.31** (−0.04)	−0.05 (0.00)
g	0.04	−0.10	−0.18**

Note: The numbers (correlations) are a measure of the strength of association between two variables. A positive correlation means that there is a tendency for one variable to be high (low) when the other is high (low). A negative correlation means that one variable tends to be low when the other is high. FFM traits are from the NEO-FFI (Costa & MacCrae 1992). Coping styles are from the Coping Inventory for Stressful Situations (Endler & Parker 1990). N = Neuroticism, E = Extraversion, O = Openness, A = Agreeableness, C = Conscientiousness. Correlations in parentheses for N, E, and C are corrected for (E, C), (N, C), and (N, E) associations, respectively. The general ability factor was obtained by combining measures of fluid and crystallized intelligence. Sample sizes range from 214 to 247. Asterisks denote levels of statistical significance: *p < 0.05; **p < 0.01; ***p < 0.001.

personality has shown that the personality trait of Openness, together with thinking style, creativity, and intelligence, all contribute to wisdom, confirming its status as a trait with both personality and intelligence components (Staudinger, Lopez, & Baltes 1997). Perhaps surprisingly, no contribution was found to wisdom from other personality dimensions, whereas the earlier discussion of the adaptive aspects of the FFM traits would suggest an overlap between wisdom and high C and perhaps low N. Wisdom also overlaps with, but is not the same as, intelligence. The contribution to wisdom that arises from social and practical skills means that an intelligent person may be "foolish" or "stupid" and a less intelligent one "wise."

SUMMARY OF THE FINDINGS ON PERSONALITY

Many of the effects of personality on quality of life are relatively small. Larger effects of personality are found for self-reported happiness and for some of the negative outcomes associated with Neuroticism. Even for these examples, situational as well as personality factors are important. Adaptive traits such as coping styles and wisdom clearly also make a contribution to quality of life, and study of these traits highlights the important role of thinking and social skills in dealing with life problems. The psychopathology of personality, to be considered in the following section, may be regarded as arising in part from a lack of such skills.

Personality Disorders

DEFINITION

"Personality disorder" is defined in the *American Psychiatric Association Diagnostic and Statistical Manual,* DSM-IV (APA 1994) as "an enduring pattern of inner experience and behavior that deviates markedly from the expectations of the individual's culture, is pervasive and flexible, has onset in adolescence or early adulthood, is stable over time, and leads to distress or impairment." This definition makes explicit both the trait-like, persistent aspect of personality disorders (in contrast to the pattern of relapse and remission characteristic of clinical syndromes such as schizophrenia) and their maladaptivity. The negative consequences of personality disorder to the patient and to others can be envisaged by reference to the examples in Table 9.3A. Given that personality disorders are quite common (estimates vary between disorders in the range of 0.5 to 7 percent in the general population; Deary & Power 1998), it can be seen that these conditions are responsible for much distress and suffering.

EXAMPLES OF PERSONALITY DISORDERS

Little evidence suggests that patients with personality disorders differ in intelligence from the general population, with the exception of some indirect evidence for Antisocial personality disorder. This disorder is linked to criminal/delinquent behavior, which is in turn associated with below average IQ (McGarvey et al. 1981; Moffitt, Gabrielli, & Mednick 1981). Studies of other personality disorders have generally found no intelligence differences between patients and healthy controls. It is, however, clear that personality disorders are associated with disordered thinking and problematic interpersonal relationships. In this section the features of three particular disorders with differing patterns of social/interpersonal dysfunction are described. A review of the literature in this area and a discussion of cognitive processes in other personality disorders are given by Endler and Summerfeldt (1995). Diagnostic criteria for the three selected disorders are given in Table 9.3B.

Paranoid personality disorder. The suspicion of the motives and actions of others that characterizes this disorder is linked to the highly efficient detection of (generally spurious) evidence that confirms the person's view of external threats, while they simultaneously screen out disconfirming evidence. This "focused scanning" gives rise to a consistent, self-reinforcing negative view of the behavior and motives of others, with consequent maladaptive effects on social relationships.

Histrionic personality disorder. The characteristics of this disorder include

TABLE 9.3(a). Brief Descriptions of the DSM-IV Personality Disorders

Paranoid	A pattern of distrust and suspiciousness such that others' motives are interpreted as malevolent
Schizoid	A pattern of detachment from social relationships and a restricted range of emotional expression
Schizotypal	A pattern of acute discomfort in close relationships, cognitive or perceptual distortions and eccentricities of behavior
Antisocial	A pattern of disregard for, and violation of, the rights of others
Borderline	A pattern of instability in interpersonal relationships, self-image, and affects, and marked impulsivity
Histrionic	A pattern of excessive emotionality and attention-seeking
Narcissistic	A pattern of grandiosity, need for admiration, and lack of empathy
Avoidant	A pattern of social inhibition, feelings of inadequacy, and hypersensitivity to negative evaluation
Dependent	A pattern of submissive and clinging behavior related to an excessive need to be taken care of
Obsessive-compulsive	A pattern of preoccupation with orderliness, perfectionism, and control

TABLE 9.3(b). Diagnostic Criteria for Paranoid, Histrionic, and Antisocial Personality Disorders

Paranoid   Meets four or more of:
1. Suspects (without sufficient basis) that others are exploiting, harming, or deceiving him or her
2. Is preoccupied with unjustified doubts about the loyalty or trustworthiness of friends or associates
3. Is reluctant to confide in others because of unwarranted fear that the information will be used maliciously against him or her
4. Reads hidden demeaning or threatening meanings into benign remarks or events
5. Persistently bears grudges, i.e., is unforgiving of insults, injuries, or slights

TABLE 9.3(b). continued

      6. Perceives attacks on his or her character or reputation that are not apparent to others and is quick to react angrily or to counterattack

      7. Has recurrent suspicions, without justification, regarding fidelity of spouse or sexual partner

Histrionic Meets five or more of:

1. Is uncomfortable in situations in which he or she is not the center of attention
2. Interaction with others is often characterized by inappropriate sexually seductive or provocative behavior
3. Displays rapidly shifting and shallow expression of emotions
4. Consistently uses physical appearance to draw attention to self
5. Has a style of speech that is excessively impressionistic and lacking in detail
6. Shows self-dramatization, theatricality, and exaggerated expression of emotion
7. Is suggestible, i.e., easily influenced by others or circumstances
8. Considers relationships to be more intimate than they actually are

Antisocial Meets three or more of:

1. Failure to conform to social norms with respect to lawful behaviors as indicated by repeatedly performing acts that are grounds for arrest
2. Deceitfulness, as indicated by repeated lying, use of aliases, or conning others for personal profit or pleasure
3. Impulsivity or failure to plan ahead
4. Irritability and aggressiveness, as indicated by repeated physical fights or assaults
5. Reckless disregard for safety of self or others
6. Consistent irresponsibility as indicated by repeated failure to sustain consistent work behavior or honor financial obligations
7. Lack of remorse, as indicated by being indifferent to or rationalizing having hurt, mistreated, or stolen from another

---

Source: Adapted from the American Psychiatric Association; *Diagnostic and Statistical Manual of Mental Disorders*

attention-seeking behavior, rapidly shifting and shallow emotions, and self-dramatization. The associated mode of thinking is "broad brush" in style, relying on rapid impression formation rather than attention to detail and on information from the outside world rather than from the person's own belief system. In comparison to paranoid thinking, it is harder to completely connect this thinking style to all aspects of the problematic social behavior associated with the disorder. An inability to perceive others and the external world realistically appears to provide a partial explanation of some aspects of these problems, although emotional factors are clearly also relevant.

Antisocial personality disorder. The aspects of this disorder that relate to irresponsible and/or criminal behavior together with a disregard for the consequences of such actions have been linked in a number of laboratory studies to insensitivity to impending punishment; this inability to learn from experience might easily be construed as stupidity. One aspect of the disorder is, in effect, a tendency to "live in the present." Antisocial personality disorder is also associated with a pattern of specific social deficits involving deceitful and manipulative behavior and a lack of empathy.

DIAGNOSTIC APPROACHES—OLD AND NEW

The psychiatric approach to personality disorder diagnosis has historically been a medical, classificatory one. Thus, either a personality disorder is present or it is not. Existing clinical scales involving the use of a questionnaire or checklist for the assessment of personality disorders reflect this binary system. This approach has, however, proved to be problematic because of the high levels of multiple diagnoses of personality disorder (Deary & Power 1998) and because of studies which have demonstrated that current diagnostic scales are of low reliability and validity (Clark, Livesley, & Morey 1997; Deary et al. 1998; Zimmerman 1994). This means that the use of these scales risks unacceptable rates of both false positive and false negative diagnoses and also that at least some personality disorders may currently not be well defined.

The problems of understanding and diagnosing personality disorders might be resolved by considering these disorders as an aspect of individual differences in personality rather than distinct clinical conditions. From this viewpoint, personality disorders might be at least partially defined by a pattern of extreme scores on a relatively small number of broad personality dimensions. This leads to the idea that personality disorders manifest themselves subclinically in the general population rather than being confined to distinct clinical groups. If this is the case, an interesting question is whether there is a relationship between the FFM dimensions of normal personality described earlier and personality disorders. A considerable amount of evidence indicates that this is indeed the case.

A number of studies have been carried out in which normal personality questionnaires and diagnostic questionnaires for personality disorders have been filled in by the same group of people. As a result, associations between scores on the two types of questionnaire can be investigated. There is still some disagreement about how many dimensions of personality disorder there are, but evidence from a large number of studies suggests that there are four, not five, such dimensions (Deary et al. 1998; Livesley, Jang, & Vernon 1998; Mulder & Joyce 1997; Schroeder & Livesley 1991; Presly & Walton 1973; Tyrer & Alexander 1979). The recent study by Livesley, Jang, and Vernon (1998) provides particularly strong evidence in favor of four "disordered personality" dimensions; in this work the same dimensions were found in both clinical sufferers and in the general population, showing that the same personality structure exists in both groups, with patients having higher scores.

The basic picture of how "disordered" and normal personalities are related is reasonably clear, with each "disordered" dimension being associated with a normal personality trait. The naming of the "disordered" traits has not yet been finalized. Two possible naming schemes have been proposed by Mulder and Joyce (1997) and by Livesley, Jang, and Vernon (1998). The names in these two schemes are Asthenic/Emotional Disregulation, Asocial/Inhibitedness, Antisocial/Dissocial Behavior, and Anankastic/Compulsive, and these are associated with high N, low E, low A, and high C, respectively. The Asthenic dimension includes a wide range of classical, medically defined personality disorders (Avoidant, Dependent, Paranoid, Schizotypal, Histrionic, Borderline) associated with personal distress/high Neuroticism. The existence of this dimension and its association with many personality disorders confirms that the distress-prone aspects of Neuroticism play an important role in personality disorder. The Asocial dimension identifies an overlapping set of personality disorders associated with problematic social interactions. Avoidant, Dependent, Schizotypal, Schizoid—all disorders that include a pattern of social avoidance and/or fear—are associated with maladaptively low Extraversion. Histrionic disorder, which also appears in this group, is by contrast associated with high Extraversion. The structure of the Asocial and Anankastic dimensions indicates that maladaptively low levels of Agreeableness are associated in particular with Antisocial personality disorder and also with Paranoid, Narcissistic, and Borderline disorders, whereas Obsessive-Compulsive disorder is associated with high levels of Conscientiousness. Reference to Tables 9.1 and 9.3 suggests the possibility that an excess of the C facets of orderliness, striving, and self-discipline might plausibly contribute to this disorder. The Antisocial/ Agreeableness association is obvious, but it is of interest that this analysis also draws attention to the importance of low Agreeableness in several other personality disorders, clarifying the cause of at least some part of the problematic social interactions reported by patients with personality disorder. The interpretation of Obsessive-Compulsive disorder in terms of maladaptive extreme Conscientiousness was discussed above. A feature of interest here is that this disorder appears in a class of its own in the FFM description.

The above findings can also be used to produce FFM profiles of personality disorders. Thus, for example, Avoidant disorder combines high Neuroticism with low Extraversion while Paranoid disorder combines high Neuroticism with low Agreeableness. These descriptions have been refined in studies in which associations between personality disorders and the FFM facets (Table 9.1) have been studied. At this level of description, Avoidant disorder is associated with high scores on anxiety, depression, and vulnerability combined with low scores on gregariousness, assertiveness, activity, and excitement-seeking. Paranoid disorder is associated with high scores on hostility combined with low scores on trust, straightforwardness, compliance, warmth, gregariousness, positive emotions, and actions (Widiger et al. 1994).

An interesting feature of these results is the conspicuous absence of the fifth dimension of normal personality, Openness. It has been suggested that both high and low Openness scores might be associated with personality disorder, with high scores corresponding to disordered thought processes and low scores corresponding to maladaptive inflexibility (Costa & McCrae 1992). In particular it has been conjectured (Widiger et al. 1994) that high scores on Openness would be associated with schizotypal personality disorder. This association has not been confirmed but appears plausible, given that one feature of schizotypal personality disorder is openness to unusual ideas (for example, belief in the paranormal).

These findings on a dimensional approach to personality disorders still leave a number of open questions. One of these is the extent to which individual FFM scores, even if taken down to the facet level, fully account for personality disorders. The previous discussion of selected disorders shows that maladaptive thinking styles and emotions are also relevant. Another key question relates to clinical applications of these findings. It has been proposed that FFM scores should be used as a tool in the diagnosis and treatment of personality disorders (Sanderson & Clarkin 1994; McCrae 1994). This appears to be a promising approach, in that trait and facet scores are clearly of value in focusing attention on the individual patient's specific problem areas. A full study of the effectiveness of this approach has not yet been performed.

Adaptive and maladaptive features of personality can be examined from alternative theoretical perspectives. Out of the mainstream of differential psychology, Cloninger and colleagues (Cloninger, Svrakic, & Przybeck 1993; Svrakic et al. 1993) have constructed a personality system with an associated measurement instrument (the Temperament and Character Inventory; TCI) to capture adaptive and humanistic aspects of normal personality and its disorders. Cloninger's "temperamental" traits of harm avoidance, reward dependence, and novelty-seeking are considered to be biologically based and construed within an evolutionary frame of reference, prompting the question of which levels are most adaptive. Given the normal distribution of peoples' scores, mean levels would be argued to be most adaptive. For example, too high a score on novelty-seeking is likely to lead an organism into danger, while too low a score may lead to missed opportunities; a "middling" score would correspond to an optimal behavioral strategy. This would contrast with the scheme devised by Buss (1993) in which extreme scores on the FFM personality traits are viewed as different and perhaps equally adaptive strategies for environmentally important tasks such as mate retention. Cloninger's more character-oriented traits recognize the contribution of humanistic psychologists and the notion of self-actualization. Though easily seen as vaguely defined, nonscientific terms, the self-actualization-oriented constructs in the TCI are in fact associated with a *lack* of personality disorder. While it can be argued that perhaps neither frame of reference is adequately founded, both Cloninger and Buss afford value systems for judging "stupidity": perhaps flouting what is adaptive is stupid; and perhaps to grow toward self-actualization is to leave stupidity behind.

Can Intelligence Protect against Maladaptive Behavior?

In this section the theme of maladaptive/"stupid" behavior is taken up more directly by addressing the question of the extent to which intelligence can protect against such behavior. Whatever definition of intelligence is adopted, it is clear that an outcome of intelligence is the ability to deal with the problems of everyday life. One such problem encountered by every individual is that of dealing with his or her own personality and in particular keeping potentially unhelpful features (for example, high Neuroticism) under control. From this viewpoint a reasonable hypothesis is that high intelligence may provide a degree of protection from the expression of maladaptive personality traits. (It should be kept in mind, however, that more complex associations exist. In particular, H. J. Eysenck (1995) has argued that a tendency to make loose and unusual associations of words, ideas, and so on is linked both to creativity and to psychopathology.) Epidemiological and clinical studies have shown that higher levels of intelligence lower the risk of a range of psychiatric conditions (see, for example, Cederblad et al. 1995; David et al. 1997). It should be noted, however, that these findings relate to clinical syndromes such as schizophrenia. The effect of intelligence on susceptibility to personality disorder is currently a neglected research area.

In this section general findings on the associations between psychometric intelligence and a range of personality variables are first considered. The idea of possible protective effects of intelligence against maladaptive behavior will then be explored in more detail using data from a longitudinal survey of elderly people conducted in Edinburgh.

INTELLIGENCE/PERSONALITY ASSOCIATIONS

Associations between intelligence and personality have been widely studied and are generally found to be small but nonnegligible. The main results are that more intelligent people are very slightly more likely to be of high Openness, high Extraversion, low Neuroticism, and low Psychoticism (P) (low P is a blend of high Agreeableness and high Conscientiousness), with the largest effect being found for Openness (Ackerman & Heggestadt 1997). There is evidence from the same study for associations between affective traits (that is, traits associated with emotional reactions) and intelligence; examples are a negative association between intelligence level and scores on alienation, aggression, and test anxiety and positive association of intelligence with scores on control. Other interesting findings on intelligence and personality relate to associations with psychopathology—for example, more intelligent people tend to have lower scores on measures of depression (see, for example, Austin et al. 2000).

The findings reviewed above are suggestive of a generally adaptive relationship between intelligence and personality, in that high intelligence has a weak association with what might be regarded as a "desirable" personality type: low N, high E, and low P (high A/C). Association with affective traits including depression/distress also appears to be in an adaptive direction, and there are similar findings for a wide range of adaptive dispositional differences (coping style, optimism, etc.), although all these effects are weak. These observations do not, of course, indicate what the cause of the association might be. Take the intelligence/Neuroticism relationship as an example. It is possible that high intelligence exerts a weak restraining effect on trait N, that high N impedes the development of high intelligence, or that both effects might operate together. It should be reemphasized that any such adaptive effect is very weak; this means that all combinations of personality scores are found in both the intelligent and less intelligent; however, there will be a small excess of, for example, low N scorers among the more intelligent.

SOME EXAMPLE DATA—THE EDINBURGH ARTERY STUDY

The Edinburgh Artery Study (Fowkes et al. 1991) is a longitudinal survey of the general population with the objective of examining the risk factors for peripheral artery disease. Participants in the survey were initially recruited from a group ranging in age from fifty-five to seventy-four, and the data gathered included personality traits, affective traits (anger, hostility, submissiveness), intelligence, and lifestyle factors such as smoking and alcohol consumption.

Table 9.4 shows the associations between intelligence and personality traits for this general population group of older people. The first part of the table shows associations with the Big Five personality traits and confirms the general findings described above. The associations between psychometric intelligence and the affective traits shown in the second part of the table are of considerable interest. It can be seen that hostility, anger control, and anger expression are all significantly associated with intelligence. It can also be argued that these correlations run in the "adaptive" direction: higher ability is associated both with lower levels of hostility, a trait associated with negative health outcomes (Deary et al. 1994), and with an increased ability to control feelings of anger.

The effects of intelligence on hostility, anger control, and anger expression were studied in more detail by constructing structural equation models. As described previously, the structural equation method allows competing models of the interrelationships among variables in a complex dataset to be tested. In the context of the findings above, three types of model can be considered: simple models in which intelligence and personality trait variables make an independent contribution to the outcome variable; models in which intelligence mediates the effect of one or more personality traits on the outcome; and models in which one or more personality variables mediate the effect of intelligence on the outcome. Mediation means that the effect of one attribute (for example, intelligence) on the outcome is indirect and is passed on via the effect of another (for example, a personality trait). The modeling was performed using the EQS package (Bentler 1995). For hostility, the best-fitting model was found to be a simple one, with intelligence, Openness, and Agreeableness acting independently to predict hostility levels, and

TABLE 9.4. Correlations Between Intelligence and Personality Traits in the Edinburgh Artery Study

N	-0.17***
E	0.02
O	0.33**
A	0.09*
C	0.00
Hostility	-0.14** (-0.15**)
Submissiveness	-0.05 (0.04)
Total anger	-0.05 (-0.02)
Anger T	-0.08 (-0.07)
Anger R	-0.03 (0.00)
Anger in	0.01 (0.09)
Anger out	-0.09 (-0.06)
Anger control	0.17*** (0.16***)
Anger expression	-0.16** (-0.11**)

Note: The interpretation of correlations is explained in the caption for Table 9.2. The group was of mean age 64.9 years, standard deviation 5.7 years. Sample sizes vary between 393 and 426. FFM traits are from the NEO-FFI (Costa & McCrae 1992). Hostility and submissiveness scales are from the Personality Deviance Scales (Deary, Bedford & Fowkes 1995). Anger scales are from the State-Trait Anger Expression Inventory (Spielberger et al., 1983). Anger T = Angry Temperament; Anger R = Angry Reaction. Asterisks denote levels of statistical significance: * $p < 0.05$; ** $p < 0.01$; *** $p < 0.001$. Correlations in parentheses are corrected for associations between Neuroticism, intelligence and other traits.

with higher hostility levels being associated with lower intelligence, higher Openness, and lower Agreeableness. However, for both anger control and anger expression the best-fitting model was found to be one in which the effect of intelligence was mediated by Neuroticism. The best-fitting model for anger expression is shown in Figure 9.2 (the anger control model has the same structure). The emergence of a mediating model for anger control and anger expression is of theoretical interest, in that it suggests the beneficial effects of intelligence on these traits operates at least in part by an indirect route.

Finally, within the Edinburgh Artery Study, the possibility of associations between intelligence and behavioral outcomes was studied. Two outcomes that were available from the survey were smoking status and number of units of alcohol consumed per week. Associations between intelligence and the behaviors of smoking and heavy drinking were studied. (Heavy drinking

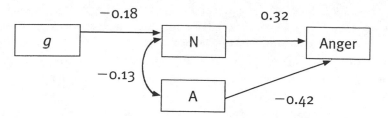

FIGURE 9.2. Mediating models for anger expression. N = Neuroticism, g = general ability, A = agreeableness. Model fit was found to be improved by including a correlation between N and A. Model details: N = 441, average off-diagonal absolute standardized residual 0.02, Normed Fit Index 0.97, Non-Normed Fit Index 0.94, Comparative Fit Index 0.98, c^2 = 5.71, df = 2. The square of the path coefficient on each linking line gives the percentage variance shared by the corresponding variables.

was defined as the consumption of more than twenty-one units of alcohol per week for males and fourteen units for females.) For smoking, a negative but nonstatistically significant association with intelligence was found, but for heavy drinking the association was found to be positive although again not statistically significant. The number of units of alcohol consumed per week, however, was found to be weakly but significantly positively associated with intelligence. There is thus an indication from this sample that intelligence may act as a protective factor against smoking, since the more intelligent tend to smoke less. However, the more intelligent both consume more alcohol than the less intelligent and have a slightly greater tendency to be heavy drinkers as defined by medical criteria; thus intelligence does not appear to protect against problem drinking in this sample. It can be argued that there is a problem with generalizing results from this study in that the relevant health-related information was not available to this elderly age cohort at the time of they started smoking or drinking, which would typically be in early adulthood. Repeating this analysis in a sample of younger adults would therefore be of interest.

Conclusion

Normal personality traits—in particular, Neuroticism and Extraversion—are associated with a range of behaviors that can lead to distress or unhappiness, and the concept of adaptivity in personality can be extended by the consideration of dispositions such as coping style and wisdom. While the effects of trait levels on quality of life are weak, they are certainly nonnegligible. By contrast, personality disorders can be severely maladaptive. There is increasing evidence that normal and disordered personalities lie on essentially the same continuum, although personality disorders display additional features of cognitive and social maladaptivity. As well as being of academic interest, this finding provides hope that the insights of personality trait theory may be deployed in a clinical context in the assessment and treatment of personality disorders.

The idea that high intelligence might sometimes operate to mitigate the negative effects of personality or to protect against maladaptive behavior has also been explored, and evidence for some protective effects has been presented. Given the established weakness of intelligence/personality associations, it is clear that any such effects must be small. Thus research findings support the commonsense conclusion anyone might draw by considering their own friends and acquaintances: even the highest levels of intelligence will not alone promote happiness or prevent maladaptive/"stupid" behavior.

NOTE

We thank Professor F. G. R. Fowkes and Dr. M. Whiteman for allowing use of the Edinburgh Artery Survey data, and the British Heart Foundation for supporting this study. The study of Scottish farmers was supported by the Scottish Office of Agriculture, Environment and Fisheries Department.

REFERENCES

Ackerman, P. L., & E. D. Heggestadt (1997). Intelligence, personality and interests: Evidence for overlapping traits. *Psychological Bulletin, 121,* 219–245.

American Psychiatric Association. (1994). *Diagnostic and statistical manual of mental disorders,* fourth edition (DSM-IV). Washington D.C.: American Psychiatric Association.

Ardelt, M. (1997). Wisdom and life satisfaction in old age. *Journal of Gerontology: Psychological Sciences, 52B,* 15–27.

Argyle, M., & L. Lu (1990). The happiness of extraverts. *Personality and Individual Differences, 11,* 1011–1017.

Austin, E. J., S. M. Hofer, I. J. Deary, & H. W. Eber (2000). Interactions between intelligence and personality: Results from two large samples. *Personality and Individual Differences, 29,* 405–428.

Austin, E. J., J. Willock, I. J. Deary, G. J. Gibson, J. B. Dent, G. Edwards-Jones, O. Morgan, R. Grieve, & A. Sutherland (1998). Empirical modelling of farmer behaviour using psychological, social and economic variables. Part I: Linear models. *Agricultural Systems, 58,* 203–224.

Barrick, M. R., & M. K. Mount (1991). The Big Five personality dimensions and job performance: A meta-analysis. *Personnel Psychology, 44,* 1–26.

———. (1996). Effects of impression management and self-deception on the predictive value of personality constructs. *Journal of Applied Psychology, 81,* 261–272.

Bartram, D. (1995). The predictive validity of the EPI and 16PF for military flying training. *Journal of Occupational and Organisational Psychology, 68,* 219–30.

Bentler, P. M. (1995). EQS Structural Equations Program Manual. Encino, Calif.: Multivariate Software Inc.

Bolger, E. A., & E. A. Schilling (1991). Personality and the problems of everyday life: The role of neuroticism in exposure and reactivity to daily stressors. *Journal of Personality, 59,* 555–586.

Brebner, J., J. Donaldson, N. Kirby, & L. Ward (1995). Relationships between happiness and personality. *Personality and Individual Differences, 19,* 251–258.

Buss, D. M. (1993). Strategic individual differences: The role of personality in creating and solving adaptive problems. In J. Hettema & I. J. Deary (Eds.), *Foundations of personality* (pp. 139–164). Dordrecht: Kluwer.

Cederblad, M., L. Dahlin, O. Hagnell, & K. Hansson (1995). Intelligence and temperament as protective factors for mental health. A cross-sectional and prospective epidemiological study. *European Archives of Psychiatry and Clinical Neuroscience, 245,* 11–19.

Clark, L. A., W. J. Livesley, & L. Morey (1997). Personality disorder assessment: The challenge of construct validity. *Journal of Personality Disorders, 11,* 205–231.

Cloninger, C. R., D. M. Svrakic, & T. R. Przybeck (1993). A psychobiological model of temperament and character. *Archives of General Psychiatry, 50,* 975–990.

Costa, P. T., & R. R. McCrae (1992). *Revised NEO Personality inventory and NEO five factor inventory professional manual.* Odessa, Fla.: Psychological Assessment Resources.

Crozier, W. R. (1982). Explanations of social shyness. *Current Psychological Reviews, 2,* 47–60.

David, A. S., A. Malmberg, L. Brandt, P. Allebeck, & G. Lewis (1997). IQ and risk for schizophrenia: A population-based cohort study. *Psychological Medicine, 27,* 1311–1323.

Deary, I. J., A. Bedford, & F. G. R. Fowkes (1995). The personality deviance scales: Their development, associations, factor structure and restructuring. *Personality and Individual Differences, 19,* 275–291.

Deary, I. J., H. Blenkin, R. M. Agius, N. S. Endler, & H. Zealley (1996). Models of job-related stress and personal achievement among consultant doctors. *British Journal of Psychology, 87,* 3–29.

Deary, I. J., F. G. R. Fowkes, P. T. Donnan, & E. Housley (1994). Hostile personality and risks of peripheral arterial disease in the general population. *Psychosomatic Medicine, 56,* 197–202.

Deary, I. J., A. Peter, E. J. Austin, & G. J. Gibson (1998). Personality traits and personality disorders. *British Journal of Psychology, 89,* 647–662.

Deary, I. J., & M. J. Power (1998). Normal and abnormal personality. In E. C. Johnstone, C. P. L. Freeman, & A. K. Zealley (Eds.), *Companion to Psychiatric Studies* (pp. 565–596). Edinburgh: Churchill Livingstone.

Deary, I. J., S. Scott, & J. A. Wilson (1997). Neuroticism, alexithymia and medically unexplained symptoms. *Personality and Individual Differences, 22,* 551–564.

Edwards-Jones, G., I. J. Deary, & J. Willock (1998). Incorporating psychological variables in models of farmer behaviour: Does it make for better predictions? *Etudes et Reserches sur les Systemes Agraires et le Development, 31,* 153–173.

Endler, N. S., & J. D. A. Parker (1990). *Coping inventory for stressful situations (CISS):* Manual. Toronto: Multi-Health Systems.

Endler, N. S., & L. J. Summerfeldt (1995). Intelligence, personality, psychopathology and adjustment. In D. H. Saklofske & M. Zeidner (Eds.), *International handbook of personality and intelligence* (pp. 249–284). New York: Plenum.

Eysenck, H. J. (1995). *Genius.* Cambridge: Cambridge University Press.

Eysenck, M. W. (1992). *Anxiety: The cognitive perspective.* Hillsdale, N.J.: Erlbaum.

Felsten, G., & C. L. Leitten (1993). Expressive but not neurotic hostility is related to cardiovascular reactivity during a hostile competitive task. *Personality and Individual Differences, 14,* 805–813.

Fowkes, F. G. R., E. Housley, E. H. H. Cawood, C. C. A. MacIntyre, C. V. Ruckley, & R. J. Prescott (1991). Edinburgh Artery Study. Prevalence of asymptomatic and symptomatic peripheral artery disease in the general population. *International Journal of Epidemiology, 20,* 384–392.

Friedman, H. S., J. S. Tucker, C. Tomlinson-Keasey, J. E. Schwartz, D. L. Wingard, & M. H. Criqui (1993). Does childhood personality predict longevity? *Journal of Personality and Social Psychology, 65,* 176–185.

Furnham, A., & C. J. Brewin (1990). Personality and happiness. *Personality and Individual Differences, 11,* 1093–1096.

Furnham, A., & H. Cheng (1997). Personality and happiness. *Psychological Reports, 80,* 761–762.

Furnham, A., & M. Zacherl (1986). Personality and job satisfaction. *Personality and Individual Differences, 7,* 453–455.

Goldberg, L. R. (1990). An alternative "Description of personality": The Big-Five factor structure. *Journal of Personality and Social Psychology, 59,* 1216–1229.

Gottfredson, L. S. (1997). Why g matters: The complexity of everyday life. *Intelligence, 24,* 79–132.

Gustavsson, J. P., R. M. Weinryb, S. Goransson, N. L. Pedersen, & M. Asberg (1997). Stability and predictive ability of personality traits across 9 years. *Personality and Individual Differences, 22,* 783–791.

Livesley, W. J., K. L. Jang, & P. A. Vernon (1998). Phenotypic and genetic structure of traits delineating personality disorder. *Archives of General Psychiatry, 55,* 941–948.

Magnus, K., E. Diener, F. Fujita, & W. Pavot (1993). Extraversion and neuroticism as predictors of objective life events: A longitudinal analysis. *Journal of Personality and Social Psychology, 65,* 1046–1053.

Matthews, G., & I. J. Deary (1998). *Personality Traits.* Cambridge: Cambridge University Press.

Matthews, G., & K. Oddy (1993). Recovery of major personality dimensions from trait adjective data. *Personality and Individual Differences, 15,* 419–431.

Mayer, J. D., & P. Salovey (1993). The intelligence of emotional intelligence. *Intelligence, 17,* 433–442.

McCrae, R. R. (1994). A reformulation axis

II: Personality and personality-related problems. In P. T. Costa & T. A. Widiger (Eds.), *Personality disorders and the Five Factor Model of personality* (pp. 303–309). Washington, D.C.: American Psychological Association.

McGarvey, B., W. F. Gabrielli, P. M. Bentler, & S. A. Mednick (1981). Rearing, social class, education and criminality: A multiple indicator model. *Journal of Abnormal Psychology, 90,* 354–364.

Moffitt, T. E., W. F. Gabrielli, & S. A. Mednick (1981). Socioeconomic status, IQ and delinquency. *Journal of Abnormal Psychology, 90,* 152–156.

Mulder, R. T., & P. R. Joyce (1997). Temperament and the structure of personality disorder symptoms. *Psychological Medicine, 27,* 99–106.

O'Leary, K. D., & D. A. Smith (1991). Marital interactions. *Annual Review of Psychology, 42,* 191–212.

Presly, A. S., & H. J. Walton (1973). Dimensions of abnormal personality. *British Journal of Psychiatry, 159,* 463–471.

Sanderson, C., & J. F. Clarkin (1994). Use of the NEO-PI personality dimensions in differential treatment planning. In P. T. Costa & T. A. Widiger (Eds.), *Personality disorders and the Five Factor Model of personality* (pp. 219–235). Washington, D.C.: American Psychological Association.

Schaubroeck, J., & D. C. Ganster (1991). Associations among stress-related individual differences. In C. L. Cooper & R. Payne (Eds.). *Personality and stress: Individual differences in the stress process* (pp. 33–66). Chichester: Wiley.

Schroeder, M. L., & Livesley, W. J. (1991). An evaluation of DSM-III-R personality disorders. *Acta Psychiatrica Scandinavica, 84,* 512–519.

Spielberger, C. D., Jacobs, G., Russell, S. & Crane, R. S. (1983). Assessment of anger: The State-Trait Anger Scale. In J. N. Butcher & C. D. Spielberger (Eds.), *Advances in personality assessment* (Vol. 2) (pp 159–187). Hillsdale, N.J.: Erlbaum.

Staudinger, U. M., D. F. Lopez, & P. B. Baltes (1997). The psychometric location of wisdom-related performance: Intelligence, personality and more? *Personality and Social Psychology Bulletin, 23,* 1200–1214.

Svrakic, D. M., C. Whitehead, T. R. Przybeck, & C. R. Cloninger (1993). Differential diagnosis of personality disorders by the seven-factor model of temperament and character. *Archives for General Psychiatry, 50,* 991–999.

Tett, R. P., D. N. Jackson, & M. Rothstein (1991). Personality measures as predictors of job performance: A meta-analytic review. *Personnel Psychology, 44,* 703–742.

Tyrer, P., & J. Alexander (1979). Classification of personality disorder. *Journal of Psychiatry, 135,* 163–167.

Watson, D., & J. W. Pennebaker (1989). Health complaints, stress and distress: Exploring the central role of negative affectivity. *Psychological Review, 96,* 234–54.

Whiteman, M. C., A. Bedford, E. Grant, F. G. R. Fowkes, & I. J. Deary (in press). The Five Factor Model (FFM-FFI) and the Personality Deviance Scales—Revised (PDSR): Going around in interpersonal circles. *Personality and Individual Differences, 31,* 259–67.

Widiger, T. A., T. J. Trull, J. F. Clarkin, C. Sanderson, & P. T. Costa (1994). A description of the DSM-III-R and DSM-IV personality disorders with the five-factor model of personality. In P. T. Costa & T. A. Widiger (Eds.), *Personality disorders and the Five Factor Model of personality* (pp. 41–56). Washington, D.C.: American Psychological Association.

Willock, J., I. J. Deary, M. J. McGregor, A. Sutherland, G. Edwards-Jones, O. Morgan, J. B. Dent, R. Grieve, G. J. Gibson, & E. J. Austin (1999). Farmers' attitudes, objectives, behaviours and personality traits: The Edinburgh study of decision making on farms. *Journal of Vocational Behaviour, 54,* 5–36.

Zeidner, M., & N. S. Endler (Eds.) (1996). *Handbook of coping: Theory research, applications.* New York: Wiley.

Zeidner, M., & D. H. Saklofske (1996). Adaptive and maladaptive coping. In M. Zeidner & N. S. Endler (Eds.), *Handbook of coping: Theory research, applications* (pp. 505–531). New York: Wiley.

Zimmerman, M. (1994). Diagnosing personality disorders. *Archive of General Psychiatry, 51,* 225–245.

10 When "Stupid" Is Smarter Than We Are

MINDLESSNESS AND THE ATTRIBUTION OF STUPIDITY

The stupid should wear signs so we know not to rely on them. It's like before my wife and I moved from Texas to California, our house was full of boxes and there was a U-Haul truck in our driveway. My neighbor comes over and says, "Hey, you moving?" "Nope. We just pack our stuff up once or twice a week just to see how many boxes it takes. Here's your sign."

A couple of months ago I went fishing with a buddy. We pulled his boat into the dock, I lifted up this big ol' stringer of bass and this idiot on the dock says, "Hey, y'all catch all them fish?" "Nope. Talked 'em into giving up. Here's your sign."

Language is used literally by some and more figuratively by others. When we ask a person "How are you?" we may care to know or we may simply want to signal that we are polite. If the person takes the question literally, discord may result when we barely wait for an answer. The person may then feel stupid for thinking that we care. Perhaps we do, but that is not what the interaction was about for us. As demonstrated in the opening lines of this chapter, words spoken by the "stupid" are not meant literally. They are meant to convey a friendly nod.

Stupidity is an unkind but not infrequent attribution made by observers of behavior. Our behavior makes sense to us or else we would not engage in it. Nevertheless, when we consider our behavior in retrospect or when others observe us and they do not see the sense the behavior made to us at the time, the conclusion is that it was senseless and we should have known better. Some people are slower to grasp concepts than others, but it is difficult to know whether this is because they are processing the same information less well or because they are processing different information or the same information differently. This chapter considers these latter instances, wherein people process information using different models from those of their interlocutors.

The attribution of stupidity frequently is based on the unquestioned and naive realism of the person making that attribution. Consider the case of someone not getting a joke that everyone else present seems to appreciate. Take the following joke to illustrate the point: A young woman was very sad and when asked why, she said "because my boyfriend gave me a golf club for my birthday." When further asked why that made her sad, she said, "Because it didn't have a swimming pool." Those who find the joke funny first think of a golf club as a piece of equipment, perhaps a wood or a putter, and then realize the other meaning of golf club, a place with a golf course, and perhaps tennis courts and a swimming pool.

If we heard this joke in the presence of golfers and the two meanings did not occur to us, they would laugh, we would not, and we would look stupid. However, if we were in the presence of very wealthy people who owned things like golf courses, they also might not find it funny and might even feel compassion for the young woman. If we laughed in the presence of these people, we might be seen as stupid and probably even unkind, if it did not occur to them to think of a golf club as a piece of equipment, as an alternative to their understanding of "golf club." Further, the person who thinks of both meanings of golf club at the very beginning of the joke will not find it funny. Far from being stupid, this person is clever. So what does it mean when someone doesn't laugh? The same analysis may be given in any situation where the person seems not to "get it."

"Stupidity" as a Mindless Cognitive Commitment

By implicitly assuming there is "one world out there" and only one way to think about it, we remain oblivious to the difference between actors and observers. Not only do we see different things, we frequently see the same things differently. As such, it may be that the attribution of stupidity follows more from the mindlessness of the *observer* than from the actor's lack of mental acuity. When we are mindless we are responding to the present situation based on a "frozen" previous understanding of it, oblivious to the subtle ways the situation may have changed or how it may look different from different perspectives. The mindlessness of the observer is often confused with the stupidity or cognitive incompetence of the actor.

Before the airport in Provincetown, Massachusetts, was renovated, a large glass wall looked out over the runway. Waiting for a friend to arrive, a visitor asked the airline receptionist behind the counter when the flight from Boston was expected. She said it was expected to arrive on time. There was no one else in the airport or the surrounding area. The visitor was less than two feet from the receptionist when the plane arrived in full view. Rather than lean over and tell the visitor that the plane had arrived, she announced it over the public address system, filling the empty room with the information. Was she stupid for doing so? In a different context her behavior would have made sense. Here it seemed mindless.

People who learned to drive many years ago were taught that if they needed to stop the car on a slippery surface, the safest way was to slowly, gently pump the brake. Today most new cars have anti-lock brakes. To stop on a slippery surface, now the safest thing to do is to step on the brake firmly and hold it down. Most of us caught on ice will still gently pump the brakes. What was once a safety measure is now a dangerous act. The context has changed, but our behavior remains the same. If I see you pumping the brake and I know you should hold it down firmly, I may think you're stupid. If I see you holding it down firmly and I learned to drive years ago, I may think you are stupid. A more accurate attribution in both cases, again, is mindlessness, not stupidity.

THE UBIQUITY OF MINDLESSNESS

Why does it sometimes seem like there are so many stupid people out there? Because, much of the time, we are mindless. Of course we are unaware when we are in that state of mind—we are "not there" to notice. To notice, we would have had to have been mindful. Yet over twenty-five years of research reveals that mindlessness may be pervasive and very costly to us. In these studies we have found that an increase in mindfulness results in an increase in competence, health and longevity, positive affect, creativity, charisma, and reduced burnout, to name a few of the findings (for reviews of this work, see Langer 1989, 1997).

When we are mindless, we are trapped in rigid mindsets, and we are oblivious to the context or perspective of the person we observe. When we are mindful we are actively drawing novel distinctions rather than relying on distinctions drawn in the past. This makes us sensitive to context and perspective. When we are mindless, our behavior is rule- and routine-governed.

In contrast, when mindful, our behavior may be guided rather than governed by rules and routines.

Mindlessness comes about in one of two ways: either through repetition or by a cognitive commitment made on a single exposure to information. The first case is the more familiar. Most of us have had the experience, for example, of driving and then realizing, only because of the distance we have come, that we made part of the trip on "automatic pilot," as we sometimes call mindless behavior. Another example of mindlessness through repetition is when we learn something by practicing it so that it becomes "second nature" to us. We try to learn the new skill so well that we don't have to think about it. The problem is that if we've been successful, it won't occur to us to think about it even when it would be to our advantage to do so.

We can also become mindless instantly, when we hear or see something and accept it without questioning it. Most of what we know about the world or ourselves we have mindlessly learned in this way. For example, when Susan was at a friend's house for dinner and the table was set with the fork on the right side of the plate, she felt like some natural law had been violated. The fork "goes" on the left side! Susan knew this was ridiculous—it really doesn't matter where the fork is placed. Yet it felt wrong to her, despite the fact that she could think of many reasons why it would be better to place the fork on the right. She thought about how she had learned that the fork belongs on the left side of the plate. She hadn't memorized information about how to set a table. When Susan was a child, her mother simply said to her that the fork goes on the left. Forever after, that is where she was destined to put it, no matter what circumstances might suggest otherwise. Her behavior in this respect became fixed, and she was unaware that the information itself would remain fixed in the future.

Whether we become mindless over time or on initial exposure to information, we unwittingly lock ourselves into a single understanding of that information. For example, Susan had once learned that horses don't eat meat. One day at an equestrian event someone asked her to watch his horse while he went to get the horse a hot dog. Susan shared her "fact" with the horse's owner. She had learned the information in a context-free, absolute way and never thought to question whether it was true. This is the way we learn most things. It is why we are frequently in error but rarely in doubt. So, what happened? The owner got the hot dog anyway—and the horse ate it.

When information is given by an authority, appears irrelevant to the problem at hand, or is presented in absolute language, it typically does not occur to us to question it. This is particularly important in situations where we make attributions about ourselves on the basis of cognitive commitments: "I was born stupid," we might think upon reading the latest treatise on the genetic origins of intelligence after having performed poorly on the latest flavor of IQ test. Authorities are sometimes wrong or overstate their case, and what is irrelevant today may be relevant tomorrow. Nevertheless, virtually all the information we receive is given in absolute language. For example, a child may be told, "A family consists of a mommy, a daddy, and a child." All is fine until Daddy leaves home. Then, just like where the fork goes, it won't feel right to the child when told, "We are still a family." Instead of using absolute language, if a parent told a child that *one* possible understanding of a family is a mother, father, and child, the problem might not arise if the circumstances change.

In an experiment conducted to test this, Benzion Chanowitz and Ellen Langer (Chanowitz & Langer 1981) gave people information about a perceptual disorder. Several of the groups were given a reason to think about the information they were to read. The target group was simply given the information. After taking tests and scoring them, all subjects concluded that they had the disorder. On follow-up tests that required abilities presumably stunted by the disorder, the target group performed less than half as well as the groups initially given a reason to think about the information they read. There was no difference in what subjects had learned about the disorder, only a difference in *how* they had learned it. Even when the context changes, our understanding of it does not. When we learn mindlessly, it does not occur to us to question the information when the context changes.

LANGUAGE AS A COGNITIVE TRAP

Language too often binds us to a single perspective, with mindlessness as a result. As students of general semantics tell us, the map is not the territory. In one of our studies (see Langer 1997), we introduced people to a novel object in either an absolute or conditional way. They were told that the object "is" or "could be" a dog's chew toy. We then created a need for an eraser. The question we considered was: who would think to use the object as an eraser? The answer: only those subjects who were told that it "could be" a dog's chew toy. The name of an object is only one way it can be understood. If we learn about it as if "the map and the territory" are the same thing, creative uses of the information will not occur to us. Most aspects of our culture currently encourage us to reduce uncertainty: we learn so that we will know what things are. This way of learning sets the stage for us to look and feel stupid once circumstances change and the facts we have learned are no longer to be trusted. Instead, we should consider exploiting the power of uncertainty so that we can learn what things can become.

The validity of information depends on the context in which it is embedded and understood. Even the "simple" facts we think we know have this property. If a student is asked "How much is the sum of one plus one?" it may be tempting to conclude that the student is stupid if her answer is not "Two." Consider: "How much is one wad of chewing gum plus one wad of chewing gum?" Answer: "One wad of chewing gum." If a person observes me and does not understand the reason for my behavior, that person will likely conclude that my behavior was stupid and that I should have known better.

When Researchers Conclude "Cognitive Incompetence"

In the same way that we mindlessly learn our facts, researchers may mindlessly produce those facts. Many cognitive "biases" and "fallacies" that psychologists have uncovered through lengthy experimentation may reflect the mindless attributions of the observers (researchers) rather than the cognitive incapacities of the subject. For the past three decades, researchers have exposed the layperson's purported stupidity by showing the way in which we misuse heuristics and arrive at "wrong" answers to contrived problems and decision scenarios.

However, as we have already seen, what is correct from one perspective may be incorrect from another perspective. Consider the following inclusion fallacy. The inclusion rule states that if one class of events is logically subsumed under another class of events, then the probability of the inclusive class cannot be smaller than the probability of the included class. Consider the question "Which is more likely to happen—spilling coffee, or spilling hot coffee?" Many people will answer "Spilling hot coffee." To those who know the inclusion rule and believe it is applicable in this case, these people may seem stupid. "Clearly," they would argue, "the category 'coffee' includes hot coffee and iced coffee and coffee that we have allowed to run cold, so that spilling coffee includes spilling all forms of coffee including hot coffee. Therefore spilling coffee must be more likely than spilling hot coffee." From this perspective, "Spilling coffee" is the right answer.

One could, however, come to this "right" answer by a wrong line of reasoning. One person said that spilling coffee is more likely than is spilling hot coffee, and then explained that when you want hot coffee, you drink it right away, but "coffee" stays around longer, so there is more opportunity to spill it. It is also possible to come up with the "wrong" answer by another line of reasoning that is a relevant alternative to a straight application of the inclusion rule. One may handle the decision problem by dividing "coffee" into two categories—"hot coffee" and "every other kind of coffee"—rather than viewing "coffee" as one category that includes many different kinds of coffee. A person may assume that the "coffee" in question refers to any coffee that is not hot. The experimenter, after all, may have forgotten to label it specifically as non-hot coffee. By equating probabilities with frequencies (Gigerenzer 1996), the person then—correctly—reasons that she more frequently drinks hot coffee than she does cold, iced, or lukewarm coffee—and gives the normatively "stupid" answer: "hot coffee." Nevertheless, she has reasoned by valid deductive steps from plausible premises—and can hardly be condemned as incompetent.

Stupidity as Mindlessness of the Observer

Before returning to everyday uses of the word *stupid*, let us consider the findings of behavioral decision theorists (Dawes 1998) and those who study the psychology of judgment and attribution (Tversky & Kahneman 1982) which aim at identifying cognitive shortcomings and incapacities of the actor. These studies, in which the actor is the experimental participant, confront us with a dilemma. On one hand, we have come to believe that people are unable to follow the very basic axioms of probability theory (Dawes 1998; Plous 1993) and elementary first order logic in making judgments about uncertain situations and predicaments (Nisbett & Ross 1980). On the other hand, we know that the scientists who carry out the experiments and interpret the data are themselves just as prone to making the same cognitive "errors" that their participants are purported to make (Tversky & Kahneman 1982).

One way to resolve the dilemma is to throw up our hands and admit that cognitive science may contain a fatal logical inconsistency in its entrails. Cognitive psychologists are essentially saying: "Using logic, we have come to show that we are incapable of using logic." At the core, the inconsistency is the same as that of someone standing on a stage and saying, "I am telling a lie." The statement is true if it is false, and false if it is true. Kurt Godel (1931) parlayed this simple riddle—dating back to an epistle of St. Paul—into an overarching critique of logic which proves that no logical system can be both complete and consistent.

Similarly, cognitive science seems to be predicated on a whole set of results purporting to document the cognitive shortcomings of the layperson. It also usually extends these results, arguing that biases are "hardwired" (genetically determined) into our cognitive processes, which leads us to the paradoxical conclusion that the very people on whom we depend to use the rules of logic and the axioms of probability theory in order to produce objective knowledge are *themselves* subject to the same biases as those their experiments seem to support and document (Tversky & Kahneman 1982). "I," the cognitive scientist seems to say, "am cognitively incompetent to render a judgment on my own cognitive capacity"—which is structurally similar to the paradox of the liar: "I am telling you a lie."

A solution to this dilemma is to argue that experimental results can be interpreted in many different ways, some of which do not entail any kind of cognitive incapacity on the part of the participant. Take, for example, the famous "Linda" experiment that Tversky and Kahneman (1982) used to argue that people fail to obey the "conjunction rule" of the probability calculus. Participants are presented with a text that describes a young woman. She is described as having attended a liberal arts college, and as being bright and outspoken. The participants are then asked to rank, in order of likelihood of being correct, several one-sentence descriptions of "Linda."

One sentence ("Linda is a bank teller") is meant to describe a class of objects (bank tellers) that includes bank tellers who dance, bank tellers who are active in the feminist movement, more generally bank tellers of any kind. Any sentence that begins with "Linda is a bank teller *and* is (something else)" should be ranked as less likely than the simple sentence "Linda is a bank teller," because, by the conjunction rule, if two events are statistically independent, the probability that both events will be realized simultaneously is less than the probability that each event will be realized on its own. To test their application of the conjunction rule, participants to the experiment are also given the sentence ("Linda is a bank teller who is active in the feminist movement") as one of the sentences which could be true of Linda. It is meant to be a "subsumed" sentence, which should, because of this status, be judged to have a lesser likelihood than the sentence "Linda is a bank teller."

Participants seemed to systematically ignore the conjunction rule, and most of them ranked the compound sentence as more likely to be a true description of Linda than the simple sentence. Moreover, they resisted experimenters' attempts to "correct" this bias by teaching them the conjunction rule. One interpretation of these results is that people are simply unable—or hardwired—to break out of the conjunction fallacy. They are not only stupid for violating the rule but also bullheadedly stupid—for resisting attempts to teach the "right" approach to the rule. We (Moldoveanu & Langer 2001) have produced at least two alternative interpretations of the same findings that are (1) normatively "correct" (albeit according to different norms of reasoning), and (2) exculpatory of the verdict of Kahneman and Tversky. They run as follows:

- *First Interpretation:* Subjects interpreted the problem as one of finding the description of Linda that is most likely to be true, given the description of Linda they were presented with in the opening paragraph. The textual description of Linda was the "evidence," and the statements about Linda that they were asked to rank in order of likelihood were the "models" or hypotheses being tested against the evidence. They, in other words, acted as perfectly reasonable *Bayesian* statisticians, who wanted to maximize the posterior probability that the sentence they chose was a true description of Linda, given some prior probability about who Linda was and the "data" about Linda they were presented with. The relevance of the data to the theory is a key ingredient of the Bayesian conditionalization procedure (Jeffrey 1983). According to this interpretation, "Linda is a bank teller who is active in the feminist movement" can be reasonably judged to be more likely to be true than "Linda is a bank teller," given that we already know that "Linda is bright, outspoken, and a former liberal arts major," because the fact that Linda is an outspoken former liberal arts major is *relevant* to her being active in the feminist movement, whereas her being outspoken and a former liberal arts major is not generally considered to be relevant to her being a bank teller.

- *Second Interpretation:* In the second interpretation we advanced (Moldoveanu & Langer 1997), people are assumed to treat the experiment as a learning situation, and are using a logic of scientific discovery that calls for them to treat the various descriptions of Linda as hypotheses to be tested against a "data" set that includes the researcher's feedback. Famously, Popper (1959) believed that the prior probability of any general statement is zero. He advised that we should test hypotheses with the greatest possible "empirical content" through our actions (i.e., we should pick the statement (a & b) over the statement (a) for testing purposes because compound hypotheses provide the greatest opportunity for a theory to be "falsified," even though, from a probabilist standpoint, (a & b) will have a lower prior probability than will (a) or (b) alone). Thus, if participants in the "Linda" study behaved like Popperian scientists, they would pick, for testing purposes, the compound statement "Linda is a bank teller who is active in the feminist movement" over the statement "Linda is a bank teller" because they would be choosing the statement with the greatest empirical content, for testing purposes. It matters not that they were asked for the statement "Most likely to be true of Linda." They may have simply encoded the statement as "The statement you would most want to test" in the situation at hand.

Many other cognitive biases and fallacies can be similarly questioned by alternative interpretations that make the behavior of the participants seem justified (Moldoveanu & Langer 2001). From an attribution of "stupid lay-people," we arrive at attributions of "people following different norms" for arriving at choices over alternative judgments. The key, in each case, to making the attribution of stupidity—or cognitive incapacity—disappear is to introduce the possibility of an alternative interpretation.

This leaves open the possibilities that (1) people may indeed attempt to be intuitive statisticians but may fail in their attempts, despite their best intentions, or (2) people may have developed approaches to conceptualizing the same predicament other than that which the experimenter assumes they are using to operate with. We know that people are generally prone to attributing their own knowledge and interpretation of a situation to others (Nickerson 1999), and there is no reason to assume that researchers are immune from this sort of attribution. It is likely, therefore, that conclusions of cognitive incompetence of the subjects reveal researchers' mindless attribution of their own interpretation of the test problem to the subjects.

How can we intervene to ease the grip that the current set of attributions has on our minds as investigators of the mind? Langer (1997) has shown that presenting information in a conditionalized way (e.g., using phrases like " X could be Y" or "X can be thought of as Y," rather than " X is Y" or "X can only be Y") actually *enhances* individual performance results on tests that stimulate extensions of the knowledge presented in novel situations, *and* increases the enjoyment that people report having while learning. These results provide a basis for teaching people about individual cognitive "fallacies" in a conditional way (i.e., people "could be poor Bayesian decision makers"), which would allow them to test the hypothesis of cognitive incompetence against their own experiences and to compare it with alternative explanations for observed behavior rather than as a foregone conclusion. We conjecture that such a conditionalized approach to learning will also diminish the propensity of researchers in the field to make the attribution of stupidity about their subjects. The happy result may be that increasing the mindfulness of the observing researcher may decrease the "stupidity" of the actor.

Stupidity as Mindlessness of the Interaction

We now turn our attention to situations in which the attribution of stupidity is mutual and self-reinforcing, and the process can be traced to interactants' mindless following of "scripts" (Langer & Abelson 1972) or roles (Goffman 1959) that lead to the vicious spiral of mutually pejorative attributions. Langer and Abelson found that scripted social behavior can explain social behaviors such as "mindless" requests for help and other people's acquiescence to them. Writing from the micro-interactionist tradition in sociology, Goffman argued that the "self" is no more than a collection of social "roles" that are selectively activated by different social environments but that, once activated, regulate the behavior of the individual person. According to this view, there is no "being" of the self independent of the social context in which behavior is situated, and role-regulated behavior is difficult—if not impossible—to change. The theory of "scripts" can be seen as a natural extension of the theory of "roles," wherein the script is an interpersonal and social—rather than individual—action plan. A script regulates interpersonal behavior in the same way a role regulates individual behavior. Often, scripts are enacted mindlessly.

Some scripts are based on an a priori established mutual attribution of cognitive jurisdiction or of cognitive incapacity. Take, for instance, the teacher-student script. "My teacher's a jerk, and he thinks I'm a fool"—goes an old rap line. The teacher teaches. In his own mind, he has cognitive jurisdiction over the subject matter. His "script" calls for him to be correct all of the time, for the student to be "stupid" or "incapable of giving the right answer" some of the time. In the teacher's script, the student is in the classroom to learn, to be evaluated, and to fail some of the time. Otherwise, there would not be much that the teacher could teach the student. Forced grading curves beautifully reinforce the student-teacher script. They legislate, *ex ante,* that most students must receive a grade that is less than the "top" grade in the class.

Langer (1997) has analyzed in more detail the "teacher script" that governs most modern education, boiling it down to seven principles: (1) the basics must be learned so well that they become second nature; (2) paying attention means staying focused on one thing at a time; (3) delaying gratification is important; (4) rote memorization is necessary in education; (5) forgetting is a problem; (6) intelligence is knowing "what's out there"; (7) there are right and wrong answers.

Having figured out the teacher's script, the student proceeds to game it quite beautifully, by producing behavior targeted at reinforcing that script in order to achieve maximum results. The student's script calls for behavior designed to produce not necessarily the greatest amount of knowledge, skill, or wisdom for the student, but the most favorable impression on the teacher. These two goals are not always (if ever) identical. The student realizes that the "teacher must teach." She also realizes that the quickest way to a teacher's heart (and to good grades, consequently) is to play the game of repeating back to the teacher what the latter has presented as "knowledge" to the classroom. Of course, the student counts on the fact that the teacher is too self-deceived to see through the student's strategy of appeasement. With every action the student takes, she reinforces the teacher's "teachers must teach" script. With every reward and punishment the teacher metes out to students, he reinforces the student's "the teacher is stupid enough to be flattered" script. The result is a mutually reinforcing spiral of actions that jointly perpetuate the two scripts.

Matching the teacher's script, the student's script can be thought of also in terms of a few "axioms" of behavior, matched to the axioms of the teacher's script:

1. Do not question the basic assumptions of the teacher's argument, lest the teacher hate and punish you for disrupting the "show."
2. Demonstrate focus in your work and attitude, and hide from the teacher your many interests and endeavors.
3. Show the teacher how much you are working on his class material; refer to the class material as difficult or demanding.
4. Memorize the teacher's precise words in talking about a problem relevant to the class.
5. Do not bring up any subject from the class that you have forgotten; focus only on what you remember and blow it up out of proportion in order to impress the teacher with your prodigious memory.
6. Show the teacher how informed you are by fitting other events from the media and work or family life into the same framework as that presented by the teacher in the classroom.
7. Beam at the teacher when he praises you for a good answer; show contrition and concern when he chides you for a poor answer; explain poor answers using self-admonitions and excuses that only reinforce how right the teacher was in giving the right answer to the class.

The mindlessness of the teacher is a key ingredient in the student's script. The core axiom of this script seems to be the teacher's own stupidity in not seeing the game the student is playing.

Let us watch how mutually reinforcing negative attributions work to produce a particularly mindless experimental result, beautifully described in Ritchhart and Perkins's work (2000). In this study, students are told that seventeen sheep and sixteen goats are on a boat. They are then asked: "What is the age of the captain?" Most of them answer, without batting an eyelash: "Thirty-three." At first, we are sorely tempted to explain the result as typical of the stupidity of schoolchildren who do not pay attention to the problem statement. The cognitive failure in this case comes in not realizing that the number of animals on the boat may be irrelevant to the captain's age. The teacher script kicks in and condemns the students as stupid for not paying close attention. "There are right and wrong answers" is combined with "Forgetting is a problem" to produce the teacher's verdict.

How does the result look from the vantage point of the student script? Quite different indeed. The student obeys axiom (1) of the student's script (having previously been punished for questioning a problem statement in class: problem statements are part of the "basic assumptions that are not to be questioned"). Axiom (1) is then combined with the "teacher is stupid" axiom (underlying all the other axioms; otherwise, they could not possibly work in the classroom because they would be transparent to an intelligent teacher) to produce something like the following explanation that the student may give for her own behavior: "He has previously given us silly and confusing questions that make no sense ['teacher is stupid'], and I got punished for saying the question made no sense ['don't question assumptions']. So, I will cut straight to the chase and assume this is an 'addition' problem [to which there are always 'right' and 'wrong' answers]. It cannot be any other kind of problem, since addition and subtraction problems [these were second graders] are the ones most likely to have right or wrong answers. Therefore I will just ignore the [stupid] errors that the [stupid] teacher might have made, and I will simply add the number of goats to the number of sheep to give him the [stupid, but 'correct') answer." "QED," we might say to this little feat of deductive logic. Whatever else it may be, it is hardly stupid!

In their recent essay, Ron Ritchhart and David Perkins (2000) review several interventions aimed at making classroom interactions more mindful. They argue, for instance, that teaching elementary algebra to schoolchildren by starting from the epistemological foundations of knowledge of a number or of the result of an equation can increase the involvement of the students with the material presented. Their work aims to increase the cognitive "availability" of students in the classroom by including ability, sensitivity, and inclination (rather than ability or inclination alone) in the definition of a disposition that the "mindful classroom" could aim to cultivate. They show how students in mindful classrooms come to question problem statements, and in particular how the infamous "age of the captain is the sum of the numbers of animals" result gets reversed in a classroom schooled in the questioning ways that typify the mindfulness interventionist literature pioneered by Langer (1989).

Langer (1997) shows how each of the axioms of the teacher script can lead to counterproductive results in real life, and shows how each of the axioms can be uprooted by interventions aimed at cultivating mindfulness. She demonstrates how the conditional presentation of information (refuting the "learn the basics" axiom) can increase both enjoyment and performance; how varying the focus of attention (refuting the "focus on one thing at a time" axiom) can increase awareness and sensitivity to context; how getting people to mix work and play (refuting the "delay of gratification") axiom can lead to greater enjoyment of and performance on a set of tasks; how unfreezing the pre-set ways in which knowledge has been learned (by presenting information in a disorganized way, *contra* the "forgetting is a problem" axiom) can increase the ingenuity and creativity of a solution to a specified problem; how introducing uncertainty into the presentation of information (refuting the "right and wrong answers" axiom) can increase people's sense of control over a task. These challenges to the axioms of the teacher script are easy to replicate and implement in the classroom, give unambiguously positive results for the students, and call into question most—if not all—of the entrenched educational practices that characterize our education system. They are apt to turn the "teacher's a jerk and he thinks I'm a fool" spiral of mutual deception and attribution of stupidity into a positive spiral where students and teachers push each other to deepen their understanding of the subject matter and of one another.

Stupidity as Mindlessness of the Actor

We have thus far examined two contexts in which attributions of stupidity can be understood as processes reflecting the mindlessness of the observer: the cognitive science laboratory, where the participant is judged on the basis of a preselected interpretation of the "facts of the case," and the classroom, where mutual attributions of stupidity can fuel an interpersonal, destructive, and deceptive spiral wherein teachers and students are individually reinforced in their respective attributions about one another's cognitive incompetence. Now we turn to the process by which the actor herself internalizes the judgments of others about her performance, and turns the "attribution gun" upon herself, arriving at the verdict "I am stupid" on the basis of perceived reactions that others have to her behavior and work.

The process of individual trial and error—which Popper (1959) convincingly argued underscores individual learning—is fraught with opportunities to make pejorative self-attributions. After all, the world is a confusing place, where our expectations are often refuted by observation statements, as the following tale from Rupert Riedl (1984) (a friend of Popper's) illustrates:

> It is late in the day and the shadows have fallen. The house we enter is unknown to us, but the situation is familiar. It is too dark in the entrance hall to read the name plates. Where is the light switch? There—three buttons. It's probably the top one. We push it and immediately jump back:

for as long as the finger was on the switch, a bell shrilled through the whole house (and then the fluorescent light flickers on as well). Embarrassing! It must have been the doorbell (or did we also cause the light to come on?) A door opens behind us. Have we roused the tenants too? But no! It is the front door. "Excuse me" says the person coming in, "I thought the door was already locked." Did he then cause the bell to ring and did we turn the light on after all? Apparently. But why do we expect to be the cause of an unexpected coincidence, namely, the simultaneous occurrence of the touching of the switch and the sound of the bell?

At any point in the above adventure, the protagonist could have harmed himself by losing faith in his own cognitive ability to cope with the situation. "I am stupid," he could have said to himself when the loud bell rang, "I am stupid," he could have argued to himself when the front door opened. "I am stupid for thinking I was stupid," he could say to himself at the end of the whole, frightening sequence. While the failure of our expectations in the face of events in the world is sometimes terrifying—and frequent—the attributions we make on the basis of these failed expectations are not determined by the failures themselves.

How do we end up calling ourselves stupid, especially given the very high subsequent costs in individual performance of doing so? The literature on self-attribution and self-efficacy (Bandura 1997) contains many examples in which self-attributions of stupidity result from failed expectations about one's own behavior or performance. Having once failed at ice-skating, one might deduce that one is a poor ice-skater—rather than that one did not have the right instructor or the right ice conditions or the right skating partner. Such self-disparaging reactions are common when one is outperformed by others on a task at which one considers oneself competent (Bandura & Jourden 1991).

Saying "I'm stupid" is often a consequence of performing poorly on tests of cognitive skill in relation to others. People's beliefs about their own cognitive efficacy can—not surprisingly—be raised or lowered by presenting them with information about the cognitive performance of other people (Davis & Yates 1982). Thus, despite the famous propensity of people to make "situational" attributions for their own failures and dispositional attributions for the failures of others (Nisbett & Ross 1980), they also readily take in the "verdicts" of the external world when it comes to interpreting performance results on tasks that are meaningful to them.

What kind of attribution will make one mindful about being stupid? It is well known that most people respond to *constructive* criticism (Baron 1988) with an increased sense of self-efficacy, and to disparaging criticism with a decreased feeling of self-efficacy. The difference between constructive and disparaging criticism is precisely that the former makes statements about the performance of the individual that leave open the possibility of improvement the next time that individual attempts to perform the task. It is precisely the difference between a mindless cognitive commitment that forecloses possibilities ("I screwed up—therefore I'm stupid") and a mindful attribution that leaves open the possibility of improvement ("Under these conditions, I achieved these results—here are some possible hypotheses about the links between my effort, these conditions, and my performance"). The attribution "I did not sing well this time around because of . . ." leads to very different emotions about oneself than the attribution "I'm not a good singer."

Perhaps conditional learning from one's own experience can turn dispositional, incompetence-reinforcing self-criticism into constructive self-criticism and higher self-efficacy. This may be because conditional learning stresses the particular *conditions* under which an attribution is valid and therefore focuses the attention of the actor on the particular circumstances that led to a mismatch between her expectations and her results. For example, if someone learns from a negative experience learning to dance that *under some conditions* he will not feel comfortable on the dance floor, then he is more likely to focus on further experimentation with dancing—with different partners, with different lighting, different music, and so forth than is someone who learns from her negative experience with dancing that "I'm no good at it" or that "There's something about dancing itself that is ill-suited to my temperament."

From a cognitive perspective that teaches that we are not good at processing complicated information in order to arrive at more informed judgments (Slovic, Fischhoff, & Liechtenstein 1977), constructive self-criticism through situation-specific, conditional learning from failure may seem difficult to achieve. Dispositions ("I am stupid") may function as precisely the kinds of heuristics that people use to cut through the complexity of a cognitively complicated predicament (Tversky & Kahneman 1982). However, the work of Ellen Langer (1997) shows that uncertainty and ambiguity (often used to model cognitive complexity) can have highly beneficial effects on people's ability to process information with clarity and sensitivity, as evidenced by their improved performance on cognitive tasks where the information presented was either ambiguous or conditional. The mindfulness interventions developed for the facilitation of individual mindful learning may also facilitate the production of constructive self-criticism. In particular, increasing uncertainty and ambiguity about the causes of failed self-expectations and presenting the reasons for the failed expectations (to oneself) as conditional upon a wide selection of unknown variables can *increase* the amount of control that an individual feels, by making the self-criticism produced by that person more constructive. Mindfulness treatments generally decrease people's propensity to concentrate on context-independent facts, models, and categories, and to tune in to the detail of a situation. We conjecture that more mindful individuals are more likely to produce constructive self-criticism and are also more proficient at changing their behavior in the face of performance failures.

Mindlessness versus Stupidity and Mindfulness versus Intelligence

This chapter has focused on identifying the ways in which the attribution of stupidity gets constructed, both interpersonally and intrapersonally. To show that a characteristic is socially constructed (rather than given, or objectively "there"), we have followed a particular strategy. First, we proposed a plausible interpersonal or intraperson model or theory that explains how people can think of themselves or of each other as "stupid," and then we showed how the premises on which the model rests can be invalidated by interventions aimed at increasing mindfulness in the actors. We argued that stupidity is essentially an observer's phenomenon. It can become an actor's phenomenon as well through internalization of someone else's perspective, through well-documented processes of self-attribution and self-criticism. It can be made to disappear by changing the processes of (1) interpersonal attribution or (2) self-attribution.

Mindfulness research can have a useful place in the public debate and academic research on intelligence, provided that the relationship between mindfulness, mindlessness, intelligence, and stupidity is made clear. In particular: Is mindfulness to mindlessness what intelligence is to stupidity? The answer is both "Yes" and "No." First, it is clear that we use the words *intelligence* and *stupidity* as antonyms, in the same way we use the words *mindful* and *mindless*. So far, the two pairs of concepts seem to be alike. However, while it is not generally possible to approach a problem both stupidly and intelligently at the same time, it is possible to be mindful with respect to the formulation of a problem, and mindless in the solution of that problem. To understand why this is the case, we need to understand how mindfulness and intelligence differ.

According to the "linear" conception of intelligence, the intelligent individual assumes there exists a pre-set, always-already-there correspondence between word and object (or word and perception, or word and event) and proceeds to calculate an optimally adaptive solution or plan that will link the current state of the world to a desired state of the world. This, indeed, is the algorithmic structure of all plans and problem-solving sequences, and is the classical model of problem-solving skill used by cognitive psychologists such as Herbert Simon and Alan Newell (Newell 1990). It is important to note that the categories in which perceptions are organized are assumed to be constant and unchanging. Herein lies the Platonist heritage of the classical view of intelligence.

Now, it becomes clear why it is that one can be intelligent only to the extent that one is not stupid in the solution of the problem. At their core, all problems based on a determined set of conditions or axioms have the architecture of a set of consistency checks among the axioms in question (or, to put it in Simonesque terms, between the goals and the constraints of the problem statement). If one carries out all the required consistency checks in question, one "gets" the answer. In the classical, linear view of intelligence, one is intelligent, or as intelligent as possible, given the problem statement. If one carries out only some of the consistency checks, then one gets only "partial credit" for being intelligent. One is considered to be cognitively unable, or "stupid" the rest of the way. Hence, we have that intelligence and stupidity are traded off in equal amounts in the case of "partial deductively valid" approaches to problem solving.

The mindful individual, in contrast, is one who "shapes reality by identifying several possible perspectives from which any situation may be viewed" (Langer 1997). The innovation of the mindful kicks in before the assumptions, or the problem statement itself, has been determined. Mindfulness rests on the Bergsonian insight that we should consider not the ways in which people resolve problems and the validity of their answers, but rather on the kinds of problems they choose to resolve (Deleuze 1990). Mindfulness, then, refers not to a finite capacity for consistency checks, but rather to a process or phenomenon by which new thought-shapes (ideas, categories, mental images) that organize perception are generated. Mindlessness refers to the unquestioning acceptance of any one set of constraints or axioms that algorithmically "determine" the problem-solving steps one needs to take in order to produce the desired behavior. Mindfulness and mindlessness cannot, therefore, be traded off linearly against each other. The moment we have accepted—unconditionally—a set of constraints or objectives, we have ceased to become mindful and have instead become mindless.

Mindfulness also bears an interesting link to the theory of multiple intelligences developed by Howard Gardner (1991). Gardner's significant contribution is to extend the classical, linear notion of intelligence to multiple dimensions, so that many different cognitive and emotional skills and traits can be positively counted as intelligence-enhancing factors. While the idea of multiple intelligences represents a great advance over the concept of a single intelligence, each individual kind of intelligence, however, remains defined as an optimal-plan or optimal-activity-producing capability, starting from a particular problem statement or kind of problem statement. However, as the number of possible different kinds of intelligence becomes infinitely large, different problem formulations begin to morph into one another, leading to different ways of conceptualizing the world, different categories for organizing perceptions, and different links between words and objects, in which case infinitely multiple intelligences are a form of mindfulness. The interesting consequence of this extension to the stupidity/mindlessness discussion we have carried out above is that the replacement of intelligence—even of multiple intelligences—with mindfulness leads to the exclusion of "stupidity" as a meaningful term from public discourse. Since we can admit to being mindless far more easily than to being stupid, this replacement has the happy consequence of promoting the kind of constructive self-criticism and mutual criticism that breeds greater control and a sense of competence in dealing with the world.

REFERENCES

Bandura, A. (1997). *Self-efficacy: The exercise of control*. New York: Freeman.

Bandura, A., and F. J. Jourden (1991). Self-regulatory mechanisms governing the impact of social comparison on complex decision making, *Journal of Personality and Social Psychology, 60,* 941–951.

Baron, R. A. (1988). Negative effects of destructive criticism: Impact on conflict, self-efficacy and task performance, *Journal of Applied Psychology, 73,* 199–207.

Davis, F. W., and B. T. Yates (1982). Self-Efficacy expectancies versus outcome expectancies as determinants of performance deficits and depressive affect, *Cognitive Therapy and Research, 6,* 23–25.

Dawes, R. (1998). Behavioral decision theory. In D. Gilbert and R. Lindzay (Eds.), *Handbook of social psychology*. New York: Oxford University Press.

Deleuze, G. (1990). *Bergsonism*. Cambridge: Zone Books, MIT Press.

Fiske, S., and S. Taylor (1991). *Social cognition* (second edition). New York: McGraw-Hill.

Gardner, H. (1991). *Multiple intelligences*. New York: Free Press.

Gigerenzer, G. (1996). On narrow norms and vague heuristics: A reply to Kahneman and Tversky, *Psychological Review, 103,* 592–596.

Godel, K. (1931 (1955)). On provably undecidable propositions in the *Principia Mathematica*. New York: Dover.

Goffman, E. (1959). *The presentation of self in everyday life*. New York: Anchor Books, Doubleday.

Jeffrey, R. (1983). *The logic of decision*. New York: McGraw-Hill.

Langer, E. J. (1997). *The power of mindful learning*. Reading, Mass.: Addison Wesley.

—— (1989). *Mindfulness*. Reading, Mass.: Addison Wesley, 1989.

Langer, E. J., and Abelson, R. (1972). The semantics of asking a favor: How to succeed in getting help without really suffering, *Journal of Personality and Social Psychology, 24,* 26–32.

Moldoveanu, M. C., and E. J. Langer (2001). False memories of the future: A critique of the applications of probabilistic reasoning to the study of cognitive processes. Forthcoming, *Psychological Review.*

Newell, A. (1990). *Unified theories of cognition.* Cambridge: Harvard University Press.

Nickerson, R. (1999). How we know—and sometimes misjudge—what others know: Imputing one's knowledge to others, *Psychological Bulletin, 125,* 737–759.

Nisbett, R., and L. Ross (1980). *Human inference.* Englewood Cliffs, N.J.: Prentice Hall.

Plous, S. (1993). *The psychology of judgment and decision making.* New York: McGraw-Hill.

Riedl, R. (1984). The consequences of causal thinking. In P. Watzlawick (Ed.), *The invented reality.* New York: Norton.

Ritchhart, R., and D. Perkins (2000). Mindfulness in the classroom: Nurturing the disposition of mindfulness. *Journal of Social Issues.*

Slovic, P., B. Fischhoff, and S. Liechtenstein (1977). Behavioral decision theory, *Annual Review of Psychology, 28,* 1–39.

Tversky, A., and D. Kahneman (1982). Judgments of and by representativeness. In D. Kahneman, P. Slovic, and A. Tversky (Eds.), *Judgment under uncertainty: Heuristics and biases.* New York: Cambridge University Press.

ROBERT J. STERNBERG

11 Smart People Are Not Stupid, But They Sure Can Be Foolish

THE IMBALANCE THEORY OF FOOLISHNESS

According to the *American Heritage Dictionary of the English Language* (1992), a person who is *stupid* is "1. Slow to learn or understand; obtuse; 2. Lacking or marked by lack of intelligence" (pp. 1784–1785). A person who is *foolish* is "1. Lacking or exhibiting a lack of good sense or judgment; silly. . . 2. Resulting from stupidity or misinformation; unwise . . . 3. Arousing laughter; absurd or ridiculous . . . 4. Immoderate or stubborn, unreasonable" (p. 707). The two definitions refer to quite different kinds of entities.

Consider what became the classic case of the 1990s: President Clinton's affair with Monica Lewinsky. Did Clinton know and understand what he was doing? By all means. He understood all too well, which was part of the reason people were reluctant to forgive him. His splitting hairs regarding the meanings of words such as "sexual relations" showed that he was keenly aware of the nature of his actions. Clinton was not acting stupidly. But he certainly was acting foolishly, showing a lack of good sense and being generally unwise in his course of behavior.

If we go back a political generation, we find another very intelligent president acting foolishly. Richard Nixon was absolutely determined to have the scoop on his enemies, and to strike back at them. The Watergate burglary was an opportunity to learn key facts about Democratic practices and plans. Nixon's role in the burglary remains unclear. But what is clear is that Nixon was at the center of the cover-up of that burglary. The president even tried to

232

perpetuate the secrecy while the walls of the cover-up were falling down around him. Nixon wasn't stupid, by any reasonable standard. But he was foolish.

If we go back yet another generation to a very different context and a very different political leader, we see the same pattern. Was Neville Chamberlain stupid to keep appeasing Hitler? Not in any dictionary sense. Chamberlain was able to give any number of reasons why he was acting cautiously, and he was able to convince many people that he was taking the intelligent course of action. But he was being foolish. He was lacking in good sense and judgment. The question at hand was whether Hitler would continue with his imperialistic quest; all signs were that he would.

If we can agree that Clinton, Nixon, and Chamberlain were not stupid or otherwise mentally deficient, then we need to view their puzzling actions in a different way. I propose here that their actions be viewed as foolish. Yet, precisely speaking, neither the individuals nor their actions were foolish in and of themselves. Rather, foolishness occurs in the interaction between a person and a situation. These world leaders behaved foolishly in certain contexts. In other contexts, their behavior was anything but foolish. Nixon, for example, opened doors to China. Clinton presided over the strongest economy in U.S. history. People who are very effective in some domains can prove to be foolish in others.

The *imbalance theory of foolishness* builds on my earlier balance theory of wisdom (Sternberg 1998). The proposed theory views foolishness as the opposite of wisdom. The large majority of behaviors that we refer to as *stupid* are not stupid as opposed to intelligent, but, rather, foolish as opposed to wise. The beginnings of foolishness lie in a defect in tacit knowledge.

A Tacit-Knowledge Approach

THE NATURE OF TACIT KNOWLEDGE

The view of foolishness proposed here has at its core defects in the acquisition or utilization of tacit knowledge (Polanyi 1976). *Tacit knowledge* can be defined as action-oriented knowledge, usually acquired without direct help from others, that allows individuals to achieve goals they personally value (Sternberg et al. 1995; Sternberg et al. 2000). Tacit knowledge has three main features: it is procedural; it is relevant to the attainment of goals people value; and it is acquired with little or no help from others.

When we refer to tacit knowledge as being procedural, and as intimately related to action, we are viewing it as a form of "knowing how" rather than of "knowing that" (Ryle 1949). In our work, we view condition-action sequences (production systems) as a useful formalism for understanding the mental representation of tacit knowledge. For example, if one needs to deliver bad news to one's boss and if it is Monday morning and if the boss's golf game was rained out the day before and if the boss's staff seems to be "walking on eggshells," then it is better to wait until later to deliver the news so as not to spoil the boss's week. Note that tacit knowledge is always wedded to particular uses in particular situations or classes of situations.

Suppose, though, that one has a defect in the acquisition or utilization of tacit knowledge. Perhaps one never learned one of these elements, for example, the significance of Monday morning for the boss (bad news spoils her week). Or perhaps one never learned that the boss tends to be in a bad mood when she misses her Sunday golf game. Alternatively, one may have learned these things but decided not to act despite knowing them. So one spills the bad news at the wrong time, the boss blows up and takes out her anger on the messenger who brought the bad news. The messenger has acted foolishly and pays the price.

Tacit knowledge also is practically useful. It is instrumental to the attainment of goals people value. Thus, people use this knowledge in order to achieve success in life, however they may define success. Abstract academic knowledge about procedures for solving problems with no relevance to life would not be viewed, in this perspective, as constituting tacit knowledge.

Finally, tacit knowledge is acquired without direct help from others. Ideally, others can guide one to acquire this knowledge. Often, environmental support for the acquisition of this knowledge is minimal, and sometimes organizations actually suppress the acquisition of tacit knowledge. For example, an organization might not want its employees to know how personnel decisions are really made, as opposed to how they are supposed to be made. From a developmental standpoint, this view suggests that wisdom is not taught so much as indirectly acquired. Similarly, foolishness is acquired not from formal courses in foolish patterns of behavior, but from defects in reading the cues in the environment. One can provide the circumstances for the development of wisdom and case studies to help students develop wisdom, but one cannot teach particular courses of action that would be considered wise, regardless of circumstances. No matter how much one is placed in an environment that enables one to acquire tacit knowledge, it is almost always the individual's responsibility to acquire it. And if it is not acquired and then utilized effectively, one opens the door to foolish patterns of behavior.

Tacit knowledge is wedded to contexts, so that the tacit knowledge that would apply in one context would not necessarily apply in another. People may not see things in this light, however. They may believe that if they make wise judgments in one domain, they are generally wise across domains. This belief in their own wisdom is often what brings them down.

The tacit knowledge Clinton would have needed in order to avoid the Monica Lewinsky crisis was not subtle or somehow hidden. The question then becomes: How could someone as obviously smart as Clinton have failed to acquire or implement that knowledge? The answer is that people in positions of great power often acquire three dispositions that dispose them to foolishness: a sense of omniscience, a sense of omnipotence, and a sense of invulnerability.

The *sense of omniscience* results from having available at one's disposal essentially any knowledge one might want that is, in fact, knowable. With a phone call, a powerful leader can have almost any kind of knowledge made available to him or her. At the same time, people look up to the powerful leader as extremely knowledgeable or even close to all-knowing. The powerful leader may then come to believe that he or she really is all-knowing. So may his or her staff, as illustrated by Janis (1972) in his analysis of victims of groupthink. In case after case, brilliant government officials have made the most foolish of decisions, in part because they believed they knew much more than they did.

The *sense of omnipotence* results from the extreme power one wields. In certain domains, one essentially can do almost whatever one wants to do. The risk is that the individual will start to overgeneralize and believe that this high level of power applies in all domains.

The *sense of invulnerability* comes from the presence of the illusion of complete protection, such as from a huge staff. People, especially leaders, seem to have many friends ready to protect them at a moment's notice. The leaders may shield themselves from individuals who are anything less than sycophantic. The solution, suggested by Harry Truman, is for high-powered (Washington) leaders craving friendship to buy a dog. As soon as things turn bad, friends can prove to be anything but loyal friends—whereas a dog's loyalty is unconditional.

MEASUREMENT OF TACIT KNOWLEDGE

In a series of studies (summarized in Sternberg, Wagner, & Okagaki 1993; Sternberg et al. 1995; and Sternberg et al. 2000), we have sought to develop assessments of tacit knowledge in real-world pursuits. The methodology for constructing assessments is rather complex, involving interviewing individuals for how they have handled critical situations on their jobs. We then extract the tacit knowledge implicit in these interviews. Next, assessments are constructed that ask people to solve the kinds of problems they find in managing themselves, others, and tasks on the job. Each of these problems typically presents a scenario about a job-related problem along with possible options for dealing with that problem. Test-takers are asked to evaluate the quality of the problems on a Likert scale. Their response profiles for all items are then typically scored against the averaged profile of a nominated expert group.

FOOLISHNESS AS TACIT KNOWLEDGE BALANCING INTERESTS

The definition of foolishness proposed here draws both upon the notion of tacit knowledge, as described above, and on the notion of imbalance. Consider first the definition of the opposite of foolishness, wisdom.

Wisdom is defined as the application of tacit knowledge as guided by values toward the achievement of a common good, through a balance among intrapersonal, interpersonal, and extrapersonal interests of the short and long term, in order to achieve a balance among (1) adaptation to existing environments, (2) shaping of existing environments, and (3) selection of new environments.

Foolishness, in contrast, is defined as the faulty acquisition or application of tacit knowledge as guided by values away from the achievement of a common good, through an imbalance among intrapersonal, interpersonal, and extrapersonal interests of the short and long term, resulting in a failure in balance among (1) adaptation to existing environments, (2) shaping of existing environments, and (3) selection of new environments. Foolishness is an extreme failure of wisdom.

If we return to our earlier examples, we see how imbalance functions in foolish decisions. In his involvement with Monica Lewinsky, President Clinton obviously put his own interests well above those of his wife, family, or country (of which he was serving as chief executive). He also placed the short-term gratification of the situation above the potential long-term consequences. But, of course, he did not expect to be caught, feeling relatively omniscient, omnipotent, and invulnerable from the threats that would face others engaging in the same behavior. And his shaping of the situation was deficient by almost any standard: few people found credible his hair-splitting definitions of what he did and did not do.

Similarly, Nixon, in his cover-up, placed his self-interest and perhaps the interests of his co-involved cronies well above the interests of the country. His attempt to shape the situation, too, was distorted by semantic hair-splitting. Eventually, having lost the remainder of his dwindling constituency, Nixon resigned the presidency of the country.

Thus, wisdom is not just about maximizing one's self-interest, but about balancing various self-interests (intrapersonal) with the interests of others (interpersonal) and the interests of other aspects of the context in which one lives (extrapersonal), such as one's city, country, environment, or even God. Foolishness is about an imbalance in these elements. The imbalance is usually not subtle. Rather, the combination of feelings of omniscience, omnipotence, and invulnerability leads people to believe that they will not be caught in a trap of their own making.

Wisdom is different from practical intelligence. When one applies practical intelligence, one deliberately may (although will not necessarily) seek outcomes that are good for oneself and bad for others. In wisdom, one certainly may seek good ends for oneself, but one also will seek good outcomes for others. If one's motivations are to maximize certain people's interests and minimize other people's, wisdom is not involved. In wisdom, one seeks a common good, realizing that this common good may be better for some than for others. An evil genius may be academically intelligent; he or she may be practically intelligent; he or she cannot be wise.

Foolishness can involve seeking bad outcomes for others. A New York State judge became involved in an ill-fated affair. When he was jilted, the judge tried to do everything in his power to cause harm to the woman who had jilted him. Eventually, he was found out and imprisoned. The judge gained little from his attempts to hurt his former lover—except, perhaps, some perverse kind of personal satisfaction. In putting this satisfaction over the interests of the woman, his career, and the judiciary system that he was supposed to represent, he sacrificed a great deal. Once again, a sense of omniscience, omnipotence, and invulnerability undermined the good judgment that the judge had shown in past dealings, at least in other domains.

I refer in this discussion to "interests," which are related to the multiple points of view that are a common feature of many theories of wisdom (as reviewed in Sternberg 1990). Diverse interests encompass multiple points of view—thus the use of the term "interests" is intended to include "points of view." Interests go beyond points of view, however, in that they include not only cognitive aspects of divergences, but affective and motivational divergences as well. Sometimes differences in points of view derive not so much from differences in cognitions as from differences in motivations. For example, executives in the tobacco industry for many years have defended their products. Their point of view may be divergent from those of many others, but the motivation of maintaining a multi-million dollar business may have more to do with the divergences in points of view than do any kinds of cognitive analysis. Economic interests no doubt motivate these executives to adopt a point of view favorable to the continued use in society of tobacco products. As the lawsuits mount, the behavior of these executives seems increasingly foolish. They have failed to balance the long-term interests of other people and of society against the short-term interests of their companies.

Problems requiring wisdom always involve at least some element of each form of interest: intrapersonal, interpersonal, and extrapersonal. For example, one might decide that it is wise to go to college, an issue that seemingly involves only one person. But many people are typically affected by an individual's decision to go to college—parents, friends, present or future significant others and children, and the like. And the decision always has to be made in the context of the whole range of available options. Similarly, a decision about whether to have an abortion requires wisdom because it involves not only oneself but the baby who would be born, others to whom one is close such as the father, and the rules and customs of the society.

Foolishness always involves interests going out of balance. Usually, the individual places self-interest way above other interests. But not always. Chamberlain may truly have believed he was doing the best thing for Great Britain. But in ignoring the interests of all the other countries that were being crushed under Hitler's brutal reign, Chamberlain was ignoring the common good, and, as it turned out, the long-term good of his own country.

Similarly, occasionally people sacrifice everything for another individual, only to be crushed by their own foolishness. The "classic" case is that of the prolonged war between Greece and Troy. Was Helen of Troy worth the war? Many wars have started over slights or humiliations, and the interests of the slighted or humiliated have taken precedence over the interests of the thousands who have then been sacrificed to avenge the slight. There are those who believe that the war in Chechnya resulted in part from the humiliation suffered by the Russian army in the earlier war in Chechnya. Certainly events after World War I contributed to Germany's humiliation after that war.

Wisdom involves a balancing not only of the three kinds of interests, but also of three possible courses of action in response to this balancing: adaptation of oneself or others to existing environments; shaping of environments in order to render them more compatible with oneself or others; and selection of new environments. In adaptation, the individual tries to find ways to conform to the existing environment that forms his or her context. Sometimes adaptation is the best course of action under a given set of circumstances. But typically one seeks a balance between adaptation and shaping, realizing that fit to an environment requires not only changing oneself, but changing the environment as well. When an individual finds it impossible or at least implausible to attain such a fit, he or she may decide to select a new environment altogether, leaving, for example, a job, a community, or a marriage.

Foolishness results in action that represents poor use and balance of these processes. Wars are examples of shaping of the environment that often have proved to be of little avail. What, for example, did the Hundred Years' War have to show for itself in the end? Or, for that matter, the more recent Cold War? National leaders have shaped environments in ways that have caused great harm, suffering, and distress. In much of the world, they are continuing to do so.

Foolishness derives not only from inappropriate shaping of the environment. One can adapt to a tyrannical environment to save one's skin, only to find oneself paying the ultimate price. An example of this principle is shown in the poem by Pastor Martin Nïemoller (1945):

In Germany first they came for the communists
and I did not speak out—
because I was not a communist.

Then they came for the Jews
and I did not speak out—
because I was not a Jew.

Then they came for the trade unionists
and I did not speak out—
because I was not a trade unionist.

Then they came for the Catholics
and I did not speak out—
because I was a Protestant.

Then they came for me—
and there was no one left
to speak out for me.

Selection also can be foolish, as when older individuals leave good or at least acceptable marriages for much younger partners whose main goal appears to be to share the financial success of their newly found, more established partners. The selection can be with respect to environments rather than people. An individual may love the idea of living in a place, move to that location, and then find that the reality bears little resemblance to the ideal. An American living abroad commented to me somewhat bitterly that the reasons one moved to the country in which he lived were inevitably different from the reasons for which one stayed. Those who continued to hope to find what they came for almost inevitably returned to the United States, because they never found it.

PROCESSES OF WISDOM AND FOOLISHNESS

Wisdom manifests as a series of processes, which are typically cyclical and can occur in a variety of orders. These processes are related to what I have referred to as "metacomponents" of thought (Sternberg 1985), including (1) recognizing the existence of a problem, (2) defining the nature of the problem, (3) representing information about the problem, (4) formulating a strategy for solving the problem, (5) allocating resources to the solution of a problem, (6) monitoring one's solution of the problem, and (7) evaluating feedback regarding that solution. In deciding whether or not to leave a spouse, for example, one first has to see both staying and leaving as viable options (problem recognition), then figure out exactly what staying or leaving would mean for oneself (defining the problem), then consider the costs and benefits to oneself and others of staying or leaving (representing information about the problem), and so forth.

In foolishness, the problem-solving process is defective. Most often, I believe, one misdefines the problem one is facing. Clinton perhaps defined his relationship with Lewinsky as a harmless flirtation. Nixon perhaps defined the cover-up as the withholding of information that was no one else's business. It is interesting to compare Nixon's definition of the situation to those of others who have more successfully negotiated similar situations. When Johnson & Johnson faced a disaster over the poisoning of extra-strength Tylenol, the top executives quickly decided to temporarily remove all of the product from the marketplace. The disaster quickly passed. The executives at A. H. Robbins, in contrast, tried to hide the damage caused by a birth control device, the Dalkon Shield, ultimately resulting in the bankruptcy of the company.

The balance theory suggests that wisdom is at least partially domain-specific, in that tacit knowledge is acquired within a given context or set of contexts. It is typically acquired by selectively encoding new information that is relevant for one's purposes in learning about that context, selectively comparing this information to old information in order to see how the new fits with the old, and selectively combining pieces of information in order to make them fit together into an orderly whole (Sternberg, Wagner, & Okagaki 1993).

Foolishness often results from knowledge acquisition gone awry or poorly utilized. The history of malevolent dictators such as Hitler shows that they rarely stop until they are stopped. Genghis Khan was not satisfied with what he would have perceived as half a loaf. Usually, the information is there to be had. The individual avoids seeking or fully processing the information that is so readily found, in what Moldoveanu and Langer (in Chapter 10 of this volume) refer to as "mindlessness."

As noted above, however, our research has found significant correlations on scores of tacit knowledge across domains. For example, we have found that scores on tests of tacit knowledge for academic psychology and management correlate significantly (Wagner & Sternberg 1986), as do scores on tests of tacit knowledge for management and military leadership (Sternberg et al. 2000). Thus, although one's development of wisdom might be somewhat domain-specific, the tacit knowledge one learns in one domain might potentially extend to other domains. At the same time, the wise individual necessarily would have to know the limits of his or her own tacit knowledge. Wisdom may also show some correlations across domains, although such correlations have yet to be shown empirically.

I suspect that actualized foolishness, as opposed to the potential for foolishness, shows some degree of domain specificity. People who are foolish in one domain certainly possess the potential to be foolish in others. The question is whether they are able to find the incentive to do so. Foolishness results when people let down their guard as a result of feelings of omniscience, omnipotence, and invulnerability. People who make themselves vulnerable in one domain may well do so in other domains, but only if there is a reason to do so.

Unfortunately, one domain can be enough. The financial chicanery of the Yeltsin administration in Russia, the Mobutu administration in Zaire, or the Abacha administration in Nigeria was enough to send whole countries into soaring debt and near ruin. How many domains of foolishness were necessary for great harm to be done? In each of these cases, the foolishness of the leaders showed up in multiple domains, but one domain was enough largely to cause great harm to their countries.

The costs of foolishness can be very high. In order to avoid it, we first need to understand it. Such an understanding can be achieved by viewing foolishness as an imbalance that results from feelings of omniscience, omnipotence, and invulnerability.

NOTE

Preparation of this article was supported by Grant REC-9979843 from the National Science Foundation and by a grant under the Javits Act Program (Grant No. R206R000001) as administered by the Office of Educational Research and Improvement, U.S. Department of Education. Grantees undertaking such projects are encouraged to express freely their professional judgment. This article, therefore, does not necessarily represent the position or policies of the National Science Foundation, Office of Educational Research and Improvement, or U.S. Department of Education, and no official endorsement should be inferred.

REFERENCES

The American Heritage dictionary of the English language (third edition, 1992). Boston: Houghton Mifflin.

Janis, I. L. (1972). *Victims of groupthink.* Boston: Houghton Mifflin.

Polanyi, M. (1976). Tacit knowledge. In M. Marx & F. Goodson (Eds.), *Theories in contemporary psychology* (pp. 330–344). New York: Macmillan.

Ryle, G. (1949). *The concept of mind.* London: Hutchinson.

Sternberg, R. J. (1985). *Beyond IQ: A triarchic theory of human intelligence.* New York: Cambridge University Press.

—— (Ed.) (1990). *Wisdom: Its nature, origins, and development.* New York: Cambridge University Press.

——. (1998). A balance theory of wisdom. *Review of General Psychology, 2,* 347–365.

Sternberg, R. J., G. B. Forsythe, J. Hedlund, J. Horvath, S. Snook, W. M. Williams, R. K. Wagner, & E. L. Grigorenko (2000). *Practical intelligence in everyday life.* New York: Cambridge University Press.

Sternberg, R. J., R. K. Wagner, & L. Okagaki (1993). Practical intelligence: The nature and role of tacit knowledge in work and at school. In H. Reese & J. Puckett (Eds.), *Advances in lifespan development* (pp. 205–227). Hillsdale, N.J.: Erlbaum.

Sternberg, R. J., R. K. Wagner, W. M. Williams, & J. A. Horvath, J. A. (1995). Testing common sense. *American Psychologist, 50,* 912–927.

Wagner, R. K., & R. J. Sternberg (1986). Tacit knowledge and intelligence in the everyday world. In R. J. Sternberg & R. K. Wagner (Eds.), *Practical intelligence: Nature and origins of competence in the everyday world* (pp. 51–83). New York: Cambridge University Press.

CONTRIBUTORS

Elizabeth J. Austin, *University of Edinburgh*

Ozlem Ayduk, *Columbia University*

Carol S. Dweck, *Columbia University*

Ian J. Deary, *University of Edinburgh*

Diane F. Halpern, *California State University*

Ray Hyman, professor emeritus, *University of Oregon*

Elena L. Grigorenko, *Yale University,* PACE *Center, and Moscow State University*

Ellen Langer, *Harvard University*

Donna Lockery, *Yale University,* PACE *Center*

Walter Mischel, *Columbia University*

Mihnea Moldoveanu, *Joseph L. Rotman School of Management*

David N. Perkins, *Harvard University*

Keith E. Stanovich, *Ontario Institute for Studies in Education, University of Toronto*

Robert J. Sternberg, *Yale University,* PACE *Center*

Richard K. Wagner, *Florida State University*

INDEX

California Psychology Inventory, 54
Campos, Paul, 181
Carl Perkins Vocational and Applied
    Technology Act (P.L. 101–392), 177,
    185n4
Carter, Jimmy, 106–7
Center for Creative Leadership study, 53, 54
Challenger case, folly and, 83
Chamberlain, Neville, 233, 238
Chanowitz, Benzion, 216
Charly (film), 171, 173–74
A Child Is Waiting (film), 174
child prodigies, 35
Children of a Lesser God (film), 171, 175, 176
Chiu, C. Y., 28, 30
City of Manchester Democratic Party
    Committee, 168
Clark, Walter Le Gros, 12
Cleveland, Grover, 111–12
Clinton, Bill: decision making and, 109, 121–
    22; failure to adapt to environmental
    changes, 116–17; feminist support for,
    118–19; foolish behavior of, 236;
    impeachment and, 86; prior learning and,
    110–11, 117; problem-solving defects in,
    240; psychology of explaining and, 117;
    understanding of actions of, 232; wishful
    thinking and, 115, 120. *See also* Clinton-
    Lewinsky scandal
Clinton, Hillary, 87, 109–10
Clinton-Lewinsky scandal, 3, 8, 100;
    changing nature of evidence and, 115–16;
    Clinton's view of, 87; lies and denials in,
    120–21; machismo of United States
    presidency and, 111–12; mindlessness
    and, 216; moral issues of, 107; public
    office in post-Watergate era and, 114–15;
    Starr spotlight and, 119–20; US social
    mores and, 112–13
Cloninger, C. R., 203
cockney, definition of, 165, 185n1
cognitive-attentional strategies, in rejection
    sensitivity, 96–97
cognitive capacities, versus thinking
    dispositions, 130–31
cognitive incompetence, 217–18, 221
cognitive science: biases of researchers in,
    218–19, 221; levels of analysis in, 127–29,

131–32, 134–35, 137, 140, 142; logical
    inconsistency in, 218; open-minded
    thinking and, 140–42; predictors of
    rational thinking, 131–37; process models
    of, 142–44; sure-thing principle, 124–25;
    terminology in, 128–29, 133–34
The Coming of the Fairies (Doyle), 18
confirmatory factor analysis, 54
conjunction rule, 219–20
conscientiousness, 191, 192, 195
conscious intentions, 78–79
convoluted action, 50
cool system processing, in delay of
    gratification, 91–92, 95, 97, 100–101
coping strategies: beliefs and, 99; in
    neuroticism, 189–90, 195; personality
    traits and, 194–95, 196; in rejection
    sensitivity, 96–97
covariation detection literature, 148
cripple, definition of, 165, 185n2
critical thinking, 116–17, 132. *See also* rational
    thinking; thinking dispositions
criticism, constructive versus disparaging,
    226–27
current performance, importance of, 39. *See
    also* performance

Dalkon Shield case, 240
Darke, Paul, 164, 165
Darwin, Charles, 11, 34
Davey, S. J., 14–18
Dawson, Charles, 9
de Groot, A. D., 57
delay of gratification paradigm: definition of,
    88; hot/cool system analysis of, 91–92,
    93, 95, 97, 100–101; mental
    representations and, 89–90; rewards and,
    89, 90, 94; self-distraction in, 92, 93, 97,
    98–99
Dennett, D. C., 128, 129
depression: effort and, 33–34; intelligence
    and, 204
desires, 101–2, 131
Differential Aptitude Tests, 53
digit span task, 55–56
disabilities: actors with, 171–72; attitudes of
    disabled towards, 178–79; base-rate fallacy
    of, 166–67; conjunction/asexuality fallacy

management, rational (*continued*)
of, 44–45; decline and limitations of, 45–
46, 48; emergent activity switching and,
70–71; processing biases and information
in, 47–48; responses biases and
information in, 48
managerial competence: expertise and, 55–
60; nonlinear problem solving and, 50;
reflection-in-action, 50–51; tacit
knowledge and, 51–55; thinking in action,
49
managerial incompetence: characteristics of
failed managers and, 59; personality and
temperament in, 58–60; provost case and,
42–43, 61
Manktelow, K., 147
The March of Folly (Tuchman), 82
Marks, D., 172, 173, 177
Marr, D., 128, 129
mass media, role in disabilities stereotype
formation, 164–66, 171–77, 183–84
Matthew effects, 148, 149
McCall, M. W., 50
McCauley, C. D., 58
measurements, of tacit knowledge, 51–52,
235–36, 241
The Men (film), 174–75
MENSA, 108
The Mentality of Apes (Köhler), 4–5
mental representations, in delay, 89–90
Mercer, Lucy Page, 111
Meredith, B., 160
Merton, R. K., 148
Mighty (film), 184
Mill, John Stuart, 34
Milliken, F. J., 83
Mills, John, 171
mindfulness: cultivation of, 79, 226–28;
versus intelligence, 228–30; Langer on, 80
mindlessness: of actor and attributions of
stupidity, 225–28; Clinton-Lewinsky
scandal and, 216; cognitive commitment
to, 213–17; cognitive incompetence and,
217–18, 241; folly as, 80; of interaction/
scripts and mutual attributions of
stupidity, 221–25; language as trap for,
216–17; of observer, 213–14, 218–21,
228; of researchers, 213–17, 221; as result

of authoritative information, 215–16; as
result of repetition of information, 215;
scripted social behavior and, 221–22; as
stupidity, 3, 13, 20; teacher-student script
example, 222–25; ubiquity of, 214–16;
wisdom and, 20
Mintzberg, H., 45, 50
The Miracle Worker (film), 171
Mischel, Walter, 2, 98
mistuning, folly and, 66, 75–76, 83
Mitterand, François, 113
Mitsubishi, 118
Moldoveanu, Mihnea, 3, 4, 9, 20, 241
Mooney, Jonathan, 184
Morton Thiokol, 83
Moshman, D., 129–30
motivation, genius and, 32, 34
movies, stereotypes of people with disabilities
in, 164–66, 169, 171–77, 183–84
Mozart, Wolfgang, 35, 183
Mueller, Claudia, 26, 36–37
Mulder, R. T., 201
Murray, C., 25
musicians, patterns of genius in, 34–35
Myers, D., 114
Myers-Briggs Type Indicator, 54
My Left Foot (film), 171

NAEP (National Assessment of Educational
Progress), 162
narcissists, 59–60, 201
NASA, 83
National Assessment of Educational
Progress (NAEP), 162
National Center for Policy Analysis, 160
National Collegiate Athletic Association, 180
neglect, folly and, 71
Neisser, U., 43
Nemeth, S. A., 175
neuroticism, 189–90, 192, 195, 196, 201,
204–5, 207
Newell, Alan, 128, 129, 229
Nickerson, R., 132
Nisbett, R., 135, 136
Nitzberg, Greg, 169
Nixon, Richard, 106–7, 116, 232–33, 236,
240
Noon, S. L., 56

177; "Somnolent Samantha" case and disabilities, 167–68

Sternberg, Robert J., 3–4, 9; definition of intelligence, 138–39; on development of expertise, 56; on intellectual styles, 129; on tacit knowledge, 51, 52, 53; Triarchic theory of, 65; on wisdom, 20 (see also wisdom)

Stone, Jeremy, 28

street smarts, versus book smarts, 43–44

strength of intention, 78

stupidity: ambiguity of terminology for, 4, 137–38; attribution of, 213, 220–21; cognitive and moral implications of, 19–20; definition of, 1–2; as foolishness, 3–4, 9, 13–14; as lack of information and resources, 20–21; mindlessness as, 3, 13, 20 (see also mindlessness); multiple determinants of behavior of, 87; mutual attribution of, 221–25; rationality as opposite of, 3, 20; self attribution of, 225–28; theories of, 2–5, 19–22

sure-thing principle, definition of, 124–25

Tabachnik, N., 148

tacit knowledge: definition of, 233; factors undermining effective acquisition and use of, 235; IQ and, 53–54; managerial competence and, 51–55; measurement of, 51–52, 235–36, 241; nature of, 233–35; role in foolishness, 236–40

task-focused coping, 194–95

task mastery, 29

teacher-student script, mindlessness and, 222–25

Temperament and Character Inventory, 203

theoretical rationality, 126

thinking dispositions. See also rational thinking: versus cognitive capacities, 130–31; definition of, 131; diversity in terminology for, 129–30, 133–34; education and, 140–42; epistemic goals and, 135; intentional level psychological structure and, 129, 131–32, 134, 137, 140, 142; normative issue and open-minded, 136, 140–42; as predictors of rational thought, 132–37; prior beliefs and, 132–33; theories of, 133–34

thought, metacomponents of, 240. See also critical thinking; rational thinking; thinking dispositions

Tim (film), 176

tipping points, 68

Tolstoy, Leo, 34

trait theory, of personality, 188–96

Tregoe, B. B., 44, 45, 46

Triarchic theory, Sternberg's, 65

trigger events, 68, 69, 70

Tripp, Linda, 116

Tuchman, Barbara, 82

Tversky, A., 124–25, 135–36, 219–20

Tylenol case, 240

underachievement, 36–39

undermanagement, folly and, 66, 76, 83

Underwood, J., 160

United States Department of Education, 160, 161

United States Supreme Court, 181

vacillation, folly and, 73

ventromedial damage, to prefrontal cortex, 146

Verbal Reasoning subtest, of Differential Aptitude Tests, 53

Vernon, P. A., 201

violence, against people with disabilities, 169–71

Vulcan case, as example of stupidity, 6–9

Wachtler, Sol, 86, 87, 100

Wagner, Richard K., 3, 4, 51, 52, 53, 54

walking the edge, folly and, 74

Wallace, Alfred Russel, 14–18

Walt Disney Corporation, 165

Wan, Wendy, 28, 30

wars, foolishness and balance in relationship to, 238–39

weakness of will, folly and, 78–79, 87–88

Weiner, J. S., 11–12

West, R. F., 135

Westling, Joe, 167–68

What's Eating Gilbert Grape (film), 172, 173

Wiener, Norbert, 34

Willey, Kathleen, 114

willpower, demystification of, 87–88